Slipping Through the Cracks

"Exceedingly difficult philosophical and theological issues deserve very careful explanations. Zach Breitenbach steers a very careful path through one of the thorniest of these issues, clearing a potential trail through the obstacle course of how Jesus Christ could be the only way to salvation. Being additionally sophisticated and exhibiting well-written clarity are side benefits. Very highly recommended."

—GARY R. HABERMAS
Liberty University

"I am grateful for Breitenbach's carefully reasoned analysis of Molinism, the unevangelized, and 'the problem of the contingently lost.' He presents important clarifications and arguments worthy of further engagement. *Slipping through the Cracks* provides a model that is not only faithful to Scripture and rationally coherent but also stands out as a valuable contribution to the literature on an important perennial topic."

—PAUL COPAN
Author of *True for You, But Not for Me*

"Seamlessly interweaving academic precision and charitable sensitivity, Breitenbach offers a combination rarely found in substantive works dealing with weighty topics. Neither simplistic nor inaccessible, *Slipping Through the Cracks* should be required reading for anyone seeking to better understand the soteriological problem of evil."

—T. J. GENTRY
Cofounder of Good Reasons Apologetics

"Zach Breitenbach has done the Christian, philosophical, apologetic, and theological community a wonderful service. Unafraid to tackle prohibitively difficult questions, the prodigiously gifted author has the expansive mind and requisite skill and aptitude to navigate their contours, often with penetrating profundity. Breitenbach's original theodicy offered here is both extremely thoughtful and eminently worthy of careful consideration ... With lucid prose and crystal-clear explanations, he has written a wonderful book."

—DAVID BAGGETT
Houston Baptist University

"Dr. Breitenbach is a maestro, creating and conducting a sophisticated theological and philosophical symphony. He meticulously scrutinizes and adapts alternative works and themes to arrange a brilliant harmony of God's classical attributes, Christian exclusivism, and the reality of the contingently lost. His composition deserves an attentive audience. He doesn't allow much, if anything, to slip through the cracks."

—**RICHARD A. KNOPP**
Lincoln Christian University

"With clear language and critical insight, Zach Breitenbach offers a fresh theodicy in the form of reasoned proposal for addressing the theological topic of the contingently lost. He does not avoid the hard issues but offers a biblically faithful response to a variety of perspectives dealing with this philosophical issue. Breitenbach astutely works through a multitude of possible viewpoints and addresses topics like God's love, God's sovereignty, and the problem of those who may be considered contingently lost. This approach will no doubt encourage fresh discussion and raise new questions to pursue."

—**LEO PERCER**
John W. Rawlings School of Divinity

"Zach Breitenbach presents us here with a carefully argued treatment of one of the tougher questions arising for the Christian believer who thinks that some stripe or flavor of Molinism is the best model for reconciling divine sovereignty and human freedom. His summary and analysis of contemporary molinistic theories is worth the price of the book alone; his further work on how to be a Molinist and address the soteriological problems of evil is remarkable, providing a series of strong arguments for his model. Highly recommended!"

—**EDWARD N. MARTIN**
Liberty University

Slipping Through the Cracks

Are Some Lost Who Would Have Been Saved
in Different Circumstances?

Zachary Breitenbach

Foreword by David Baggett

WIPF & STOCK · Eugene, Oregon

SLIPPING THROUGH THE CRACKS
Are Some Lost Who Would Have Been Saved in Different Circumstances?

Copyright © 2021 Zachary Breitenbach. All rights reserved. Except for brief quotations in critical publications or reviews, no part of this book may be reproduced in any manner without prior written permission from the publisher. Write: Permissions, Wipf and Stock Publishers, 199 W. 8th Ave., Suite 3, Eugene, OR 97401.

Wipf & Stock
An Imprint of Wipf and Stock Publishers
199 W. 8th Ave., Suite 3
Eugene, OR 97401

www.wipfandstock.com

PAPERBACK ISBN: 978-1-7252-9469-1
HARDCOVER ISBN: 978-1-7252-9470-7
EBOOK ISBN: 978-1-7252-9471-4

03/26/21

Scripture quotations taken from the (NASB®) New American Standard Bible®, Copyright © 1960, 1971, 1977, 1995, 2020 by The Lockman Foundation. Used by permission. All rights reserved. www.lockman.org

Written permission has been granted by the editor of *Philosophia Christi* to draw upon material from an article that the author of this book published with them: "A Case for How Eschatological and Soteriological Considerations Strengthen the Plausibility of a Good God." This essay first appeared in *Philosophia Christi* 22 (2) 2020.

To my parents, Larry and Sheri Breitenbach, who have been crucial supporters of my spiritual and academic growth and have always been living examples to me of what it means to be a committed follower of Christ.

Contents

Foreword by David Baggett | ix

Introduction | 1
1. The Soteriological Problem of Evil and the Contingently Lost | 12
2. An Explanation and Defense of Molinism | 54
3. Assessment of Existing Molinist Theodicies | 100
4. A New Molinist Theodicy Against the Problem of the Contingently Lost | 157
5. The Applicability of This Theodicy to the Broader Problem of Evil | 184

Conclusion | 205

Bibliography | 215

Foreword

OVER THE COURSE OF my long friendship with Zach Breitenbach, he has consistently shown a remarkable willingness to keep struggling with an issue until clarity comes. I recall that he used to be a wrestler, and it would appear that he still is! Like many of the luminaries in the history of apologetics, he is willing to sit with an issue, live and wrestle with questions, and give a topic the time and effort required to do it justice.

This delightful book is a product of such laudable patience, tenacity, and labor, and the result does not disappoint. To the contrary, he has done the Christian, philosophical, apologetic, and theological community a wonderful service. Unafraid to tackle prohibitively difficult questions, the prodigiously gifted author has the expansive mind and requisite skill and aptitude to navigate their contours, often with penetrating profundity. He is unrelenting in his search for a theory that is at once both philosophically rigorous and biblically sound.

One of the significant challenges assailing those who believe in a wholly good and loving God is to make sense of the category of the "contingently lost" (i.e., those who are lost but would have been saved in other circumstances that God could have brought about). Indeed, this problem is intractable enough that some insist that no sense can be made of it at all, and that no one is ultimately unredeemed in the actual world if they are redeemed in some other world that is feasible for God to make. This deep existential issue of whether some people "slip through the cracks," as it were, can hardly be overstated, shedding light by turns on the human condition and questions of ultimate meaning and significance, the nature of reality and the very character of God.

Breitenbach's original theodicy offered here is both extremely thoughtful and eminently worthy of careful consideration. Canvassing and digesting, integrating and synthesizing an array of disparate discussions—from Reformed epistemology to Molinism, from exclusivism to theodicy—he makes accessible and brings to life wide, important, and difficult literatures, deftly navigating their nuances and generating real clarity in the process.

With lucid prose and crystal clear explanations, he has written a wonderful book that is both philosophically astute and historically informed, and both theologically sophisticated and biblically faithful. He does not make the job he carves out for himself an easy one. He aims to effect a rapprochement of nothing less than the conjunction of exclusivism and the possibility of some people being contingently lost, a God of perfect love (for all) and substantive doctrines of sovereignty—albeit decidedly non-Calvinist variants of election and predestination. His interlocutors may agree or disagree with his analysis, but they will be unable responsibly to ignore it.

David Baggett
Professor of Philosophy and
Director of the Center for Moral Apologetics
at Houston Baptist University.

Introduction

Overview of the Issue

STANDING BEFORE THE SANHEDRIN and facing a hostile audience, the Apostle Peter refuses to back down from proclaiming the message that he knows to be true: The only road to God and salvation goes directly through Jesus Christ. Pressed to provide an explanation for his involvement in God's healing of a crippled man, Peter does not fail to capitalize on the evangelistic opportunity to assert that, besides Jesus, "there is no other name under heaven that has been given among men by which we must be saved" (Acts 4:12).[1] In the same way, Jesus himself insists that he is "the way, and the truth, and the life" and the only means we have of coming to the Father (John 14:6); moreover, he is clear that many will enter through what he calls the "wide gate" that leads to destruction rather than accessing God through faith in him (Matt 7:13–14).

In view of the pluralistic mindset that is so prevalent today, the biblical teaching that salvation is offered only through faith in Christ is met by many with scorn and indignation. It is often seen as too narrow and unworthy of the Christian God, whom Scripture depicts as omnibenevolent and perfectly holy. We are now more aware than ever of the vast diversity of religions in the world, and it is clear that many people do not even hear the Christian gospel during their lifetimes. Indeed, it may seem that the opportunity one has to respond to the gospel is largely contingent upon whether one has the good fortune of being born into the right circumstances. Although Christianity has more adherents than any other world religion, the majority of people alive today have not accepted Christ as their Savior and a significant portion of the world's people have not been reached with the Christian message. There are

---

1. All quotations of the Bible will be from the NASB unless otherwise indicated.

thousands of world religions, and approximately two-thirds of the world's seven billion people are not Christians; in addition, it is estimated that around one-fourth of all people alive today have never heard the gospel and remain unevangelized.[2] While some are born in twenty-first century America where freedom of religion is permitted and Christianity is widely preached and accepted, others are not so fortunate. Some are born in a time and place where the gospel does not reach during their lifetimes. Others are born into a culture where the gospel is at least known, but it is not tolerated. For example, a person born into a devout Muslim family in Saudi Arabia, an Islamic state that allows only the public practice of Islam and has a population that is almost entirely Muslim, will be heavily encouraged to adopt Islam. It is easy to imagine that many who are born into such a culture might have accepted Christianity if only they were placed into different circumstances.

It is therefore not difficult to recognize the significant challenge that is raised against Christianity's claim that Jesus is the only path to an eternity of blessedness in the presence of God and to the avoidance of eternal punishment in everlasting separation from God. If salvation is exclusively through Christ, how could an omnibenevolent, omnipotent, and omniscient God allow so many people to be lost who have never even so much as heard the Christian gospel? Even if God does somehow offer all people an opportunity to be saved, is God not unloving to those lost persons who are provided with minimal revelation of God but would have chosen to be saved if placed into better circumstances? This problem, which is one of the most pressing questions related to the so-called "soteriological problem of evil," primarily calls God's omnibenevolence into question. This difficulty might be dubbed the "problem of the contingently lost," and the central concern behind it is as follows: How could an omnibenevolent, omnipotent, omniscient God allow certain people to be lost when they would have freely accepted God's grace and been saved if only God had placed them into different circumstances? How

---

2. Barrett and Johnson, *World Christian Trends*, 24. While a bit old, this statistic cannot be far from accurate today. The statistics in this source are still cited widely in the literature. The following source from 2011 estimates that somewhere close to a third of the world population may be unevangelized: Johnstone, *Future of the Global Church*, 161. It is safe to estimate that somewhere in the range of a quarter to a third of the world has not heard the Christian gospel. More statistics will be given in the next chapter, indicating the percentage of the world that is estimated to have been unevangelized at various points over the course of church history.

could God allow anyone's lost state to be contingent upon circumstances beyond that person's control?

Core Hypothesis of the Book

The aim of this book is to flesh out and defend a theodicy[3] against the problem of the contingently lost. This theodicy may be summarized as follows. God has sovereignly arranged the world in such a way that nobody is lost due to lack of information (e.g., not hearing the gospel) or due to the sin and corrupting influences of those around them (i.e., being in the wrong circumstances to accept the gospel when they hear it). It is possible that every lost person remained lost as a consequence of his or her *own* sinful rejection of God and not epistemological or circumstantial limitations, and this theodicy aims to show how this may be the case even if one must hear the gospel and respond to it in this life to be saved (i.e., even if Christian exclusivism is true). The theodicy proposes that there may only be two types of contingently lost persons (i.e., two

---

3. It is useful to clarify what I mean by a "theodicy" and how it differs from a "defense." When it comes to the problem of evil, a defense (as I use the term) only requires giving some possibly true statement (even one that may be false) that shows that God and evil are not inconsistent. So a defense is very modest in this sense and merely aims to show the logical consistency of God and evil. A theodicy (as I use the term) gives an account that tries to reconcile God and evil in a way that is plausible and consistent with Scripture. I am calling what I am doing in this project a soteriological theodicy. The problem of the contingently lost claims that God's attributes entail that God would not allow anyone to be contingently lost and yet there are some who are contingently lost. As would be required in a defense, I will aim to show that God's attributes do not necessarily entail that God would never allow anyone to be contingently lost. But I want to go beyond merely showing that it is possibly true that God would allow some to be contingently lost. I want to weave together a plausible account that suggests what God may well be doing. I want to show that it is not just possible but reasonable and consistent with Scripture (even if not explicitly taught in Scripture) to think that an omnipotent, omniscient, perfectly good and loving God would allow some people to be contingently lost in certain ways. There is no doubt that plausibility is to some degree in the eye of the beholder, and readers will have to evaluate the plausibility of my proposal for themselves. Nevertheless, my aim is to relieve the tension that is caused by the problem of the contingently lost as much as possible by offering more than a mere possibility. I will strive to offer an account that, if true, logically undercuts the problem of the contingently lost and also is likely to leave one feeling comfortable that the solution that was offered is neither unbiblical nor implausible. A description of how a theodicy differs from a defense that is in line with what I have described above may be found at: Moreland and Craig, *Philosophical Foundations*, 538. See also: Murray and Rea, *An Introduction to the Philosophy of Religion*, 170.

types of persons who are lost in the actual world but would have been saved in other worlds of free creatures that were feasible for God to create). It makes room for these two types because there is biblical support for them. The first type is one who would not accept the gospel under any *sufficiently non-pressured* circumstances; that is, the person would have to be shown in a way that is (for that person) unduly overt that the gospel ought to be accepted before that person would repent and accept God's grace. The second type is anyone who willfully rejects God's grace after previously accepting it (i.e., apostatizes). In both of these cases, such persons are contingently lost. I will propose, however, that these may be the only two types of contingently lost persons that God allows and that God's omnibenevolence is not undermined even if he allows these two types. In this way I will seek to defend God's omnibenevolence despite allowing that some may be contingently lost.

Before laying out the above core hypothesis of the book, some foundational topics will have to be addressed. First, the soteriological problem of evil (POE), which is mentioned above, must be carefully explained. As part of doing this, I will evaluate a couple of challenges that are sometimes alleged to show an incompatibility between the Christian God's attributes and the fact that many people will be eternally lost, and I will briefly offer a solution to these. After clearing away these initial objections, I will contend that a key remaining objection—the one described above concerning the contingently lost—seems to be the most pressing difficulty. That will set the stage for focusing on the problem of the contingently lost for the remainder of the book and offering a theologically consistent and philosophically plausible theodicy that shows why this problem does not bring God's attributes into conflict with the Bible's teaching on soteriology. As I examine the soteriological POE, I will also point out how concern over the unevangelized has fueled rejection of Christianity in the form of religious pluralism. Anxiety over the unevangelized has also led many Christians to adopt Christian inclusivism and abandon the idea that one must hear the gospel and respond to it to be saved. I will explain that my theodicy accepts the truth of Christian exclusivism because there is strong evidence that this view is biblical and because it is useful to show that one can offer a reasonable theodicy against the problem of the contingently lost even if one does not appeal to inclusivism.

Second, I will introduce Molinism and provide a defense of this doctrine's philosophical and theological viability. This is necessary because my proposed solution to the problem of the contingently lost depends upon the validity of Molinism. The concept of Molinism, which was put forth by the sixteenth-century Jesuit Luis de Molina, holds that God's omniscience—even logically prior to God's decree to create the world—includes not only knowledge of all possible worlds, but also knowledge of all feasible worlds.[4] God's "middle knowledge" involves God knowing logically prior to his creative decree what all creatures with libertarian freedom would do in any circumstances into which God might place them.[5] I will take time to explain Molinism, briefly discuss the history behind the rise of this view, and offer biblical and philosophical support to show that it is defensible. As part of my biblical defense of Molinism, I will also note how Molinism makes it possible to capture key insights from both Calvinism and Arminianism. It allows one to hold that God is sovereign over human affairs and even elects individuals to salvation in a real sense; meanwhile, it also allows one to hold that Christ died for all people to have the opportunity to be saved and that all humans are entirely free in the libertarian sense to accept or reject God so that "whosoever believes" will be saved.

Third, given the viability of Molinism, I will explore some Molinist solutions to the problem of the contingently lost that have already been put forth, and I will contend that these solutions suffer from various theological and/or philosophical difficulties such that it is desirable to provide a better solution. This will pave the way for me to reveal an alternative proposal that leverages the power of Molinism to address the problem of the contingently lost without falling prey to any significant theological or philosophical stumbling blocks. There are numerous possible ways that Molinism could be employed in developing a soteriological theodicy. Of those that have been proposed, the one that is most prominent and most promising is William Lane Craig's proposal. My own theodicy draws heavily upon key concepts in Craig's clever theodicy but also departs

---

4. A feasible world is one that can be actualized by God. Some logically possible worlds are not feasible. An example of a logically possible world that is not feasible is the following: a world W that is identical to the actual world (and let us assume that both W and the actual world contain free creatures) up until the exact moment that I am typing this sentence but instead of finishing my typing of this sentence I freely choose to punch myself in the face. W is not a feasible world because I simply would not freely make that choice in these circumstances.

5. An agent has libertarian freedom if, when given a choice between multiple options, the agent is not determined to opt for any of the particular options. There are no circumstances in place that determine which option the agent will choose. Regardless of what option the agent selects, she could have chosen a different option.

from it at significant junctures. For this reason, I will focus particularly on explaining Craig's theodicy and identifying its merits and its drawbacks. I will disagree with Craig's theodicy primarily because there are multiple ways in which Scripture seems to contradict his crucial proposal that nobody is contingently lost. I will also highlight the fact that his appeal to Christian inclusivism is difficult to support on biblical grounds. In addition, when I eventually unpack my own theodicy, I will show how God plausibly has various goals for the world besides soteriological optimality that may place limitations on the balance of saved versus lost that is feasible for God to bring about—a possibility that Craig does not explore. That is, I will suggest that God may optimize the soteriological balance within the bounds of certain restrictions that are important to God—restrictions that, if removed, may have allowed for an even more favorable ratio of saved versus lost.

At this point, the necessary groundwork will have been laid so that I can put forth and defend my Molinist theodicy against the problem of the contingently lost. The theodicy will propose a process by which the Holy Spirit might break down a person's sinful resistance to accepting the gospel, utilizing a slightly modified version of Reformed epistemology as well as Molinism.[6] This process will allow that all people have an opportunity to be saved and that nobody is contingently lost aside from those who require unduly overt revelation in order to accept the gospel and anyone who commits apostasy. I will suggest that God creates the best soteriological balance that is possible given counterfactual truths concerning what all possible humans would freely do in all possible circumstances into which God might place them and given at least two key parameters (a certain degree of divine hiddenness and God allowing Satan to tempt us) that may limit the soteriological balance from being as favorable as it otherwise would be.[7] Although God desires as many

---

6. I will suggest two modifications to Reformed epistemology. First, I will specify that only one's own sin is ultimately decisive in one's failure to accept the gospel. Second, I will stress that arguments, evidences, and certain life experiences may be a crucial part of the Holy Spirit overcoming the sin barrier that prevents a person from recognizing in a properly basic way that the gospel is true. This epistemology will play a key role in the proposed process by which God ensures that all those who would freely and without undue pressure accept the gospel will come to accept it.

7. Counterfactual conditionals are conditional statements in the subjunctive mood. They state what would be the case if a hypothetical antecedent were true. The following offers a good explanation of the concept of counterfactual conditionals: Moreland and Craig, *Philosophical Foundations*, 46.

people as possible to be saved and as few as possible to be lost, God also desires that those who are saved make that decision without excessive pressure and that they are sufficiently tempted by sin (though God himself does not tempt anyone to sin). In this way, God ensures that those who are saved must make a significant moral decision in choosing to love God rather than remaining a slave to sin. For this reason, though it may result in a less optimal balance of saved versus lost than would otherwise be feasible for God to bring about over the course of human history, God keeps enough of an epistemic distance from us so that our decision to love him and enter into a saving relationship with him will be free from excessive pressure. God also allows Satan to tempt us with his lies so that our affections might be drawn away from God if we allow them to be. I will show that these two parameters—God's hiddenness and God allowing Satan to tempt us—are consistent with God's goodness and love because they ensure an environment that allows humans to make a free and morally significant choice to love God, and this is presumably a great good. The soteriological outcome God brings about on this view is purposeful, loving, and consistent with God's omnibenevolence. It takes divine sovereignty and providence seriously while preserving human freedom. It also accounts for the reality of spiritual warfare and the biblical teaching that God desires the salvation of all people. In addition, it is consistent with the biblical evidence that exclusivism is true and that some are contingently lost.

Finally, after unpacking my proposed theodicy against the problem of the contingently lost and completing my defense of it, I will briefly show how my theodicy—although it is intended to deal with an aspect of the soteriological POE—also offers benefits in responding to the broader POE as it relates to the amount of suffering and evil and the apparent gratuitousness of suffering and evil in our present earthly existence. If Molinism is true and God's sovereign activity in directing the world is aimed largely at achieving the best soteriological outcomes (both of which are key ingredients in my theodicy), it will be shown how this can reduce the perplexity that often arises from the seemingly excessive amount of evil that occurs in this world and the fact that so much of it seems pointless so far as we can tell. In addition, I will suggest how the truth of my proposed soteriological theodicy (or one like it) would help to bolster two prominent responses to the broader POE that make an appeal to soteriological outcomes—those of Eleonore Stump and John Hick.

Significance of the Book

This proposal is significant for soteriology as well as Christian apologetics. With regard to soteriology, it is useful to provide a coherent perspective that: (1) accounts for God's classical attributes; (2) upholds Christian exclusivism; and (3) does not require a denial of the biblical evidence that some will be lost who would have been saved in different circumstances. I believe my project offers insights for Christian theology by putting forth a biblically consistent and philosophically reasonable soteriological proposal that accomplishes all of the above.

From a practical, apologetic standpoint, offering a defensible theodicy against the soteriological POE—and specifically against the problem of the contingently lost—can be a valuable tool for removing barriers that may prevent some non-Christians from accepting the Christian faith. Religious pluralism is a powerful enemy of Christian evangelism, and the soteriological POE might be the most significant impetus that drives people to religious pluralism—a position exemplified perhaps most notably by John Hick in which all religions are considered equally valid paths to ultimate reality and a generic form of "salvation." Offering a plausible theodicy against the problem of the contingently lost helps to defuse much of the concern that many have about accepting Christianity as the only entirely true religion. This soteriological theodicy also strengthens the response that one can give to the broader POE in terms of the amount and apparent gratuitousness of evil. Since the POE is the most significant challenge to theism in the eyes of many, this has much apologetic value. Furthermore, offering a good answer to this problem will also strengthen the faith of those who are already Christians and will make them better-equipped witnesses for Christ. It will allow believers and non-believers alike to see that the doctrine of Christian exclusivism is not incompatible with the omnibenevolent Christian God. By removing the concerns raised by the problem of the contingently lost, perhaps this project might be a small part of God's eternal plan of ensuring that as many people as possible are brought into a saving relationship with Christ.

Scope of the Book

The primary goal of this project is to argue that Molinism is a viable doctrine concerning God's omniscience, that Reformed epistemology is also viable, and then to offer a philosophically and theologically sound soteriological theodicy concerning the problem of the contingently lost that makes use of these two perspectives. Although much has been written concerning the soteriological POE and how one might respond to its multifaceted concerns, I will focus primarily on the question of how an omnibenevolent God who is said to desire the salvation of all people could allow some to be lost who would have been saved in different circumstances (i.e., the problem of the contingently lost). My proposal is intended to improve upon Craig's Molinist theodicy in key ways.

It is important to make clear what is meant by "contingently lost." The focus of this book is on the eternal fate of those who are of a sufficient age and cognitive capacity to engage in sin and to understand the concepts of sin and repentance and accepting divine grace. It is beyond the scope of this project to examine the fate of the following sorts of unevangelized persons: the unborn who die in the womb; those dying as small children who lack an awareness of sin and have no ability to understand the concepts of repentance and grace; and the severely mentally handicapped who never develop the ability to understand sin and the need for grace. While these groups may rightly be considered unevangelized, Scripture never directly addresses what God will do with such people. There is certainly no clear biblical teaching that such individuals cannot be saved or will not be saved. If anything, there are hints to the contrary—at least with regard to those who die as infants. King David, for example, believed that he would once again be reunited with his infant son who died (2 Sam 12:23).[8] In any case, at the very least there is no basis for thinking that such persons are lost simply because they lack the cognitive ability to understand moral accountability, repentance, and grace. The concern of this work is with the contingently lost; since Scripture lacks any clear indication that the above-mentioned categories of unevangelized persons are lost at all, their fate does not fall within the problem of the contingently lost. Scripture does, however, indicate that those who have the cognitive capacity to sin and understand moral guilt and the need for God's grace will be held responsible for their evil

---

8. In addition, some Christian theologians have argued persuasively that children are born in a state of original grace until they reach a cognitive ability in which they have sufficient understanding to be responsible for their personal sins. Jack Cottrell makes this case, focusing especially on Romans 5:12–19 and arguing that this passage teaches that whatever spiritual condition all of humanity would have inherited from birth as a result of Adam's sin is cancelled by what Christ did on the cross; nevertheless, he still rightly holds that faith in Christ is needed to remove our guilt for our own personal sins. See: Cottrell, *The Faith Once for All*, 179–90.

and for suppressing the truth about God. In the book of Romans, the Apostle Paul teaches that, ever since the beginning of creation, God has made plain to all such people through what he has made his "invisible attributes, His eternal power and divine nature" (Rom 1:20). Guilt for violating God's moral law applies to all people who have the minimal capacities needed for recognizing it. Even those who have never received God's moral law via special revelation are guilty when they violate this moral law because the law is written on their hearts (Rom 2:12–16). So the focus of my theodicy is only on those who are "contingently lost," and I will consider the contingently lost to be only those who: (1) have the capacity in the actual world to recognize the basic truths about God and the moral law that God has made plain via general revelation in nature and conscience; (2) ultimately die in an unsaved state and are lost in the actual world; and (3) would have been saved in at least one other feasible world of significantly free creatures in which they attain a cognitive capacity that allows them to understand the basic truths mentioned in (1) concerning moral guilt and the reality of God.

The following are the ten most crucial questions addressed in this book: (1) Is it possible to offer a biblically-faithful proposal for how all people may have an opportunity to be saved? (2) Does the Bible indicate that some people are contingently lost? (3) Is it possible that any person who never hears the gospel or is in disadvantageous circumstances for accepting the gospel could nevertheless be solely responsible for not accepting God's grace even if Christian exclusivism is true? (4) What good reasons might an omnibenevolent God have for allowing some people to be contingently lost? (5) What is Molinism, and what are biblical and philosophical reasons to think it is true? (6) What is Reformed epistemology, and what are biblical and philosophical reasons to think that it is true? (7) What is Craig's Molinist theodicy to answer the problem of the contingently lost, and is this theory plausible? (8) How can Reformed epistemology and Molinism be leveraged to propose a better Molinist theodicy against the problem of the contingently lost? (9) Why would God be as hidden as he is and allow Satan to tempt humans if God wants as many as possible to be saved? (10) How might the truth of Molinism and appealing to God's possible soteriological aims for this world help to explain why God might allow the amount of suffering and evil and the apparent gratuitousness of so much evil that is observed in this present earthly existence?

I will only briefly address other questions related to the soteriological POE, since I believe (in agreement with Craig) that the problem of the contingently lost is the most significant and challenging one. Of course, in the first chapter I will need to justify carefully why I believe this. Many of the topics that arise in this book are complex, and theologians and philosophers have long struggled to resolve the questions surrounding them. For example, this project touches upon God's omniscience, omnipotence, and sovereignty. It also runs squarely into the centuries-old controversy concerning determinism and human free will. The need to limit the scope of this book will prevent me from investigating in great depth certain matters that, while relevant and important, are more peripheral to what I aim to accomplish. For example, my position affirms that humans possess libertarian free will, and this seems to require that humans have souls. Entire books have been written on the subjects of libertarian free will and the existence of the soul; thus, the support that I will give to such issues must be limited.

Finally, it is important to recognize that my proposal is put forth merely as a *possible and plausible* solution to the problem of the contingently lost. I do not claim that my proposal is necessarily true or that it can be "proven" to be true. Nevertheless, so long as my proposal provides a theologically and philosophically defensible justification of God, then it is a good theodicy.

1

The Soteriological Problem of Evil and the Contingently Lost

Salvation is Found Only in Jesus

IN THE HOURS BEFORE his betrayal, Jesus assures his disciples that his return is as certain as his upcoming departure, and he encourages them by pointing toward the hope that awaits them of being with him in his "Father's house." His disciple Thomas then asks him to explain the way to get to this place. In response, Jesus boldly declares, "I am the way, and the truth, and the life; no one comes to the Father but through Me" (John 14:6). The Greek text places focus on the "I" in "I am" (ἐγώ εἰμι) by the emphatic use of the personal pronoun. Jesus is emphasizing that *he himself* is the one and only path to God.

Jesus is certainly not alone in professing that he is the only provision God has given to humans by which we might enjoy eternal life with God and escape the condemnation that our sins deserve. Indeed, the unanimous testimony of the New Testament writers is that there is no salvation apart from Christ and his atoning death. The uniqueness of Christ's sacrifice and its necessity for salvation have been recognized since the beginning of the church.

Peter pointedly affirms the soteriological centrality of Jesus, declaring that "there is salvation in no one else; for there is no other name under heaven that has been given among men by which we must be saved" (Acts 4:12). Paul likewise insists that "there is one God, and one mediator also between God and men, the man Christ Jesus, who gave Himself as a ransom for all, the testimony given at the proper time" (1 Tim 2:5–6). The Apostle John's teaching further adds to Scripture's unwavering consistency on this point. John raises the question: "Who is the one who overcomes the world?" His answer is that it is only "he who believes that Jesus is the Son of God" (1 John 5:5). John asserts that "God has given us eternal life, and this life is in His Son. He who has the Son has the life; he who does not have the Son of God does not have the life" (1 John 5:11–12). John preached the universal applicability and soteriological necessity of what Jesus accomplished on the cross, pronouncing that Jesus "is the propitiation for our sins; and not for ours only, but also for those of the whole world" (1 John 2:2).

The biblical testimony on this point is decisive. Nobody can be saved apart from Jesus and what he accomplished in dying for our sins.[1] This simple truth, however, ushers in a number of difficult questions.

Definition of the Soteriological Problem of Evil

Although Jesus offers the hope that he is the gate (John 10:9) by which one accesses salvation, his unsettling affirmation that those who accept this salvation "enter through the narrow gate" does not paint an optimistic picture for the majority of mankind. Not only is salvation obtained through Christ alone, but the teaching of Jesus himself seems to be that a significant portion of humanity will enter through the "wide gate" that "leads to destruction" while only a relative "few" will find salvation (Matt 7:13–14).

Perhaps Jesus' statement that many will be lost should not be surprising given the biblical teaching that salvation is only through Christ and given what we know about the world's religious diversity and the historical spread of the Christian faith. The fact that there is a vast assortment of religions in the world is far more widely known than ever before. As noted previously, only about one in three people alive today call themselves Christian (even though more people adhere to Christianity than any other world religion), and there are almost as many unevangelized persons in the world as there are Christians. Indeed, down

---

1. We will examine the controversy concerning Christian inclusivism and exclusivism, which has to do with whether or not one must hear the gospel of Christ and respond to it in order to be saved; however, the fact that Jesus is at least *ontologically* necessary for salvation is an uncontroversial doctrine that lies at the core of Christianity.

through the history of the Christian church, it has always been the case that most people alive at any given time did not know Christ, and there has always been a large percentage of the world population that is unevangelized. At the start of the second century (roughly seventy years after the death of Christ), it is approximated that well under one percent of the world was Christian and ninety-four percent of the estimated 180 million people alive at that time were unevangelized. By the start of the eleventh century, about seventeen percent of the world was Christian and seventy-nine percent of the roughly 264 million people alive at that time were unevangelized. Although close to one-third of the world's 1.6 billion people were likely Christians by the turn of the twentieth century, over half of the world still remained unevangelized. The world population has exploded in the more than one hundred years since that time, yet Christians have steadily comprised only about one-third of that population. Although the percentage of the world that is unevangelized has been cut in half since the year 1900, it remains that over 4.5 billion people that are alive today are not Christians and around 1.7 billion of those people are unevangelized.[2]

These statistics help to demonstrate why the biblical teaching that Jesus is the only path to salvation raises challenging problems for Christians and provokes skepticism among some who are outside of the Christian faith. Why does God create anyone who fails to believe and is lost to hell? Why does God not ensure that all people hear the gospel? Why are some people placed into circumstances that are much more conducive to accepting Christ and his salvation than others? These are prominent issues within the so-called "soteriological problem of evil."

The soteriological POE is a particular aspect of the broader POE. The broader POE is a challenge to theism—and thus to Christian theism—which contends that the existence of God (i.e., the God of classical theism, a being who is omnipotent, omniscient, and omnibenevolent) is inconsistent with—or at least made unlikely by—the existence of evil in some way. The "deductive" or "logical" version of the POE is the claim that there is a logical incompatibility between the existence of God and the existence of evil such that evil disproves theism. By contrast, the "inductive" or "probabilistic" version of the POE holds that the existence of God is unlikely given the features of evil that are observed in the world (e.g., its intensity, its pervasiveness, and its apparent gratuitousness in

---

2. Barrett and Johnson, *World Christian Trends*, 24.

many cases). Philosophers have widely abandoned the deductive version in light of Alvin Plantinga's Free Will Defense, though the inductive version still garners much support. Within this broader POE, the soteriological POE specifically focuses on the challenge of reconciling the above-mentioned attributes of God with the biblical teaching concerning soteriology. It alleges an incompatibility between the following propositions:

> P_1. God possesses the attributes of omniscience, omnipotence, and omnibenevolence.
>
> P_2. Some persons do not accept the forgiveness that is available via receiving Christ and are thus damned.[3]

In assessing the soteriological POE,[4] William Lane Craig rightly points out that the above two propositions "are not explicitly contradictory, since one is not the negation of the other, nor are they logically

---

3. Craig rightly points out that these two allegedly inconsistent premises are at the heart of the soteriological POE. See Craig, "No Other Name," 180.

4. One important challenge that is outside the scope of this paper is that God should not send anyone at all to an eternity in hell. This challenge is not directly part of the soteriological POE (at least insofar as the soteriological POE is considered to be an inconsistency that arises between P_1 and P_2) because this challenge concerns God's justice rather than God's omnibenevolence or love. The concern raised by the objector is that God's attribute of justice is incompatible with God determining that anyone should receive an eternal punishment (or that severe of a punishment) for committing a finite amount of sins. The claim is that the crime does not fit the punishment. If, however, it is just to send anyone to an eternal hell, then the question arises as to whether the provision indicated in Scripture that God has lovingly provided to humans for avoiding their just punishment is loving enough to be worthy of an omnibenevolent God. This concern is the essence of the soteriological POE (at least as it is defined here), and it will be my focus. In brief, though, it is worth noting three common responses to the objection that it is unjust for God to send anyone to an eternal hell. David Clotfelter examines each of them. First, he notes that even if a person can commit only a finite number of sins in this life, the lost may continue to sin while in hell so that their sins are ongoing just as their punishment is ongoing. If one's sins are ongoing, it seems just that the punishment is as well. Second, he notes the response given by W. G. T. Shedd that the guilt of the lost is eternal and is never removed; thus, it merits eternal punishment. Clotfelter finds positive and negative aspects to both of these types of responses. Third, Clotfelter examines his preferred response (that of Jonathan Edwards), which holds that an offense against an infinite Being (God) demands an infinite punishment. God is infinite in perfection and goodness and beauty. We are utterly dependent upon God and owe God our complete obedience and allegiance. So offending a God of infinite dignity and greatness demands a punishment of infinite duration. See: Clotfelter, *Sinners in the Hands*, 88–94.

contradictory, since a contradiction cannot be derived from them using first order logic." Therefore, the objector's only hope of showing that P_1 and P_2 are inconsistent is to show that they are "inconsistent in the broadly logical sense, that is, that there is no possible world in which both are true."[5] Since there is no explicit contradiction, the only way to demonstrate the inconsistency of P_1 and P_2 is to add more propositions to this set of propositions such that an inconsistency is revealed. This chapter will handle two such arguments that are designed to uncover an alleged inconsistency. After putting to rest these preliminary objections, I will reveal that there is still a residual problem—one that will be addressed in the remaining chapters. We begin with the objection that God ought to ensure that all people are freely saved.

First Preliminary Objection: Should Not God Ensure Universal Salvation?

In defending the broader POE, J. L. Mackie has argued for two premises that, if true, would show that the existence of evil is incompatible with the existence of an omnibenevolent, omnipotent, omniscient God. First, Mackie claims that "there are no limits to what an omnipotent being can do" (i.e., an omnipotent God can literally do anything). Second, he asserts that "a being who is wholly good eliminates evil as far as he can" (i.e., an omnibenevolent God would necessarily want to prevent evil entirely if he could).[6] If God would want to prevent evil and would be able to prevent it, then evil would not exist if God exists. Since evil clearly exists, Mackie's contention is that God must not exist. In a similar way, the proponent of the soteriological POE can argue for the incompatibility of propositions P_1 and P_2 listed above by adding to them the following two premises:

> P_3. God is able to actualize a possible world in which all persons freely [in the libertarian sense] receive Christ.
>
> P_4. God prefers a world in which no persons fail to receive Christ and are damned to a world in which some do.[7]

---

5. Craig, "No Other Name," 180.
6. Mackie, *The Miracle of Theism*, 150.
7. These two premises are adapted from Craig. See Craig, "No Other Name," 180. Of course, in order for God to choose to actualize a certain world of free creatures from among all possible worlds of free creatures so as to achieve a desired end, God's "middle knowledge" is presumed. This concept will be fully developed in the next

If God's omnipotence and omniscience in P_1 entail the truth of P_3 and God's omnibenevolence in P_1 entails the truth of P_4, then God must be both able and willing to ensure that all people freely choose to be saved. That, however, means that P_2 must be false, since P_2 recognizes that some will be damned. So, if that is the case, P_3 and P_4 may seem to bring out a contradiction between P_1 and P_2.

This argument, however, is undermined by multiple problems. Craig offers an effective response by casting doubt upon both P_3 and P_4. Regarding P_3, he points out that it may not be "feasible for God to actualize any possible world."[8] Just as Mackie erred in thinking that God's omnipotence entails that God can actualize all possible worlds (including ones in which all humans freely choose to do only good and no evil), the proponent of the soteriological POE errs in thinking that an omnipotent God can necessarily actualize a world in which all of humanity freely accepts the salvation offered by Christ.[9] Just because it is logically possible to conceive of a world in which all persons have libertarian freedom of

---

chapter; in short, if God possesses middle knowledge, then God knows logically prior to creation what any free creature would freely choose to do in any possible circumstance into which God could place him.

8. Craig, "No Other Name," 180.

9. Plantinga, *God, Freedom, and Evil*, 34–44. Plantinga makes this point well. Plantinga's response to Mackie's aforementioned claim that God should be able to create a world in which all creatures freely choose not to do evil (since it is broadly logically possible that there be a world of free creatures in which all of the creatures freely choose to do only what is right throughout their lives) is to argue that God's omnipotence does not entail that God can necessarily create such a world. Plantinga makes it clear that omnipotence does not entail being able to actualize just any possible world. God is free to actualize a world with free creatures or free to refrain from doing so, but if God does actualize a world of free creatures then it is up to the free creatures to choose what actions they will perform in the various circumstances in which they find themselves. Plantinga thus rejects Mackie's claim, which Plantinga terms "Leibniz' Lapse," that an omnipotent God "could have created any possible world He pleased" (see p. 44). Plantinga names this lapse after Leibniz because Leibniz, like Mackie, thought that God could create any possible world—though Leibniz thought that our world is the best of all possible worlds and Mackie, of course, denies this. In the same way, the defender of P_3 falls into Leibniz' Lapse by assuming that God can actualize a possible world in which all persons have libertarian freedom and freely choose to receive Christ. Just because such a world is conceivable and is broadly logically possible, that does not mean that such a world is feasible for God to create; that is, given counterfactual truths concerning the choices that all free creatures whom God could create would make, God may not be able to bring about such a world. That is the sort of point that Craig is rightly making here in suggesting that God may not be able to actualize a world in which all people freely choose to be saved.

the will and freely choose to be saved, that does not mean it is feasible for God to actualize such a world. The actions of creatures possessing libertarian freedom, given the very definition of what it means to have such freedom, cannot be causally determined by God; thus, given counterfactual truths concerning the choices that all free creatures whom God could create would make, God may not be able to actualize the world described in P_3. For one thing, Craig suggests that some persons might possess what Craig calls "transcircumstantial damnation." This is "a contingent property possessed by an individual essence if the exemplification of that essence would, if offered salvation, freely reject God's grace and be lost no matter what freedom-permitting circumstances God should create him in."[10] Note that if one is transcircumstantially damned, then he is also "transworldly damned"; that is, this individual would freely choose to reject God and be lost in any world that God could actualize.[11] Even an omnipotent God is unable to create a world in which a transcircumstantially damned person is freely saved. It may be argued, however, that God could simply choose not to create a world that contains any such persons. God could choose to create only persons who would freely choose to be saved in some possible world. Nevertheless, Craig contends that "even if it were the case that for any individual God might create, God could

10. Craig, "Middle Knowledge and Christian Exclusivism," 128. For an explanation of the concept of an "essence," see Plantinga, *God, Freedom, and Evil*, 49–53. Basically, an essence is the "complete set of world-indexed properties" that are uniquely possessed by an individual. One's essence is "the set of properties essential to him." For example, although others may share some of the world-indexed properties possessed by Napoleon's essence (e.g., being born in France in 1769 in the actual world or having six fingers in a particular world), no other essence shares all of the world-indexed properties that Napoleon possesses.

11. Craig adapts this idea of transworld damnation from Plantinga's concept of "transworld depravity," a condition that a person P has in which P would err with regard to at least one morally significant action in every world in which God could create P with libertarian freedom. If P suffers from transworld depravity, then in every world W in which "is significantly free in W" and "never does what is wrong in W" are included in P's essence, God could not actualize W. So if all creaturely essences suffer from this condition, then there is no world that is feasible for God to create that is composed entirely of free creatures who never sin. Even though worlds of free creatures who never sin are logically possible, Plantinga points out that the fact that it is at least possible that all creaturely essences suffer from transworld depravity means that there may be no way that God could bring about such worlds. See Plantinga, *God, Freedom, and Evil*, 51–53. In a similar way, Craig's concept of transworld damnation may be understood as follows: If a person Q suffers from this condition, then in every world W in which "has libertarian freedom in W" and "freely chooses to be saved in W" are included in Q's essence, God could not actualize that world.

actualize a world in which that person is freely saved, it does not follow that there are worlds which are feasible for God in which all individuals are saved."[12] This is because the circumstances in which numerous different individuals freely choose to be saved may not be "compossible"; that is, they may not be able to exist together in the same world. Moreover, even if they are compossible, the combination of these various circumstances in the same world might not yield the same results that occur when the circumstances are actualized apart from each other in isolation. In other words, even if it is true that "in circumstances C_1, individual S_1 would do action a and that in circumstances C_2 individual S_2 would do b and that C_1 and C_2 are compossible," Craig points out that one would commit the counterfactual fallacy of "strengthening the antecedent"[13] if one claims that it follows that "in $C_1 * C_2$, S_1 would do a or that in $C_1 * C_2$, S_2 would do b."[14] So the fact that P_3 may well not be feasible for God is enough to show that adding P_3 and P_4 to P_1 and P_2 does not bring out a clear contradiction between P_1 and P_2.

Beyond the above problem with P_3, however, Craig also shows that P_4 is dubious. He proposes, contrary to P_4, that it may be the case that "God prefers certain worlds in which some persons fail to receive Christ and are damned [as opposed] to certain worlds in which all receive Christ and are saved."[15] Craig points out that even if God could create worlds in which everyone is freely saved, such worlds might have certain "overriding deficiencies that make them less preferable" than the actual world in which some freely reject Christ and are lost. For example, it is possible that "the only worlds in which everybody hears and freely believes the gospel are worlds with only a handful of people in them, say, three or four. If God created any more people, then at least one of them would not believe and so would be lost."[16] If so, it seems reasonable that God may prefer well-populated worlds in which some are lost to minimally-populated

---

12. Craig, "No Other Name," 182.

13. Moreland and Craig, *Philosophical Foundations*, 48. Again, counterfactual conditionals are conditional statements in the subjunctive mood. They state what would be the case if a hypothetical antecedent were true. The authors rightly explain that the counterfactual fallacy of strengthening the antecedent states that one cannot conclude that Q would be true if (P & R) is true just because Q would be true if P were true. Such reasoning does not hold for counterfactuals.

14. Craig, "No Other Name," 182. Note that $C_1 * C_2$ indicates that both C_1 and C_2 occur in a world.

15. Craig, "No Other Name," 183.

16. Craig, *Hard Questions, Real Answers*, 158.

worlds in which all are saved. Though it seems plausible that God would ideally prefer to create a world in which everyone is freely saved, the possibility exists that counterfactual truths concerning creaturely freedom[17] may be such that all of those worlds would be deficient in some way that is unacceptable to God. It is, therefore, not at all clear that it is incumbent upon an omnibenevolent, omnipotent, and omniscient God to prefer a world in which all are freely saved over a world in which some freely choose to be lost.

It is also worth noting that, for the same reason, there is no way that we can be confident that God ought to prefer creating no world at all to creating a world in which some people are damned. As Craig puts it, those "who would willingly reject God and forfeit salvation should not be allowed to have a sort of 'veto power' over which worlds God is free to create."[18] God may prefer to actualize a world in which many freely choose to be lost because it is only in such a world that many people freely choose to enjoy the unfathomable benefit of an eternity with him. So P_4 appears to be neither necessarily true nor required by Christian theism. Thus, given the difficulties with both P_3 and P_4, we may conclude that the above argument reveals no clear contradiction between P_1 and P_2.

Second Preliminary Objection: Should Not God Provide Universal Access to Salvation?

Despite the failure of the previous argument, the advocate of the soteriological POE may still appeal to an even more vexing challenge for Christians. As evidenced by the statistics given previously, a massive number of people throughout history have never even heard of Jesus. Accordingly, instead of P_3 and P_4, the defender of the soteriological POE might

---

17. The concept of a counterfactual of creaturely freedom will be explored later. Counterfactual conditionals express what would be the case if a different antecedent state of affairs were to be actual. For example, "If it were raining today, then my lawn would be wet." It is not raining today, but if it were then my lawn would be wet. A counterfactual of creaturely freedom is a counterfactual concerning what a free creature would do. A good definition of a counterfactual of creaturely freedom is that it is a counterfactual "of the form If S were in C, S would freely do A, where S is a created agent, A is some action, and C is a set of fully specified circumstances including the whole history of the world up until the time of S's free action." See Craig, "Middle Knowledge, Truth-Makers," 338.

18. Craig, *Hard Questions, Real Answers*, 161.

conjoin the following three premises to P_1 and P_2 in order to demonstrate a contradiction between them:

P_5. Some people never hear the gospel.

P_6. Anyone who never hears the gospel has no opportunity to accept God's forgiveness through Christ.

P_7. God, if he exists, would be willing and able to ensure that everyone has an opportunity to be saved.[19]

Now if P_5 and P_6 are true, then it follows that some people have no opportunity to accept God's forgiveness through Christ. Given that P_2 entails that one who does not accept God's forgiveness through Christ is damned, it follows that some people have no opportunity to avoid being damned. Yet, if God's attributes in P_1 entail that P_7 is true, then God should not allow it to be the case that some people have no opportunity to avoid being damned. Thus, one may allege that there is an inconsistency between P_1 and P_2.

To overcome this charge of inconsistency, one must make a plausible case that at least one of the added premises is neither a necessary truth nor a premise that is required by orthodox biblical theology. Since the truth of P_5 is uncontroversial,[20] the question becomes whether P_6 and P_7 are either necessarily true or required by orthodox biblical theism. I will argue that P_6 is the flawed premise. I will aim to show that it is at least possible that all people do have an opportunity to accept God's forgiveness through Christ and be saved and that there is biblical evidence that all people have at least an opportunity to be saved. If I can make this case successfully, then P_6 is neither necessarily true nor required by orthodox biblical theism.

I will not dispute P_7 and will consider it to be in agreement with biblical teaching. It should be noted that Calvinist Christians generally deny the truth of P_7 because Calvinism holds that God only wills and ensures the salvation of the elect. Indeed, a person's "opportunity"

---

19. See Table 1.1 at the end of this chapter for a summary of all the premises that are introduced in this chapter.

20. Some argue that all people hear the gospel and have the chance to respond to it while in a postmortem condition, but this speculation is not well supported in the Bible. Biblical arguments will be given later against there being postmortem opportunities to accept Christ for those who failed to accept God's offer of salvation in this lifetime. An assumption of P_5 is that hearing the gospel after death is irrelevant. I will not dispute this assumption.

to choose to accept the salvation God offers has no place in Reformed doctrine because it holds that human corruption entails that no human has any role in making a free choice to accept God's grace and be saved. *God alone* determines who is elect apart from any choices made by the individual and wholly apart from any qualities or abilities possessed by the individual (unconditional election). Moreover, Calvinism views the atoning sacrifice of Jesus as salvifically efficacious only for the elect (limited atonement). Nobody who is elect can resist God's grace (irresistible grace), and nobody who is determined by God to be reprobate can ever accept it.[21] Nevertheless, contra these Reformed views, I will accept that the biblical data does support the truth of P_7. As I will later argue, the strong case that can be made that the Bible upholds unlimited atonement and declares God's desire for all people to choose to be saved provides good reason to think that God is *willing* to supply every person with an opportunity to be saved. Furthermore, by showing that P_6 is not necessarily true and arguing that the unevangelized do have an opportunity to be saved, I will make the case that God is also *able* to provide everyone with an opportunity to be saved even if Christian exclusivism is true.

Practical Relevance: Concern for the Unevangelized Fuels Religious Pluralism

Before proceeding with a critique of P_6, it is worth highlighting the practical significance of this premise. Anxiety over the issue of whether those who are unevangelized lack the opportunity to be saved is a crucial factor that has driven some people to adopt religious pluralism. Religious pluralism rejects the truth of Christianity—and all claims to exclusive religious truth—and holds that there are many valid paths to "salvation" or some sort of ultimate religious outcome.

The pull toward religious pluralism over some form of religious exclusivism began growing in the West in the Enlightenment, but it has especially taken off in the last century. Although Christianity emerged within a milieu that included Judaism as well as the philosophies and pagan religions of the Greco-Roman world, by the fourth century Christianity was the dominant religion of the Roman Empire. It remained

---

21. These points are consistent with the standard Calvinist position, though not all Calvinists accept all of them. For a concise overview of Calvinist doctrine (as it is typically understood) from a Reformed author, see Spencer, *Tulip*.

dominant in the West for centuries, but a shift began during the Enlightenment. Charles Taylor notes how the eighteenth century saw for the first time in the West a "viable alternative to Christianity in exclusive humanism" (i.e., the belief that ultimate meaning is found only in humanity and not in a transcendent reality).[22] The diversification of new positions in the nineteenth century resulting from the various critiques of orthodox Christianity, Deism, and the emerging humanism led to what Taylor calls a "nova effect" that has spawned "an ever-widening variety of moral/spiritual options" among the social elite. In the twentieth century, however, the "fractured culture of the nova" has expanded from the elites to "whole societies" and produced a "generalised culture of 'authenticity', or expressive individualism, in which people are encouraged to find their own way."[23] We now live in what Taylor calls a "spiritual super-nova" in which there are many religious options.[24] After World War II there was greater wealth in the West and more people lived in the suburbs and on their own. A culture of "authenticity" and being one's "true self" emerged.[25] The 1960s, in particular, ushered in an "age of authenticity" in the West in which this individualism became widespread and entrenched.[26]

Although these developments contributed to a twentieth century milieu in which it became more acceptable to many people living in Western society to consider religious options other than Christianity, one key development over the course of the last century has been especially influential in driving Westerners toward a greater openness to a variety of religious options. That development is the fact that technology, immigration, and the ability to travel quickly over vast distances has led to greater awareness among Westerners of the religious diversity that exists in the world so that the world has become a smaller place than it has ever been before. Telephones, the internet, television, and air travel have greatly increased the contact that Westerners have with adherents of the various world religions. Increased immigration into the West has been a particularly significant factor. Harold Netland cites the significance of the 1965 Immigration and Nationality Act in the United States as a major contributor to greater awareness of religious diversity in America. This has led to a

22. Taylor, *A Secular Age*, 423.
23. Taylor, *A Secular Age*, 299.
24. Taylor, *A Secular Age*, 300.
25. Taylor, *A Secular Age*, 474–75.
26. Taylor, *A Secular Age*, 473.

huge influx of non-European immigrants to the United States so that it is no longer uncommon to have neighbors, coworkers, and classmates who practice Hinduism, Islam, Buddhism, and other non-Christian religions.[27] Other Western countries have also seen increased immigration from Eastern and Middle Eastern peoples. The weakening of Christian dominance in the West together with increased awareness of religious diversity and greater interaction with decent and respectable people who practice other faiths has given rise to a growing discomfort that there is only one true religion. In this much more diverse Western milieu, the Christian teaching that salvation is found only through Jesus Christ and that non-Christians will suffer eternal separation from God has driven more and more people to religious pluralism. The idea that many people living in the East may perish—people who are just like our kind Eastern neighbors and coworkers—without ever so much as hearing the gospel (and, presumably, lacking an opportunity at salvation) leads many to suspect that Christianity cannot possibly be the only true religion.

There may be no more prominent defender of religious pluralism in contemporary scholarship than the late philosopher and theologian John Hick. It is thus instructive to examine the shift that occurred in his view and how concern for the eternal fate of non-Christians drove him to religious pluralism. Hick once believed that salvation is found in Christ alone and that Christianity alone is true; however, he later abandoned orthodox Christianity and adopted the view that the supreme "Reality," which he terms the "Real," is unknowable. (Hick avoids using the term "God" in favor of more religiously neutral terminology like the "Real.") Moreover, he suggests that all world religions that promote a transformation from "self-centeredness" to "Reality-centeredness" are effective in achieving the ultimate religious goal—what Hick generically calls "salvation/liberation."[28] Hick came to regard all "Reality-centered" religions as equally effective "ways of salvation."[29] This salvation, of course, must not be understood in Christian terms. Indeed, since Hick's view is that we can know nothing about the Real, we clearly cannot know whether there are actual "sins" against the Real that require forgiveness.[30] In order to allow

27. Netland, *Encountering Religious Pluralism*, 9.
28. Hick, "A Pluralist View," 44.
29. Hick, *The Metaphor of God Incarnate*, 136.
30. Of course, one of the difficulties with Hick's view is that the unknowability of the Real seems to make the very concept of "Reality-centeredness" an arbitrary concept that cannot be defined.

that numerous mutually exclusive religions are equally valid paths to God, Hick felt compelled to reject the exclusivistic aspects of all religions.

What, then, is the catalyst that led Hick to abandon Christianity in favor of this pluralistic perspective? The key difficulty for Hick is that he began to regard the core Christian doctrine that salvation is found only in Christ as inconsistent with Christianity's conception of an all-loving God. Hick saw this doctrine as "a grave problem, for the eternal destiny of the large majority of the human race is at stake. The unacceptable aspect of the old exclusivist view that non-Christians are eternally lost, or eternally tormented in hell, is its dire implication concerning the nature of God."[31] In particular, Hick's unease with Christianity primarily boils down to the question raised by P_6 concerning the opportunity for the unevangelized to be saved. Hick explains:

> For understood literally the Son of God, God the Son, God-incarnate language implies that God can be adequately known and responded to only through Jesus; and the whole religious life of mankind, beyond the stream of Judaic-Christian faith is thus by implication excluded as lying outside the sphere of salvation. This implication did little positive harm so long as Christendom was a largely autonomous civilization with only relatively marginal interaction with the rest of mankind. But with the clash between the Christian and Muslim worlds, and then on an ever-broadening front with European colonization through the earth, the literal understanding of the mythological language of Christian discipleship has had a divisive effect upon the relations between that minority of human beings who live within the borders of the Christian tradition and that majority who live outside it and within other streams of religious life.
>
> Transposed into theological terms, the problem which has come to the surface in the encounter of Christianity with the other world religions is this: If Jesus was literally God incarnate, and if it is by his death alone that men can be saved, and by their response to him alone that they can appropriate that salvation, then the only doorway to eternal life is Christian faith. It would follow from this that the large majority of the human race so far have not been saved. But is it credible that the loving God and Father of all men has decreed that only those born within one particular thread of human history shall be saved?[32]

---

31. Hick, "Pluralist View," 45.

32. Hick, "Jesus and the World Religions," 179–80. Craig also cites this quote in: Craig, "No Other Name," 175–76.

As exemplified in this passage from Hick and as noted by Taylor and Netland, many have recognized how the widened cultural interaction resulting from the "colonial expansion of Europe during the last five centuries"[33] has shaken Christianity in the West as awareness has grown of "the existence of other nations, religions, and races outside of our own tiny enclave."[34] Hick's claim is that, in light of what we now know about the enormous religious diversity of mankind and the fact that most people who have ever lived have not been Christians, it is not "credible" that the omnibenevolent God described in the Bible would determine that eternal life hinges upon whether one happens to be born in a time and place where one has the opportunity to hear about Jesus and accept him as Savior. Hick recognizes that the Bible does teach that salvation is only through Christ, but he assumes that this means that salvation is not accessible to large portions of humanity. It is largely this fact that drives him away from Christianity and towards the pluralism that he finds more palatable.

Inclusivism versus Exclusivism: A Spectrum of Views among Christians

Yet is it true that, as P_6 states, anyone who never hears the gospel has no opportunity to accept God's forgiveness through Christ? Christians—including evangelical Christians—have adopted a full spectrum of views in response to this troubling question, from a strong form of Christian inclusivism to an unbending Christian exclusivism. Indeed, Daniel Strange contends that "there seems to be no consensus on what represents an 'historic orthodox' evangelical position" on this issue.[35] Let us explore the range of positions.

D. A. Carson offers a useful definition of Christian inclusivism that adheres to a typical understanding of the term, describing it as the view that "all who are saved are saved on account of the person and work of Jesus Christ, but that conscious faith in Jesus Christ is not absolutely necessary: some may be saved by him who never heard of him, for they may respond positively to the light they have received."[36] Carson likewise offers a standard definition of Christian exclusivism. Christian exclusivism

---

33. Mbogu, *Christology and Religious Pluralism*, 54.
34. Mbogu, *Christology and Religious Pluralism*, 56.
35. Strange, *The Possibility of Salvation Among the Unevangelized*, 21.
36. Carson, *The Gagging of God*, 278.

agrees with inclusivism that nobody is saved apart from the person and work of Jesus, but it requires that "only those who place their faith in the Christ of the Bible are saved."[37] So, in contrast to religious pluralists, both inclusivists and exclusivists accept the core Christian doctrine that the atoning work of Jesus is the one and only means by which anyone can be saved. The dividing line between inclusivists and exclusivists is simply the question of whether one must actually have explicit faith in Jesus as the object of one's faith.[38]

Within inclusivism there is a range of positions. Carson helpfully distinguishes between what he calls "hard" inclusivism and "soft" inclusivism. Soft inclusivists are very close to being exclusivists, but they at least allow the "bare possibility" that inclusivism is true. Soft inclusivists do not find that there is strong biblical evidence to affirm the truth of inclusivism, but they still allow that the biblical data does not necessarily preclude the possibility that the unevangelized may be saved by responding to the general revelation that they have. Hard inclusivists, by contrast, firmly hold that inclusivism is, in fact, biblically warranted and true. Hard inclusivists thus adopt a soteriological position that places "more emphasis on believing than on believing Christ."[39] As noted hard inclusivist John Sanders describes his position, Scripture decisively teaches that "the appropriation of salvific grace is mediated through general revelation and God's providential workings in human history." In this way, "the work of Jesus is ontologically necessary for salvation (no one would be saved without it) but not epistemologically necessary (one need not be aware of the work in order to benefit from it)."[40] Besides the distinction between hard and soft inclusivism, Craig and Moreland recognize another point of difference among inclusivists: inclusivism ranges from "narrow" to "broad."[41] Narrow inclusivists believe that few people will be saved apart from explicit

37. Carson, *The Gagging of God*, 278.

38. Some have defined exclusivism and inclusivism differently. For example, see: Netland, *Encountering Religious Pluralism*, 48–52. The definitions I provide for these terms, however, are common. In any case, regardless of the terminology, what is important is understanding the concepts that I am describing.

39. Carson, *The Gagging of God*, 279. Others have used different terms to describe the same concepts that Carson conveys. For example, Paul Helm uses the term "opaque exclusivism" and Terrence Tiessen uses the term "agnosticism" to describe the same position that Carson calls "soft inclusivism." See Tiessen, *Who Can Be Saved?*, 38–40. See also Helm, "Are They Few That Be Saved?," 278–79.

40. Sanders, *No Other Name*, 215.

41. Moreland and Craig, *Philosophical Foundations*, 630.

faith in Jesus. Broad inclusivists are optimistic that many will be saved in this way. One may adopt either a narrow or broad approach to inclusivism regardless of whether one is a soft or hard inclusivist.[42]

Along with the aforementioned Sanders, the late Clark Pinnock was perhaps the most outspoken evangelical theologian who advocated hard inclusivism in recent times. Indeed, more and more evangelical Protestants seem to be moving from the traditional exclusivist position and toward inclusivism.[43] Moreover, an even greater number of Roman Catholics have adopted hard inclusivism in light of the decision reached at Vatican II (1962—1965) concerning the unevangelized. The Roman Catholic Church, heavily influenced by the inclusivist ideas of Karl Rahner and continuing to move away from its long-held position that only those within the Roman Catholic Church are saved, declared at Vatican II: "Those who, through no fault of their own, do not know the Gospel of Christ or his Church, but who nevertheless seek God with a sincere heart, and, moved by grace, try in their actions to do his will as they know it through the dictates of their conscience—those too may achieve eternal salvation" (*Lumen Gentium* 16).[44]

Now it is evident that if inclusivism—a view which clearly enjoys a significant number of adherents in both Protestant and Catholic circles—is true, then P_6 is false; even the unevangelized would have the opportunity to respond to general revelation and be saved. Even if it were the case that very few of the unevangelized actually do choose to respond to general revelation and be saved (narrow inclusivism), the fact would remain that all people have an opportunity to be saved. Unfortunately, however, there does not seem to be strong biblical evidence for inclusivism. For that reason, in my judgment inclusivism should not be assumed.[45] I will proceed

---

42. Moreland and Craig, *Philosophical Foundations*, 633. For example, Craig and Moreland advocate hard inclusivism since they claim that the Bible provides positive evidence for inclusivism; yet they only advocate a very narrow inclusivism, as they believe certain passages give no hope that many people will be saved via general revelation. By comparison, Sanders and Pinnock are hard and broad inclusivists. It is also possible to be soft and broad as well as soft and narrow.

43. Nash, *Is Jesus the Only Savior?*, 106–7. The late Ronald Nash, an evangelical and a very ardent exclusivist, estimated in 1994 that the majority of evangelical leaders and at least a third of evangelical laypeople were inclusivists.

44. Flannery, *Vatican Council II*, 367–68. The Vatican II document *Lumen Gentium* is cited here.

45. If one were to offer a thorough case that inclusivism is not biblically supported, one would do well to consult the following helpful sources that critique prominent

to argue that P_6 is plausibly false even if exclusivism is accepted. Since P_6 is automatically false if inclusivism is true, attempting to offer a refutation of inclusivism is not necessary and will not be carried out here; rather, I will seek to show that P_6 should be rejected even if one assumes the truth of the more challenging position that Christian exclusivism is true.

After briefly examining some of the biblical data that supports exclusivism, I will contend that there are three biblical reasons for thinking that God has provided an opportunity for salvation to all people. I will then lay out an exclusivist position that, despite being exclusivist, still allows that all people have the opportunity to be saved. If this view is sustainable, it shows that one need not be driven to inclusivism out of an unwillingness to accept P_6.

Exclusivism: The Centrality of the Gospel in Scripture

Before proceeding with an assessment of P_6 under the assumption of exclusivism, it is useful to examine a sampling of the many biblical passages that underscore the elevated place of the gospel in the New Testament teaching concerning soteriology. The aim in doing this—for the reason given above—is not to offer here in this brief space a decisive refutation of inclusivism, as I will not in this section interact with any texts that are alleged to support inclusivism; rather, the aim is merely to highlight some of the texts that emphasize the centrality that the Scripture gives to the gospel in soteriology so that the value of defending an exclusivist position is clear.

In agreement with the exclusivist position, Scripture does indicate that a key component of saving faith is that faith is to be directed toward the correct object: Jesus Christ. Jesus himself highlights the importance of placing faith specifically in him, saying that whoever "believes in [me] is not judged; he who does not believe has been judged already, because

---

arguments given in favor of inclusivism: Carson, *The Gagging of God*, 285–314; Nash, *Is Jesus the Only Savior?*, chapters 8–9; Geivett and Phillips, "A Particularist View: An Evidentialist Approach," 239–43; Little, *The Revelation of God Among the Unevangelized*; and Kaiser, "Holy Pagans: Reality or Myth?," 249–84. Kaiser focuses on rejecting the supposed cases of "holy pagans." These are individuals in the Bible who are said to be saved apart from any sort of special revelation. Little also addresses this topic, arguing that even in the Old Testament it was necessary to have special revelation of God and be saved by grace through faith. He also argues that special revelation, which now must include the gospel about Christ, can be and has been brought to the unevangelized through a variety of means.

he has not believed in the name of the only begotten Son of God" (John 3:18). Jesus also gives the command to take the specific message of the gospel to all the people of the world and make disciples out of them (Matt 28:19–20).

Paul describes the gospel as "the power of God for salvation to everyone who believes, to the Jew first and also to the Greek. For in it the righteousness of God is revealed from faith to faith; as it is written, 'But the righteous man shall live by faith'" (Rom 1:16–17). Paul thus shows his high regard for the gospel by intimately tying saving faith to accepting the gospel and considering it "the power of God for salvation." Paul goes on in his letter to the Romans to emphasize the centrality of responding to the gospel, saying that the "word of faith" (Rom 10:8) he has been preaching is that "if you confess with your mouth Jesus as Lord, and believe in your heart that God raised Him from the dead, you will be saved; for with the heart a person believes, resulting in righteousness, and with the mouth he confesses, resulting in salvation" (Rom 10:9–10). So Paul describes saving faith as faith that is directed at Jesus Christ. He says that "whoever believes in [Jesus] will not be disappointed" (Rom 10:11) and "whoever will call on the name of the Lord will be saved" (Rom 10:13). Paul then emphasizes the importance of carrying out the commission Jesus gave in Matthew 28 by reminding his readers that one cannot respond to the gospel and be saved until one hears the gospel. Quoting Isaiah, Paul says: "How then will they call on Him in whom they have not believed? How will they believe in Him whom they have not heard? And how will they hear without a preacher? How will they preach unless they are sent? Just as it is written, 'How beautiful are the feet of those who bring good news of good things!'" (Rom 10:14–15). He concludes that "faith comes from hearing, and hearing by the word of Christ" (Rom 10:17).[46] Paul's message seems clear: One must call on the name of the Lord to be saved, and one cannot call on the Lord if one has not heard of the Lord. Now Paul's argument here does not exclude that one can hear the gospel from a source other than a human preacher in order to be saved, although he is undeniably emphasizing the importance of carrying

---

46. Despite Paul's subsequent reference in Romans 10:18 to Psalm 19:4, a passage which clearly describes how some knowledge of God is revealed to all people through God's general revelation, it would violate the context of Romans 10 to assume that this reference somehow advocates the idea that one can be saved by responding to general revelation apart from hearing the gospel. As Nash rightly argues, such an interpretation "would bring Paul's entire argument in that chapter to an abrupt halt." See Nash, *Is Jesus the Only Savior?*, 121.

out the call to evangelism. What it does do, however, is help us to see why the traditional Christian view has been that there is no assurance of salvation apart from somehow hearing the gospel and responding to it.

There are numerous examples of biblical texts that connect saving faith with hearing and accepting the gospel. The answer that is consistently given in the book of Acts to the question of what one must do to be saved involves an explicit response to the gospel (e.g., Acts 2:38-39; 11:14; 16:31). There is an information content in faith to which we are called to be "obedient" (Acts 6:7), for which we are to "contend" (Jude 3), and from which we must not "go astray" (1 Tim 6:21). Paul obviously cared very much about the specific content of the faith communicated in the one true gospel (Gal 1:6-9). Saving faith also is accompanied by the specific knowledge that one needs to repent of sins committed against God (Luke 13:3-5; Acts 2:38; 2 Cor 7:10). While I have not made an attempt to refute inclusivism, the above ought to at least indicate that there is a strong biblical basis for thinking that it is important—and may well be essential—for one to hear the gospel and respond to it in order to be saved. It is thus advantageous if one can refute P_6 despite assuming the truth of exclusivism.

Three Biblical Indicators Pointing Toward Universally Accessible Salvation

Let us now begin to critique P_6—which claims that anyone who never hears the gospel has no opportunity to accept God's forgiveness through Christ—under the assumption of exclusivism. Recall that rejecting P_6 will undercut the major objection we are examining, which centers upon the Christian God failing to provide universal access to salvation and aims to show that P_1 and P_2 are inconsistent. I will make the case that three biblical truths, especially when taken together, serve as strong indicators that God at least offers the opportunity for salvation to all. First, God wants all to be saved. Second, Jesus died for the sins of all people (i.e., there is unlimited atonement). Third, there is a desired response to general revelation implied by the facts that general revelation leaves everybody without excuse (Rom 1) and renders guilty those who ignore it (Rom 2). After examining each of the three biblical indicators that point toward God providing universal access to salvation, I will suggest a particular way that all people might have an opportunity for salvation even if Christian exclusivism is true and even though many do not hear the gospel. Let us begin with the first biblical indicator that God has provided all people with the opportunity to be saved.

First Biblical Indicator: God's Universal Salvific Will

The first biblical basis for thinking that God makes salvation universally accessible is that God wants all to be saved. Although, as previously argued, it may not be feasible for God to actualize a well-populated world of free persons in which all of them choose to be saved, Scripture affirms that God nevertheless genuinely desires that everyone would repent and accept his salvation. Paul declares that God "desires all men to be saved and to come to the knowledge of the truth" (1 Tim 2:4). Peter likewise proclaims, "The Lord is not slow about His promise, as some count slowness, but is patient toward you, not wishing for any to perish but for all to come to repentance" (2 Pet 3:9). God rhetorically asks, "Do I have any pleasure in the death of the wicked?" God insists that he prefers instead that the wicked would "turn from his ways and live" (Ezek 18:23).

Yet, if God truly does want all people to be saved, one would expect that God would provide all people with that opportunity. Inclusivist John Sanders contends that if God "has not provided an opportunity for all people to benefit from the redeeming work of the Son," then it would not seem that God does "truly love *all* people enough genuinely to desire that they be saved."[47] Sanders' point is valid. Clearly all people are lost sinners in need of God's salvation (Rom 3:23). In what sense could God, who sent his Son "to seek and to save that which was lost" (Luke 19:10), genuinely desire the salvation of every person if some people are not even afforded the opportunity for salvation?

Some do, however, dispute that God desires the salvation of all people. Christians with a Reformed soteriology, who hold that God sovereignly decrees to elect only some even though it is within God's power to save all, must wrestle with the aforementioned passages that indicate God's universal salvific will. Some Calvinists, such as David Engelsma, strongly reject that God does desire the salvation of all. Engelsma declares that the "Reformed doctrine of reprobation" is the "explicit denial that God loves all men, and conditionally offers them salvation. Reprobation asserts that God eternally hates some men; has immutably decreed

---

47. Sanders, *No Other Name*, 60.

their damnation; and has determined to withhold from them Christ, grace, faith, and salvation."[48] Yet it is difficult to see how one could deny God's desire for all people to be saved in light of the biblical passages cited above. Some Calvinists, in order to reconcile the fact that not every person is saved with a view of God's sovereignty that entails that God's desires are never thwarted, assert that these passages only indicate that God desires the salvation of *all sorts* of people rather than literally *all people*. Following the view of Augustine and Calvin, Ronald Nash contends that these passages indicating God's desire to save "all people" simply mean that God wants to save "all humans without distinction." In this way, Nash says that God desires the salvation of people from all nationalities and backgrounds, but not every individual person.[49] Many Reformed theologians attempt to show that these passages only teach that God desires the salvation of all of the elect.[50]

How, then, should these passages be interpreted? It is clear that the Greek word for "all" or "everybody" (πᾶς) that is used in 1 Timothy 2:4 (God "desires all men to be saved and to come to the knowledge of the truth") and 2 Peter 3:9 (God wants "all to come to repentance") is sometimes not intended to carry the idea of universal scope. This is evident from the context of such passages as Acts 21:28, in which the Jews accuse Paul of preaching about Jesus to "all" or "everyone" (πᾶς). The Jews clearly do not mean that Paul has literally preached to every single person in the world. Yet when Paul uses πᾶς to declare that "all" have sinned in Romans 3:23, Calvinists and non-Calvinists can agree—given the context of Romans 3:1–20 and the testimony of other Scriptures—that Paul is using this term with universal scope to affirm that all people are sinners in need of God's grace. So context must be our guide in determining the scope of this Greek word in each place that it is used.

When context is considered, the biblical texts cited in support of God's desire to save all people are best interpreted as referring to each and every person that God creates. Consider the context of 1 Timothy 2:4. Here, the connection with the prayers and petitions that Paul urges his audience to make "on behalf of all men" (the term for "all" is again πᾶς) in verse one of the chapter is key. There is no contextual basis for limiting the scope of "all men" in verse one to anything less than literally

---

48. Engelsma, *Hyper-Calvinism and the Call of the Gospel*, 58.
49. Nash, "Restrictivism," 124.
50. Wright, *No Place for Sovereignty*, 168–72.

all people. Some have claimed that the "specification of a subgroup" in verse two ("kings and all who are in authority") gives credibility to the interpretation that the "all" in verse one (as well as verse four) means "all *kinds* of people."[51] However, the problem with this view is that it does not fit with the flow of Paul's thought. As I. Howard Marshall points out, Paul actually maintains his focus on all people when he gives special attention to praying for those who are in authority in verse two. This is because, as Paul specifically says in verse two, these rulers are able to facilitate an environment in which mankind might live peaceful and godly lives. In this way, the call to prayer for rulers in verse two is not specifically for the salvation of the rulers as a subgroup; rather, this prayer is in support of Paul's command to pray for all people in verse one.[52] Paul continues his focus on all people in verses three and four by indicating that the idea of all men living a godly life pleases God, a state of affairs congruent with God's desire for all men to be saved. Paul continues the universal focus in verses five and six, emphasizing Christ's role as the sole mediator between mankind and God and stating that Christ "gave Himself as a ransom for all."[53] Thus, the context for the universal focus of "all" that is seen in these six verses is established in verse one and remains unbroken.

The other texts cited in support of God's universal salvific will also hold up well when their contexts are scrutinized. For example, 2 Peter 3:9 is set within the context of the Apostle Peter emphasizing God's patience in holding off on God's certain judgment of the world. Peter says that God's delay of judgment should not be misinterpreted as "slowness"; rather, the Lord's return is delayed because God is "patient with you" and is "not wishing for any to perish but for all to come to repentance." Some Reformed commentators have interpreted the "you" (which is the second person plural personal pronoun) in this verse as referring only to those who are already saved, since Peter addresses the letter to "those who have received a faith of the same kind as ours" (2 Pet 1:1). The references to "any" and "all" in this passage are then interpreted as only referring to those who are saved. The problem, however, is that it makes no sense "to say that God wants his saved ones to repent so they can be saved." Thus, there is no good reason to think that the context implies that a restriction

---

51. Knight, *The Pastoral Epistles*, 115.

52. Marshall, "Universal Grace and Atonement in the Pastoral Epistles," 61–63.

53. This latter statement supports the idea of unlimited atonement, a topic which will be handled next.

should be placed on the "any" (those whom God does not want to perish) or on the "all" (those whom God wants to repent).[54]

The strength of the arguments in favor of God's universal salvific will is also evidenced by the fact that they are even accepted by some Reformed theologians. John Piper, for example, embraces the biblical data affirming God's universal salvific will. Piper, however, claims that this truth is compatible with the Calvinist doctrine that God unconditionally chooses to elect only certain people to salvation even though it is fully within God's power to save everyone.[55] If he is able to show this is true and square Reformed soteriology with God's universal salvific will, then my contention that God's universal salvific will implies that God provides all people with an opportunity to be saved would be falsified. Piper's argument, however, is unconvincing.

Piper's argument involves God having two wills with regard to salvation. God sincerely wills for all to be saved, but this will is overruled by God's will to demonstrate his "glory in wrath and mercy (Rom 9:22–23) and the humbling of man so that he enjoys giving all credit to God for his salvation (1 Cor 1:29)."[56] Given the Reformed position that God is solely responsible for determining who is elect and that one's election or reprobation is not based upon the qualities of that individual (election is unconditional), Piper allows that universalism would be the case if God chose to elect everyone. Since universalism is not the case and God chooses that some will not be elect, the explanation that Piper gives for this, as seen in the previous quotation, is that God's will to show his holy wrath by not providing the gift of faith to the reprobate trumps his sincere will for all to be saved. As much as God would like to opt for universalism, Piper thinks that God's greater will is to demonstrate his righteous judgment of sin by condemning some individuals so that his glory is revealed to the elect and the reprobate. Nevertheless, in contrast to Engelsma, Piper holds that God does truly love the reprobate and sincerely wills their salvation.

Piper attempts to reinforce his point by offering an analogy that compares God's decision to condemn those God loves to a decision that George Washington once made to execute for treason an officer for which Washington had sincere love and compassion. Washington's will

54. Black and Black, *The College Press NIV Commentary*, 216.
55. Piper, "Are There Two Wills in God?," 107.
56. Piper, "Are There Two Wills in God?," 124.

to have compassion on the criminal was trumped by his will to carry out the "superior judgments" of "wisdom, duty, patriotism, and moral indignation."[57] Jerry Walls and Joseph Dongell, however, point out a significant problem with Piper's view, which is ironically made more obvious by his analogy. The problem is that, according to the Reformed perspective, it is within God's power to save any sinner. Although Washington lacked the power to ensure that the guilty officer could have avoided his fate, Calvinism requires that God has the power to "act on any sinner in such a way that the sinner will not persist in sin and unbelief."[58] If Washington had the ability to ensure that no one has to be condemned for his or her transgressions, then it would be problematic to claim that Washington truly had compassion and love for the officer he executed. While it is true that God's justice does not obligate God to save anyone, God's love and compassion (or at least love and compassion that rise to the level of omnibenevolence) do seem to be inadequate if God chooses not to save everyone when it is within his power to do so. As I have argued previously, given the (non-Calvinist) position that humans have the libertarian freedom to choose God's salvation or reject it of their own accord, it is possible that even an omnipotent God cannot ensure universal salvation in a well-populated world of free creatures. This accounts well for God truly having a universal salvific will despite the fact that there is not universal salvation. However, since Calvinism denies that libertarian human free will is involved in any human's acceptance of God's gracious offer of salvation and places election entirely within God's hands so that God could have saved all had he chosen to do so, it becomes inconsistent for Calvinists also to affirm that God truly desires the salvation of all people. Indeed, Engelsma derides any attempt made by fellow Calvinists to reconcile God's universal salvific will with unconditional election, flatly declaring this position "a fraud."[59]

Regarding the idea that God gains glory by determining that the reprobate will be lost so that God's wrath is carried out against them when God could just as easily have saved them, Walls and David Baggett argue that on this view "there is no intelligible sense in which God loves those who are lost, nor is there any recognizable sense in which he is

---

57. Piper, "Are There Two Wills in God?," 128.

58. Walls and Dongell, *Why I Am Not a Calvinist*, 176.

59. Engelsma, *Hyper-Calvinism and the Call of the Gospel*, 41. In the next chapter we will see how Molinism does justice to God's sovereignty in election while affirming that humans have libertarian freedom.

good to them." They contend that a God who would act in this way is not good in any way that is recognizable by humans, and they find it unacceptable that the goodness of God should be unrecognizable to us if it is to be meaningful at all for us to regard God as "good." Moreover, besides the fact that it seems impossible on this view to affirm God's goodness and love for the lost, Baggett and Walls also rightly find that the idea of God solely determining whether each human will accept Christ and his offer of salvation fails to do justice to any reasonable view of our love for God. If God's love and grace are irresistible for the elect and the reprobate lack the freedom to accept God's love and grace, then God's election seems to cash out to a sort of "divine love potion." This is problematic because genuine love seemingly must be a "two-way relationship" that is freely entered into by both parties.[60] Given a reasonable understanding of "goodness" and "love," it does not seem plausible that God is either good or loving on the view Piper proposes. While some biblical teachings may be hard (but not impossible) to square with our moral sense, Baggett and Walls seem to be correct in finding it impossible to square our moral sensibilities with the idea that Piper's view upholds God's perfect goodness and love and results in God genuinely gaining glory for God's self.[61]

In addition, Piper's appeal to Romans 9 (which is often viewed as a proof text for Reformed soteriology) in the quotation above to argue that God gains "glory in wrath and mercy" does not justify his view that God has an overriding will to damn some. Jack Cottrell offers an insightful interpretation of Romans 9 in which he makes a strong case that Paul is not aiming to teach unconditional election to salvation or reprobation. Cottrell contends that Paul distinguishes between *God's unconditional election to service* (i.e., God unconditionally chooses to use individuals and entire nations to serve in various roles that fulfill his sovereign plans) and *God's conditional election to salvation* (i.e., salvation is always conditional upon humans accepting the grace God offers). While it takes us too far afield to exegete in detail Romans 9–11 (which Cottrell rightly sees as a unit), it is worth briefly summarizing Cottrell's view. He recognizes that Romans 9:1–6 is a prologue to this three-chapter unit. This prologue introduces the contrast between national Israel (those who are ethnically Jewish) and spiritual Israel (those who accept God's grace and are saved), indicating that not all who are in the former are in the latter. Romans 9

60. Baggett and Walls, *Good God*, 71.
61. Baggett and Walls, *Good God*, 72–73.

aims to show that God is sovereign and can choose to elect people and nations unconditionally to serve particular roles in the divine plan wholly apart from whether those individuals will ultimately be saved. Paul is highlighting that God is not unfair in allowing some individuals within national Israel to be lost—the reality that Paul mournfully introduces in the prologue. Cottrell contends that the election described in Romans 9:7–18 has to do with unconditional election to service and not election to salvation; it is 9:19—10:21 that discusses salvation, and salvation is conditional. Finally, 11:1–32 stresses that those who are ethnically Jewish can be saved.[62] In addition to this interpretation being plausible, it is also attractive given: the moral challenges faced by double predestination; the clear biblical teachings we have noted concerning God's sincere universal salvific will; and the difficulty of reconciling God's universal salvific will with double predestination. God is sovereign and has good reasons for creating the lost, but it seems biblically and morally important to affirm that the lost freely choose to reject God's offer of salvation and that God genuinely desires their salvation (even though it is plausibly not feasible to actualize a world in which all are freely saved).

In the final analysis, it seems reasonable to agree with Piper over Engelsma that Scripture affirms God's universal salvific will, but it seems most reasonable to agree with Engelsma over Piper that God's universal salvific will is inconsistent with God withholding salvation from some

---

62. For the details of Cottrell's exegesis, see "Part Four" (which covers Rom 9:1—11:36) in Cottrell, *Romans*. Concerning Romans 9:7–18, which Cottrell argues has to do with unconditional election to service and not election to salvation, it is worth making a couple of additional points. Paul's comments concerning Jacob and Esau make no statement about the salvation of Jacob and Esau or about the salvation of anyone else. Paul is commenting on God's sovereign choice that Jacob's descendants would be God's chosen people and not Esau's and that this was chosen by God before the brothers were born. With regard to Pharaoh, Paul's focus is again not on the divine election or reprobation of Pharaoh. His focus is on God's sovereign choice to raise up Pharaoh and place him into power so that God's name would be known throughout the earth. God showed favor to Pharaoh by giving him power but chose to harden Pharaoh to achieve divine purposes. The focus here is not on soteriology. Moreover, the passage does not even say anything about whether Pharaoh had libertarian freedom when God hardened him in this way. The Scriptures are clear that Pharaoh stubbornly hardened his own heart (Exod 7:14; 8:15, 32; 9:34). There is also a very real sense in which God actively hardened Pharaoh's heart (Exod 9:32; 10:1, 20, 27; 11:10), but this is compatible with Pharaoh freely hardening his own heart. God knew that Pharaoh would stubbornly (and freely) harden his own heart if God continually brought the plagues on Egypt; thus, by bringing the plagues God ensured that Pharaoh's heart would be hardened and that God's objectives would be achieved through Pharaoh.

when God could have saved all. If God withholds salvation from some when God just as easily could have saved them, this would contradict the biblical teaching that God truly desires all to be saved. If God genuinely has a universal salvific will and humans have a role in freely choosing to accept or reject the grace that God offers as he works to draw us to him, then this seems to imply that God would provide at least an opportunity for salvation to every person. The divine will for all to be saved seems to serve as one strong indicator that in some way God has made salvation accessible to all.

Second Biblical Indicator: Unlimited Atonement

A second biblical basis for thinking that God makes the opportunity for salvation universally accessible is that the benefits of Christ's atoning death are offered to all people. If the previous contention that Scripture affirms God's universal salvific will is successful, then it seems to follow that the grace and forgiveness that God offers via Christ's atoning sacrifice would be made available for anyone. It would make little sense for God to desire that all people would choose to be saved if the only gate God provides for salvation is not intended for some people. As it turns out, the Bible does support the doctrine of unlimited atonement. Let us now survey some of the key evidence for this doctrine.

It is useful to begin by returning to Paul's comments in 1 Timothy. I have argued that the context of the first four verses of the second chapter supports interpreting "all" in the universal sense. We also saw that Paul continues his line of thinking in the subsequent verses. After urging his audience to pray for all people and confirming God's desire for all to be saved, Paul states in verses five and six that Christ, the only mediator between mankind and God, "gave Himself as a ransom for all." If my argument concerning the interpretation of the first four verses is correct, then it makes no sense to abandon the universal sense of "all" in verse six. This is especially true in light of Paul's later statement in the same epistle that God "is the Savior of all men, especially of believers" (1 Tim 4:10). Here, Paul specifically differentiates "believers" from "all men." This passage provides an especially impressive case for unlimited atonement because, as Millard Erickson says, it shows that "the Savior has done something for all persons, though it is less in degree than what he has done for those who believe."⁶³ While Christ is Savior for all people in some sense (plausibly in the sense that anyone can accept the salvation he offers), it is only believers who will be saved.

Although no Scripture explicitly teaches that Christ died only for the elect and not for others, the above evidence from 1 Timothy only scratches the surface of the numerous passages that do indicate that Christ died for all people. John says: "My little children, I am writing these things to you so that you may not sin. And if anyone sins, we have an Advocate with the Father, Jesus Christ the righteous; and He Himself is the propitiation for our sins; and not for ours only, but also for those of the whole world" (1 John 2:1–2). Jesus thus stands as the propitiation for the sins of all people, though it is true that not all will accept this gift. Peter says: "But false prophets also arose among the people, just as there will also be false teachers among you, who will secretly introduce destructive heresies, even denying the Master who bought them, bringing swift destruction upon themselves" (2 Pet 2:1–2). Here Peter states that the false teachers bring destruction on themselves by denying Jesus, the "Master who bought them." Even though they reject Christ and are lost, Christ nevertheless paid for their sins. In one of the most celebrated Old Testament prophecies, Isaiah says concerning Christ that "all of us like sheep have gone astray, each of us has turned to his own way; but the Lord has caused the iniquity of us all to fall on Him" (Isa 53:6). Paul is in agreement with Isaiah that even though "all have sinned and fall short of the glory of God" (Rom 3:23), "Christ died for the ungodly" (Rom 5:6). Since every person has gone astray and is ungodly, Christ's death must be able to cover the sins of all men. Finally, when Paul says that "the grace of God has appeared, bringing salvation to all men" (Tit 2:11), he clearly is not advocating a doctrine of universal salvation; rather, Paul is simply agreeing with Jesus' famous statement that "whoever believes in Him shall not perish, but have eternal life" (John 3:16). Christ offers salvation to all men, and only those who believe in him accept that offer and are saved.⁶⁴

Those who advocate limited atonement attempt to reject the above-mentioned Scriptures by appealing to other passages that they believe imply that Christ died only for the elect. For example, it is said that Jesus

---

63. Erickson, *Christian Theology*, 834.

64. Erickson, *Christian Theology*, 829–32. Many of the passages I referenced are identified by Erickson in these pages. I have only provided a brief survey of key texts, but Erickson provides a more detailed assessment.

"will save *His people* from their sins" (Matt 1:21). Paul says that Christ "loved *the Church* and gave Himself up for her" (Eph 5:25). In evaluating such passages, Scripture must be used to interpret Scripture. Robert Lightner nicely clarifies why such purportedly limiting passages should not govern our understanding of those passages that affirm unlimited atonement. Lightner says:

> The task of harmonizing those various Scriptures poses a far greater problem for those who hold to a limited atonement than it does to those who hold to an unlimited position. Those who hold to an unlimited atonement recognize that some Scriptures emphasize the fact that Christ died for the elect, for the church, and for individual believers. However, they point out that when those verses single out a specific group they do not do so to the exclusion of any who are outside that group since dozens of other passages include them. The 'limited' passages are just emphasizing one aspect of a larger truth. In contrast, those who hold to a limited atonement have a far more difficult time explaining away the 'unlimited' passages.[65]

We have now seen that Scripture supports God's universal salvific will and indicates that Christ died for all of mankind. These two facts point powerfully to the likelihood that God would provide all people with sufficient grace such that each and every human being has the opportunity to be saved. After all, the concept of unlimited atonement would prove quite hollow if the billions of people who do not hear the gospel have no opportunity to be saved. As Stuart Hackett puts it:

> If every human being in all times and ages has been objectively provided for through the unique redemption in Jesus, and if this provision is in fact intended by God for every such human being, then it must be possible for every human individual to become personally eligible to receive that provision—regardless of his historical, cultural, or personal circumstances and situation.[66]

Third Biblical Indicator: General Revelation

The third and final biblical basis that I will highlight in support of the universal opportunity for salvation is the fact that God wants mankind

---

65. Lightner, "For Whom Did Christ Die?," 166.
66. Hackett, *The Reconstruction of the Christian Revelation Claim*, 244.

to recognize and properly respond to general revelation. In accord with exclusivism, I will not presume that this desired response itself constitutes saving faith. Nevertheless, the fact that there is a desired response to general revelation implies that God seems to be working to draw all people in general to God's self.

Paul is clear that no person is "without excuse" when it comes to basic knowledge that God has revealed about God's self. Ever since "the creation of the world," Paul says that God's "invisible attributes, His eternal power and divine nature, have been clearly seen, being understood through what has been made" (Rom 1:20). Through God's creation, God has made these things about himself "evident" to people at large (Rom 1:19).[67] Nevertheless, despite this knowledge of God, the propensity of mankind has been to reject what God has revealed and turn to idolatry, acting wickedly and worshipping God's creations rather than God himself (Rom 1:21–32). Paul also emphasizes that "there is no partiality with God" (Rom 2:11) because "all who sin under the Law will be judged by the Law" and even those who have not received God's special revelation ("all who have sinned without the Law") will also "perish without the Law" (Rom 2:12). In this way, Paul reaffirms that everybody is without excuse—even the "Gentiles who do not have the Law" will be judged because they, too, have the law that is "written in their hearts" (Rom 2:14–15). God's revelation that is found in nature (Rom 1) and in our own consciences (Rom 2) brings some measure of knowledge about God and his moral requirements to the unevangelized, and the rejection of this knowledge makes them guilty of sin. Paul again makes the point as strongly as he can that all people are sinners and unrighteous before God, quoting a variety of Old Testament Scriptures (Rom 3:10–18). Although the bad news is that nobody will be made right with God "by the works of the Law" (Rom 3:20), Paul finally reveals the good news that "now apart from the Law the righteousness of God has been manifested, being witnessed by the Law and the Prophets, even the righteousness of God through faith in Jesus Christ for all those who believe" (Rom 3:21–22).

While it is clear that God's revelation via nature and conscience leaves the unevangelized guilty of sin when they inevitably violate this law, how do the unevangelized take advantage of Paul's good news that

---

67. David also famously proclaims that "the heavens are telling of the glory of God, and their expanse is declaring the work of His hands" (Ps 19:1). Like Paul, David declares that the knowledge of God that is revealed via creation "has gone out through all the earth" (Ps 19:4).

righteousness is found through faith in Christ? This conundrum has led inclusivists to conclude that the unevangelized must be able to attain salvation by responding to general revelation. After all, what other revelation do they have? Inclusivist Clark Pinnock finds it unacceptable that rejecting general revelation brings God's condemnation while accepting it is insufficient for salvation. Pinnock maintains that such a state of affairs

> implies that God reveals himself to all people, not to help them, but to make their condemnation more severe. It is easy to see why Barth took the logical step of denying that general revelation exists. What kind of God is it who would reveal himself in order to worsen the condition of sinners and make their plight more hopeless?[68]

Pinnock is surely correct that God's sole purpose in revealing himself to all people through nature and conscience is not to ensure their condemnation. We have seen that: God truly desires for all to be saved; Christ died for the sins of all people; and rejecting what God reveals about himself and his moral law via general revelation brings God's judgment even on the unevangelized. The strong implication of these biblical truths is that God desires some sort of a positive response from all humans to general revelation in which they are drawn to God. If God wants all to be saved and if God has made a pathway through Christ for all to be saved and reveals important truths about himself and sin to people at large through general revelation, then it seems likely that God did not merely provide general revelation to condemn people. Let us then consider whether there is a biblically-consistent way that exclusivism can be true and yet all people may have an opportunity to be saved. I will examine a possible way that this could work, and this possibility also shows how general revelation may have a positive purpose and not merely a condemnatory one.

How Might the Unevangelized Have an Opportunity to be Saved on Exclusivism?

Recall that P_6 states that anyone who never hears the gospel has no opportunity to accept God's forgiveness through Christ. The proponent of this premise assumes that the unevangelized, because they *never do*

---

68. Pinnock, "An Inclusivist View," 117.

hear the gospel, *never had the opportunity* to hear the gospel and accept Christ. This, however, need not be the case even if exclusivism is true. Although my own preferred view concerning how God might provide an opportunity for salvation to all people—including those who never hear the gospel—on the assumption of the truth of exclusivism will not be fleshed out until the fourth chapter when I offer my own theodicy, it is useful for now to examine one possible way of showing how this can be done. I explain in the fourth chapter why I opt for a more nuanced perspective than this approach—one that agrees that God uses general revelation to prepare the hearts of unbelievers, including the unevangelized, but does not require that one must respond in a certain way to general revelation in order to be brought the gospel. But the view offered at present is a widely-held view among Christian exclusivists and serves our purposes for now by at least showing why P_6 is not necessarily true even on exclusivism.

A view held by a number of exclusivists is that God will send the gospel to those unevangelized persons who respond appropriately to the general revelation that they do have. This view at least goes back to the middle ages and Thomas Aquinas,[69] and it has continued to be defended by such scholars as Norman Geisler, Robert Lightner, Christopher Little, and Robertson McQuilken.[70] The advantage of this view is that it makes sense of how the three aforementioned biblical indicators actually do point toward God giving all people an opportunity to be saved, since any unevangelized person has the opportunity to respond in faith to the general revelation that he has; moreover, this view upholds the strong biblical evidence for exclusivism because it requires that one must respond to the gospel (and not merely general revelation) to be saved. We will now see that this view also seems to be at least consistent with Scripture.[71]

---

69. Sanders, *No Other Name*, 156–62. Sanders provides a useful discussion of how Aquinas supported this view, and he identifies various proponents of the view from the Middle Ages through the Reformation.

70. A helpful list of many contemporary advocates of this view is given in Sanders, *No Other Name*, 163.

71. Other theories have been proposed that also seek to reconcile the universal opportunity for salvation with exclusivism. Some postulate that God gives the unevangelized a postmortem opportunity to accept Christ; others speculate that God somehow affords the unevangelized the opportunity to make a decision for Christ in the very last moment of their life prior to death. The biblical support for the first theory is weak (relying heavily on the controversial passage 1 Peter 3:18–22), and this theory trivializes the relevance of this life. So far as I can see, there is no evidence for

A key biblical principle that is consistent with this view is that God does not turn away from those who respond to God in faith. The writer of Hebrews declares that "he who comes to God must believe that He is and that He is a rewarder of those who seek Him" (Heb 11:6). If one who has never heard the gospel realizes, as Paul says one should, that there must be an incredibly wise and powerful Being responsible for our existence and that one is obligated to honor the moral law that is written in one's heart, and this person pursues righteousness and asks God to reveal God's truth to her, then God will surely not turn a deaf ear to such a person. David describes God's response to those who cry out to God by saying, "The Lord is righteous in all His ways and kind in all His deeds. The Lord is near to all who call upon Him, to all who call upon Him in truth. He will fulfill the desire of those who fear Him; He will also hear their cry and will save them" (Ps 145:17–19). Jesus says those who ask, seek, and knock will not be denied by the Lord. When a son asks his father for food, the father does not give the son a rock or a snake (Matt 7:7–10). Jesus concludes that if sinful humans "know how to give good gifts to [their] children, how much more will your Father who is in heaven give what is good to those who ask Him" (Matt 7:11). As Paul teaches in the first two chapters of Romans, the Holy Spirit uses general revelation to reveal certain truths, and a key role of the Holy Spirit is to "convict the world concerning sin and righteousness and judgment" (John 16:8). So, in light of the biblical principle that God does not turn away from those who respond to him in faith, it seems plausible that God would ensure that those who respond in faith to what revelation they have will receive the special revelation they need for saving faith.

Scripture also seems to include examples of God intervening at times to ensure that special revelation is given to those who lack it when they are responding in faith to the revelation that they do have. The book of Acts records the story of Cornelius, a Gentile centurion in the Roman army who was aware of the Jewish Scriptures but had not been reached with the gospel. Cornelius is described as "a devout man and one who feared God with all his household, and gave many alms to the Jewish people and prayed to God continually" (Acts 10:2). Although Cornelius earnestly sought God, he was not a saved believer. Yet God provided Cornelius with an angelic vision in which he is told that his "prayers and alms have ascended as a memorial before God" and Cornelius is given

---

the second theory. Neither theory will be defended here.

instructions for contacting the Apostle Peter. At this point, it is evident that Cornelius had not yet been saved because the angel told Cornelius that Peter will arrive and "will speak words to you by which you will be saved, you and all your household" (Acts 11:14). Peter was also given a vision to convince him that he is to go with the men sent by Cornelius and preach the gospel. In this way, God used visions and angelic messengers to orchestrate an interaction in which a devout man who responded in faith to God was delivered the gospel message so that he could accept it and be saved. As exemplified in the Cornelius account, Christopher Little rightly argues that there are many "modalities" that God can use to deliver the gospel. God is not limited to spreading the gospel solely through human messengers and the distribution of God's written Word. There is no reason that God cannot make use of visions, angels, and dreams today. God may even choose to use miraculous events, as seen when God called Paul on the Damascus road (Acts 9) and then transmitted the gospel to Paul "not according to man" but "through a revelation of Jesus Christ" (Gal 1:11–12).[72]

Scripture reveals other examples of God directing the gospel to seekers in various ways. In the account of Philip witnessing to the Ethiopian eunuch, the eunuch was a God-fearing person who "had come to Jerusalem to worship" (Acts 8:27) and was pondering the meaning of Isaiah's prophecy about Jesus as he returned home (Acts 8:32–34). God did not allow the eunuch to leave without hearing the message. Via an angelic message, God directed Philip to the eunuch (Acts 8:26) and Philip spoke the gospel to him, culminating in his decision to accept Christ and be baptized (Acts 8:35–39). Similarly, in Paul's second missionary journey recorded in the book of Acts, God intervened in directing Paul so that he would preach the gospel in Macedonia. Paul and his companions tried to enter Bithynia, but "the Spirit of Jesus did not permit them" to do so (Acts 16:7). Instead, they continued west to Troas where Paul received a vision of a man from Macedonia who pleaded with Paul to "come over to Macedonia and help us" (Acts 16:9). Paul thus preached the gospel in Macedonia instead of following his original plans. This vision may or may not have involved Paul seeing an actual man from Macedonian who was seeking God's truth, but at the very least this account shows that God is involved in directing the gospel to certain individuals and that part of

---

72. Little, *The Revelation of God Among the Unevangelized*, 116–30.

the basis for his directing the gospel to those individuals seems to be their openness to responding to the gospel.[73]

Although there is a biblical basis for thinking that God has a history of bringing the gospel to those who respond in faith to the revelation that they have, one might claim that we would see much more evidence of this if God does this in every case still today. Should there not be widespread stories of people who have come to Christian faith as a consequence of seeing visions or receiving an angelic message? In response to this concern, several points should be noted. First, there *are* numerous modern accounts of God using such unconventional means to bring the gospel to people.[74] Such anecdotal evidence is consistent with the above biblical accounts. Second, although it is impossible to know the precise frequency with which such occurrences take place, there is no reason to think they should be extremely widespread. As we have seen, the testimony of Scripture is that most people do not seek God. The general tendency of mankind is to reject God's general revelation, turning away from the light that they have (Rom 1—3). Third, it could be that God rarely provides a supernatural revelation by way of visions or angels. We have seen that God, in his providence, can simply ensure that human messengers carry the gospel to those who are seeking him. Christians are bringing the gospel to new places all the time, and God is undoubtedly involved in providentially directing the places it reaches—even in subtle ways. In addition, as the world population has exploded in the last century, mankind's technological capabilities have also leaped forward. The world population is approximately four times larger today than at the turn of the twentieth century,[75] and it is interesting that this population jump has corresponded with the emergence of electronic communication. Norman Geisler points out how recent technologies such as radio, television, and the internet help to facilitate the spread of the gospel.[76]

---

73. God is no doubt continually intervening to direct the spread of the gospel in countless ways that may be quite subtle. For example, I myself was once part of a short-term mission team that was scheduled to go to Zimbabwe before certain last-minute events forced us to change our plans and go to Haiti instead.

74. See the following for accounts of God using visions, dreams, or other unconventional means to deliver the gospel to people: Selby, *Persian Springs*; Greenlee, *From the Straight Path to the Narrow Way*; Brown, "Brother Jacob and Master Isaac," 41–42; Strong, *Outlines of Systematic Theology*, 3:844; and Keener, *Miracles*, 1:273 fn 52, 1:289 fn 168, and 2:878–79 fn 69–73.

75. Barrett and Johnson, *World Christian Trends*, 24.

76. Geisler, *Baker Encyclopedia of Apologetics*, 306.

The internet, in particular, continually makes the world a smaller place, and God certainly uses it to bring his truth to those who are seeking it. There is simply no way to prove that God is not delivering the gospel to those who have been made ready to respond to it.

We have thus seen that the universal opportunity for salvation is at least possible on Christian exclusivism. This perspective is consistent with the character of God and God's genuine desire for all to be saved; furthermore, it legitimizes the concept of unlimited atonement while remaining faithful to the biblical evidence for exclusivism. We may thus conclude that P_6 should be rejected on the grounds that it is not necessarily true and is not required by orthodox biblical theism. Consequently, the version of the soteriological POE that attempts to reveal a contradiction between God's attributes and the biblical teaching on soteriology on the presumption that some people lack an opportunity to be saved fails and should be rejected.

The Remaining Objection: God's Omnibenevolence and the Contingently Lost

At this point two key arguments in favor of the soteriological POE have been handled. First, we have seen that, due to counterfactual truths about free creaturely choices, it may be the case that it is not feasible for God to create a well-populated world of free persons in which everyone freely chooses to be saved. Thus, the objection that God should have created a world in which all people freely choose to be saved lacks force. Second, it has been shown that Christian exclusivism is compatible with universally accessible salvation and that Scripture seems to indicate in multiple ways that God would provide an opportunity for all to be saved. Thus, the objection that God has not given all people an opportunity at salvation is unconvincing. Neither of these arguments provides any compelling reason to believe that there is a conflict between P_1 (God's possession of omniscience, omnipotence, and omnibenevolence) and P_2 (some persons not accepting forgiveness through Christ and being lost), and such a conflict must be identified if the soteriological POE is to succeed. Nevertheless, one important difficulty remains. Craig describes the nature of this residual problem well, and it is worth quoting him at length:

> If God is all-knowing, then presumably he knew the conditions under which people would freely place their faith in Christ for

salvation and those under which they would not. But then a very difficult question arises: why does God not bring the gospel to people who he knows *would* accept it if they heard it, even though they reject the general revelation that they do have? Imagine, for example, a Native American—let us call him Walking Bear—who lived prior to the arrival of Christian missionaries. Suppose Walking Bear sees from the order and beauty of nature around him that a Creator of the universe exists and that he senses in his heart the demands of God's moral law implanted there. Unfortunately, like those described by Paul in Romans 1, Walking Bear chooses to spurn the Creator and to ignore the demands of the moral law, plunging himself into spiritism and immorality. Thus suppressing the knowledge of God and flouting his moral law, Walking Bear stands under God's just condemnation and is destined for hell. But suppose that if only Walking Bear were to hear the gospel, if only the Christian missionaries had come earlier, then he would have believed in the gospel and been saved. His damnation thus appears to be the result of bad luck; through no fault of his own he was born at the wrong place or time in history; his salvation or damnation thus seems to be the result of historical and geographical accident. Granted that his condemnation is not *unjust* (since he has freely spurned God's sufficient grace for salvation), nonetheless is it not *unloving* of God to condemn him? Would not an all-loving God have given him the same advantage that is enjoyed by that lucky individual who lives at a place and time such that he hears the gospel?[77]

This difficulty can be formalized as follows. We have seen that the soteriological POE claims that there is an inconsistency between the statements: P_1 God possesses the attributes of omniscience, omnipotence, and omnibenevolence; and P_2 Some persons do not accept the forgiveness that is available via receiving Christ and are thus damned.[78] The following additional premises may be added to P_1 and P_2 in order to reveal the alleged contradiction:

P_8. God will necessarily not allow persons to exist who are lost in their actual circumstances but who would have been saved if placed into different circumstances.[79]

77. Craig, "Politically Incorrect Salvation," 89–90.

78. See Table 1.1 at the end of the chapter for a summary of all the premises that are introduced in this chapter.

79. If one denies that God could have middle knowledge so that God cannot know for sure whether any of the lost would have been saved if placed into different

P_9. Some persons who freely reject the grace that God offers them in their actual circumstances and are lost would have freely accepted God's grace and been saved in different circumstances.

The truth of P_8 is considered to be entailed by God's omnipotence, omnibenevolence, and omniscience in P_1. It may be that God's omniscience includes having knowledge logically prior to creating the world of the possible circumstances under which each person that God would create would accept his grace through faith in Christ. (This is the view that God has middle knowledge, a view that I will accept and defend in the next chapter.) If God has this knowledge, then it may be claimed that God's omnipotence requires that he is able to bring it about that any person who God knows would freely choose to be saved in some set of circumstances is placed into such circumstances and is thus saved. Moreover, it is assumed that God's omnibenevolence requires that he would want to do this so that nobody is, as Craig puts it, lost due to "historical and geographical accident." Since God is maximally loving and beneficent and desires that all people choose to be saved, the assumption is that God would necessarily want to ensure that nobody is lost who would freely choose to be saved in some possible circumstances. Nevertheless, even if God does not have middle knowledge so that he cannot know *for sure* whether any of the lost would have been saved if placed into different circumstances, one could still argue for the truth of P_8. If God lacks middle knowledge, he still has overwhelming reason to believe that many of the unevangelized are contingently lost (e.g., it is overwhelmingly likely that at least some of the billions of people who never hear the gospel would have responded to it if they heard it). While I will argue in the next chapter that God does have middle knowledge, one could still argue that an omnibenevolent and omnipotent God who lacks middle knowledge should at least give everyone the chance to hear the gospel.

The truth of P_9 is considered to be entailed by P_2. Given that P_2 states that those who never place faith in Christ are lost, one may contend that P_9 is unavoidable. Again, one crucial change in circumstances that could plausibly lead to at least one person who is actually lost instead choosing to be saved is that those who are unevangelized could have been presented

---

circumstances, P_8 could instead be stated: "God will necessarily not allow persons to exist who are lost in their actual circumstances but who would have had *a significantly better opportunity to be saved* if placed into different circumstances." For example, as explained below, one could argue that an omnibenevolent and omnipotent God should at least give those who are unevangelized the chance to hear and respond to the gospel.

with the gospel. It is clear that many people who never turned to God on the basis of general revelation eventually accept God's salvation when they are fortunate enough to hear the gospel. Many such people thoroughly rejected God until coming into contact with the gospel and becoming convicted to respond to it. One may thus regard it as overwhelmingly likely that at least one person—if not many—out of the billions of people who go through life without ever hearing the gospel and are lost would have responded to it and been saved if they had heard it. Failure to hear the gospel is only one example of how one's circumstances might not be congruent with one choosing to be saved. As Pinnock points out, many people who might be considered "evangelized" because they have heard the gospel at least once in their life "have been exposed to the message of Jesus only in inadequate ways." Can we say that a Jew who only heard the details of the gospel explained by a guard at Auschwitz who was torturing him "really heard" it?[80] Moreover, consider a Muslim who was born into a devout Muslim family in present-day Saudi Arabia, an Islamic state that allows only the public practice of Islam and has a population that is almost entirely Muslim. Is it not highly likely that at least one such person would have become a Christian if born into a devout Christian family in America? So P_9 may be thought to be strongly implied by P_2 given the plausibility of there being some person who is lost but would have been saved if his or her circumstances had been altered in some way.

If P_8 and P_9 are both true, however, then we have an obvious contradiction. God's attributes would then be incompatible with the purported reality that some of the lost are contingently lost. Thus, if the above argument is to be refuted, one must show that either P_8 or P_9 (or both) should be rejected. One must show that at least one of these two premises is neither necessarily true nor required by Christian doctrine. A successful theodicy that is put forth to undercut one of these premises must be philosophically defensible, and it must also be theologically defensible (i.e., consistent with all of the biblical data).

---

80. Pinnock, *A Wideness in God's Mercy*, 174. Pinnock, an inclusivist, is making this point in the context of arguing that God must provide the unevangelized with a postmortem opportunity to accept Christ. It is curious for an inclusivist to adopt postmortem evangelism since inclusivists already allow that the unevangelized have an opportunity to be saved. The fact that Pinnock feels the need to conjoin this biblically unsupported doctrine to inclusivism points to the force of the problem at hand: Many feel that God's omnibenevolence requires more than providing the mere opportunity for salvation to all. Pinnock believes the disadvantage of the unevangelized of not having more favorable circumstances (e.g., hearing the gospel) is unacceptable.

The remainder of this book will develop a theodicy in response to the above objection (i.e., that an omnibenevolent, omnipotent, omniscient God would not allow anyone to be contingently lost). Since my ultimate proposed solution relies upon the truth of Molinism, the next chapter will describe this perspective on God's omniscience and offer a defense of its theological and philosophical credibility. That will pave the way for exploring how others (especially William Lane Craig) have applied Molinism to resolve this soteriological problem and for laying out an alternative Molinist theodicy that I believe overcomes some weaknesses in these approaches.

The Soteriological Problem of Evil and the Contingently Lost   53

Table 1.1. Summary of Premises Introduced in Chapter 1
Premises that the Soteriological Problem of Evil Attempts to Show are in Conflict
P_1. God possesses the attributes of omniscience, omnipotence, and omnibenevolence.
P_2. Some persons do not accept the forgiveness that is available via receiving Christ and are thus damned.[81]
First Preliminary Objection: Should Not God Ensure Universal Salvation?
P_3. "God is able to actualize a possible world in which all persons freely [in the libertarian sense] receive Christ."
P_4. "God prefers a world in which no persons fail to receive Christ and are damned to a world in which some do."[82]
Second Preliminary Objection: Should Not God Provide Universal Access to Salvation?
P_5. Some people never hear the gospel.
P_6. Anyone who never hears the gospel has no opportunity to accept God's forgiveness through Christ.
P_7. God, if he exists, would be willing and able to ensure that everyone has an opportunity to be saved.
The Remaining Objection: God's Omnibenevolence and the Contingently Lost
P_8. God will necessarily not allow persons to exist who are lost in their actual circumstances but who would have been saved if placed into different circumstances.[83]
P_9. Some persons who freely reject the grace that God offers them in their actual circumstances and are lost would have freely accepted God's grace and been saved in different circumstances.

81. P_1 and P_2 are the two basic premises that proponents of the soteriological POE claim are in conflict. See Craig, "No Other Name," 180. Since there is no explicit contradiction between them, we have considered various arguments that conjoin additional premises to these two basic premises in order to make the contradiction explicit. P_3 and P_4 were added to P_1 and P_2 in the formulation of the first objection that we considered and rejected. P_5, P_6, and P_7 were added to P_1 and P_2 in the formulation of the second objection that we considered and rejected. P_8 and P_9 were added to P_1 and P_2 in the formulation of the final objection that is described in this first chapter. The remainder of this project is aimed at responding to this final objection.

82. As noted previously, P_3 and P_4 are drawn from Craig, "No Other Name," 180.

83. As previously explained, if one denies that God has middle knowledge so that God cannot know for sure whether any of the lost would have been saved if placed into different circumstances, then P_8 could instead be stated as follows: "God will necessarily not allow persons to exist who are lost in their actual circumstances but who would have had *a significantly better opportunity to be saved* if placed into different circumstances."

2

An Explanation and Defense of Molinism

IN THE CLASSIC MOVIE *It's a Wonderful Life*, George Bailey wishes that he had never been born. In order to convince George of the positive impact that his life has had on others, an angel named Clarence shows George what would have taken place if he had never existed. George discovers that his town would have become run-down and many people that he cares about would have had much harder lives—or no life at all. His mother would be a widow running a boarding house. His uncle Billy would be placed in an insane asylum. His brother Harry would have died, and all of the soldiers that Harry saved in the actual world would have instead died at war. These things that Clarence shows George are examples of counterfactual conditionals.[1] Counterfactual conditionals express what would be the case if a different antecedent state of affairs (in this case, eliminating the birth of George) were to be actual. The consequences that Clarence shows George never actually happen because George was, in fact, born; however, if—contrary to what is in fact the case (hence the term counterfactual)—George had not been born, then what Clarence reveals to George would have occurred.

Although such a concept makes for an interesting movie, does God actually have this kind of knowledge about what would be the case if non-actual circumstances were actualized? Could God know the truth value of counterfactual conditionals concerning the actions of free creatures such that God's omniscience includes knowing what any free

---

1. There are a number of movies besides *It's a Wonderful Life* that illustrate the concept of counterfactual conditionals. Consider for example: *A Christmas Carol*, *Groundhog Day*, *Sliding Doors*, *Frequency*, and *Next*.

creature—both free creatures who come into existence and those who never exist—would do in any situation into which that creature might be placed? Numerous theologians throughout the history of the Christian church have held that God has counterfactual knowledge of human free choices; however, one sixteenth-century theologian named Luis de Molina made the case that God not only possesses counterfactual knowledge concerning the actions of free creatures, but that God possesses this knowledge *logically prior* to his decree to actualize the world. He held that God knows all worlds of free creatures that could be actualized and that God, in his sovereignty, could bring into existence just the world of free creatures that he wants. Armed with this idea, Molina attempted to reconcile human freedom with God's sovereign control over the world.

A Brief History of Molinism

Before explaining the details of Molinism and unpacking its central tenet, the doctrine of middle knowledge, it is useful to understand how Molinism arose. Luis de Molina (1535–1600), a Spanish Jesuit theologian and philosopher, lived during the turmoil of the Catholic Counter-Reformation and sought to tackle a thorny theological conundrum of great prominence in his day: How can God's sovereignty, providence, and grace be reconciled with human libertarian freedom? Leading Protestant Reformers, such as Martin Luther and John Calvin, were emphasizing God's sovereignty and providence at the expense of rejecting human libertarian freedom, and Molina was well aware of their views. Luther held that "God's foreknowledge and omnipotence are diametrically opposed to our free choice, for either God can be mistaken in foreknowing and also err in action (which is impossible) or we must be acted upon in accordance with his foreknowledge and activity."[2] That is, Luther considered human free will to be incompatible with God sovereignly ruling over his creatures with all power and knowledge because if God cannot be wrong in what God foreknows then we cannot act in any other way than the way God foreknew that we would act. Luther thought this meant that we are not capable of taking alternative courses of action other than those that we do in fact take and thus are not free in the libertarian sense; he thought that whatever God foreknows must happen necessarily.[3] In

---

2. Luther, "On the Bondage of the Will," 243–44.
3. Luther, "On the Bondage of the Will," 240–41. It is certainly biblical that God

much the same way (though emphasizing more that it is God's sovereign control over human affairs rather than God's foreknowledge of our actions that leaves no room for human freedom),[4] Calvin also rejected the idea that humans possess libertarian freedom. Calvin insisted that "by [God's] providence, not heaven and earth and inanimate creatures only, but also the counsels and wills of men are so governed as to move exactly in the course which [God] has destined."[5] While Molina agreed with Luther and Calvin that God is sovereign over all things and even agreed with them concerning God's unconditional election to salvation

---

foreknows all things and cannot err in his foreknowledge. Necessarily, whatever God foreknows will happen. But that does not mean that whatever God foreknows happens necessarily. This was a significant mistake on the part of Luther. If humans have free will, then God's foreknowledge is based upon what God knows people will freely do. It is our free choices that partly determine what God foreknows. (The other part is God's sovereign creative choice to bring about the free creatures in the circumstances in which they will freely act as they do.) If God's foreknowledge depends upon our free choices, that does not mean that God is at the mercy of our free will or that God loses his sovereignty. We will see that this is because Molinism shows how God can be sovereign over all things despite humans having libertarian freedom. The two are not at odds. It is also notable that Luther at one point (see Luther, "On the Bondage of the Will," 143) suggests that "in matters pertaining to salvation or damnation, a man has no free choice, but is a captive, subject and slave either of the will of God or the will of Satan"; however, with regard to other matters (i.e., "his faculties and possessions"), Luther says mankind has a sort of "free choice." Yet even with the latter, he says this is "controlled by the free choice of God alone." It is not clear what sort of freedom Luther is aiming for here even with regard to actions that are not related to salvation. As Craig rightly points out, it would be inconsistent for Luther to leave room for human libertarian freedom in any aspect of life given Luther's (flawed) argument that our freedom is incompatible with divine foreknowledge. God foreknows all that we will do and not merely choices related to salvation. See Craig, "Middle Knowledge: A Calvinist-Arminian Rapprochement?," 142–43.

4. Craig argues effectively that Calvin's view that man cannot have the ability to act differently than he acts is because of God's sovereignty over human affairs in contrast to Luther's focus on the necessity of our actions resulting from divine foreknowledge. See Craig, "Middle Knowledge: A Calvinist-Arminian Rapprochement?," 143–44.

5. Calvin, *Institutes of the Christian Religion*, 120 (I.xvi.8). With regard to sin, Calvin agreed with Luther that mankind sins necessarily; indeed, all that humans do is according to the sovereign decree of God and happens necessarily. Yet he denied that humans are compelled to sin and affirmed that we do so voluntarily. See Calvin, *Institutes*, 181 (II.iii.5). Both Luther and Calvin also insisted that the human will is not coerced by God when it comes to the changing of one's thoroughly depraved will so that one accepts the gospel. Robert Picirilli rightly points out that this seems blatantly inconsistent. Since prior to regeneration all humans are unable to will to accept God and turn from sin, it seems that "God must change us against our wills" if anyone is to come to God. See Picirilli, *Free Will Revisited*, 100.

(though, as we will see, unconditional election is not entailed by Molina's proposed doctrine of middle knowledge), Molina sharply disagreed with them concerning their rejection of our libertarian free will and their undermining of God's genuine universal salvific will. Molina held that God gives us his prevenient grace to overcome what would otherwise be our inability to respond to God's grace so that we all have libertarian freedom—and this applies even to matters of salvation so that we can freely accept or reject Christ.[6]

Meanwhile, on the Catholic side, Domingo Bañez and the Dominicans were following in the steps of Thomas Aquinas and arguing that God is able to predetermine the free will of humans. Bañez did not agree with Calvin or Luther that humans lack libertarian free will; nevertheless, he paradoxically maintained that God's divine decree physically operates on us to determine how we will freely act.[7] Of course, God's intervening on the will in this way does not seem to square with our libertarian free will as he claimed. Molina did not find the view of Bañez—who proved to be the primary Catholic opponent of Molina's efforts to reconcile divine sovereignty and human libertarian freedom—and the Dominicans to be acceptable either.

While Molina, along with the Protestant Reformers and the Dominicans, desired to uphold the sovereignty and providence of God and the need for God's grace in calling sinners to salvation, he also wanted to provide an adequate justification of human libertarian freedom (including freedom with regard to the decision to accept Christ) and God's sincere desire for all to be saved. Finding that the views of the Dominicans and the Protestant Reformers fail to do justice to libertarian freedom, Molina set out to formulate a more desirable option. He wanted to bring

6. Kirk MacGregor provides a useful discussion of Molina's view of grace. See MacGregor, *Luis de Molina*, 72. This recent work is the first biography of Molina, revealing much of the history of his life, the influences on him that led to his development of the doctrine of middle knowledge, and the controversy that emerged within Catholicism over Molinism. It also examines the legacy that Molina has left today, as many throughout all branches of Christianity have found Molinism to be a fruitful and biblical doctrine. In addition, since almost all of Molina's writings (aside from the crucial Part IV of his *Concordia* in which his theory of middle knowledge is unpacked) have never been published in an English translation, MacGregor usefully describes Molina's views on a variety of points that extend beyond his doctrine of middle knowledge and cites where Molina's comments can be found in Molina's original Latin texts. He also often cites Molina's exact words in Latin so that the reader knows the specific text to which he is referring.

7. Pohle and Preuss, *Grace, Actual and Habitual*, 232–34.

the synergistic Jesuits closer to the monergistic Dominicans and Protestants reformers, and he thought that his proposed doctrine of middle knowledge—which we will soon examine in detail—was just the way to accomplish this; indeed, he thought that if middle knowledge had been widely adopted by Christians much earlier, then Christian controversies and divisions over divine providence and human free will could have been prevented.[8] Nevertheless, despite Molina's high hopes, Molinism—although it was embraced by many (especially the Jesuits) throughout Europe after Molina described his views in his 1588 *Concordia*[9]—never resolved the monergistic-synergistic tensions among Christians. Molina was disheartened when his view was rejected by the Inquisition in 1591. It was rejected largely due to the opposition he received from Bañez and the Dominicans.[10] Yet the vast majority of Jesuits embraced Molinism and believed that the Dominicans misrepresented Molina. After a few years of intense disagreement between Dominicans and Jesuits over Molinism, Molina published his *Apologia Concordiae* in 1594 to defend the ideas he laid out in his *Concordia* and refute the objections of Bañez and the Dominicans. Yet the disagreement between the Dominicans and Jesuits raged on, leading Pope Clement VIII to threaten excommunication on anyone who debated about this controversy.[11] This did not quiet the storm, however, and Clement VIII ordered a careful investigation of Molina's ideas. This papal commission suspected that Molina had introduced innovative ideas that were not consistent with historic Catholic doctrine.[12] The Jesuits and Molina himself urged the pope to reconsider the merits of Molinism, but Molina died of dysentery in 1600 under the impression that he would likely be wrongly anathematized after his death.[13] However, Pope Paul V decided in 1607 that Molinism is accept-

8. MacGregor, *Luis de Molina*, 158.

9. The full title of Molina's work in Latin is *Concordia Liberi Arbitrii cum Gratiae Donis, Divina Praescientia, Providentia, Praedestinatione et Reprobatione*, and it is commonly referred to as the *Concordia*. In English, the title can be translated as: *The Concordance of Free Will with the Gifts of Grace, Divine Foreknowledge, Providence, Predestination, and Reprobation*. The title reflects Molina's desire to show how human libertarian freedom is compatible with God's grace, foreknowledge, providence, and election of individuals to salvation. It is in Part IV of the *Concordia* that Molina especially unpacks his key idea of middle knowledge.

10. MacGregor, *Luis de Molina*, 172–73.

11. MacGregor, *Luis de Molina*, 175–76.

12. MacGregor, *Luis de Molina*, 231.

13. MacGregor, *Luis de Molina*, 239–40.

able to believe, though he made no determination on whether it is true. He ordered that there is freedom within the Roman Catholic Church to adopt the position of the Dominicans or hold to Molinism.[14] So Molina was vindicated in the end. His position did not immediately revolutionize the church as he had hoped, but he nevertheless made an impact that continues to this day.

Molinism has experienced an explosion of renewed interest in the forty-five years since Alvin Plantinga "unwittingly reformulated the central tenets of Molinism in his free will defense against the logical problem of evil" in his book *God, Freedom, and Evil*.[15] It was not until three years after that, in 1977, that Robert Adams, an opponent of Molinism, recognized that Plantinga's ideas were consistent with Molinism, and Plantinga thus was led to discover that he is in agreement with Molinism. Plantinga then became a prominent advocate of divine middle knowledge.[16] Kirk MacGregor rightly regards William Lane Craig as the "world's leading defender of Molinism" at present, and Molinism has gained much traction and popularity among evangelicals in recent years.[17] A number of Christian philosophers and theologians have adopted Molinism, and it is starting to gain a significant following among lay people as well.[18] Contrary to the misimpression of some, Molinism is not a "Catholic doctrine." It is not entailed by any particular doctrines in Catholic theology or even regarded as definitely true by the Roman Catholic Church. MacGregor is correct to point out that "Molinism has been completely embraced by theologians representing a broad cross-section of Protestantism." Moreover, he rightly notes that "Protestant thinkers who reject Molinism in part or in whole have not done so because Catholic tendencies are somehow inherent to Molinist thought."[19] Molinism, as we will see, focuses on an aspect of God's omniscience. As such, once one accepts that God possesses the sort of knowledge that Molina proposes, one may apply this in a variety of ways in terms of what God might do with this knowledge. In terms of soteriology, for example, this allows for a variety

---

14. MacGregor, *Luis de Molina*, 241.
15. MacGregor, *Luis de Molina*, 243.
16. MacGregor, *Luis de Molina*, 243.
17. MacGregor, *Luis de Molina*, 244.
18. Some important contemporary advocates of Molinism include: Alvin Plantinga, William Lane Craig, Thomas Flint, Alfred Freddoso, Kenneth Keathley, Kirk MacGregor, Paul Copan, Eef Dekker, Jonathan Kvanvig, and Richard Otte.
19. MacGregor, *Luis de Molina*, 16.

of options, and Protestants who are more Reformed in their theology (e.g., Alvin Plantinga) and those who are more Arminian (e.g., William Lane Craig) have incorporated Molina's idea that God has middle knowledge into their theology.[20]

Having briefly surveyed the history of the rise of Molinism, let us turn to an examination of this view. In particular, we must understand the engine that drove Molina's theory of reconciling God's sovereignty and providence with human libertarian freedom: the doctrine of middle knowledge.

An Explanation of Molinism

In his 1588 *Concordia*, Molina recognized that the solution to the mystery of reconciling divine sovereignty and human freedom is ultimately found in God's attribute of omniscience. Molina proposed that there are "three types of knowledge in God,"[21] and these three types can be understood in terms of three logical moments. These logical "moments" do not have any temporal implication, as if God is ignorant of certain knowledge until he acquires other knowledge; rather, these moments must be understood in terms of logical priority. As Craig aptly describes it, one moment "serves to explain" the next moment and "provides the grounds or basis" for it.[22] Molina certainly did not deny that God knows all things eternally.

20. Plantinga, for example, holds that humans have libertarian freedom with regard to all of their actions except for choosing to accept Christ. With regard to the latter, he holds the Reformed position that God must grant one the gift of faith and that apart from God doing this one lacks the ability to turn from one's sins and accept Christ. Since Plantinga allows that humans have libertarian freedom with regard to all of their choices that do not pertain to accepting God's grace (which accounts for the vast majority of choices that humans make throughout their lives), he makes use of Molina's concept of middle knowledge to explain how God sovereignly directs a world of creatures who carry out most of their choices with libertarian freedom. This allows him to uphold Reformed soteriology, divine sovereignty, and human libertarian freedom and responsibility for sin. Plantinga explained this in a letter that he sent to my former dissertation chair, Dr. Ed Martin, in February of 1989. Plantinga wrote, "Calvinism embraces predestination," and this doctrine "implies at most that one doesn't become a Christian by way of free choice, but rather as a result of divine grace. But that is compatible with our having all sorts of libertarian freedom with respect to other matters." Plantinga stresses that the historic creeds of Calvinism affirm "that God is not responsible for sin," so he thinks it is best for Calvinists to affirm that humans have libertarian freedom with regard to matters outside of becoming a Christian so that the moral agency of humans can be justified.

21. Molina, *Concordia* 4.52.9, 168.

22. Craig, *The Only Wise God*, 127. As an example of how temporal and

Molina was not the first to suggest that there are logical moments in God's knowledge; indeed, this concept is found in the writings of such earlier theologians as Duns Scotus and Thomas Aquinas. In fact, Molina's first and third moments actually correspond with the first and last moments that Aquinas identified; moreover, Molina and Aquinas even agree that between these moments lies "a decision of the divine will."[23] Yet, despite this similarity, Molina's proposal is unique in terms of how his second moment is able to reconcile adequately God's sovereignty with human libertarian freedom.

Molina refers to the first moment in God's knowledge as "natural knowledge." This is God's knowledge of all things that *could* possibly come to be; that is, it includes knowledge of every possible world. Because natural knowledge includes every possibility, God possesses this knowledge necessarily (or "naturally"). Since God's natural knowledge of all possible worlds does not depend upon what world God chooses to actualize, Molina notes that this natural knowledge "could not have been any different in God."[24] In Molina's words, God's natural knowledge includes:

> all the things to which the divine power extended either immediately or by the mediation of secondary causes, including not only the natures of individuals and the necessary states of affairs composed of them but also the contingent states of affairs—through this knowledge He knew, to be sure, not that the latter were or were not going to obtain determinately, but rather that they were indifferently able to obtain and able not to obtain, a feature that belongs to them necessarily.[25]

Skipping over the second moment for now, Molina terms the third moment in God's knowledge "free knowledge." This is God's knowledge of the actual world—what *will* happen in the world that God has, in fact, freely decided to create. Molina explains that "*after* the free act of His will [to create the particular world that He did], God knew *absolutely*

---

chronological priority differ, Craig also points out (p. 128) how God's eternal foreknowledge that an event will happen is *chronologically prior* to the event, even though the event is *logically prior* to God's foreknowledge of it. That is, the *logical basis* for God foreknowing the event is the fact that it will occur. If the event were not to happen, God would not foreknow it.

23. Craig, "A Calvinist-Arminian Rapprochement?," 145.
24. Molina, *Concordia* 4.52.9, 168.
25. Molina, *Concordia* 4.52.9, 168.

and *determinately, without any condition or hypothesis,* which ones from among all the contingent states of affairs were *in fact* going to obtain and, likewise, which ones were not going to obtain."[26] Clearly then, unlike the necessary content of God's natural knowledge, what God knows in his free knowledge is entirely contingent; it is contingent upon God's creative will and could have been different from what it is if God had decided to actualize a different world.

Now, as Thomas Flint points out, what has been said about the first and third moments in Molina's view of God's omniscience is not especially controversial. Few theologians throughout church history would deny that some truths known by God are necessary while others are contingent upon God's free creative will. Yet Flint points out that "the picture sketched thus far is incomplete. For how, one might wonder, does it provide God with *complete* foreknowledge or control of events which are contingent?"[27] If God is sovereign in actualizing the specific world that he desires *and* the world he wishes to actualize includes creatures who possess libertarian free will, then some mechanism is needed whereby God can get from his natural knowledge of all possible worlds to ensuring that the specific world that he desires is actualized. How can God be sovereign over a world of free creatures and ensure that his plans are achieved without robbing the creatures of their genuine libertarian freedom? Molina's solution to this conundrum is that, logically between God's natural and free knowledge, God possesses "middle knowledge."

While Molina may not have wasted much creative energy in his naming of this logical moment that falls in the "middle" between God's natural and free knowledge, the concept of middle knowledge itself is ingenious and explanatorily powerful. Molina explains that God's middle knowledge, the second logical moment in God's omniscience, is God's knowledge of what each free creature that he might create "would do with its innate freedom were it to be placed in this or in that or, indeed, in infinitely many orders of things—even though it would really be able, if it so willed, to do the opposite."[28] So while God's natural knowledge includes all of the possibilities concerning what free creatures *could* do (e.g., if Judas is placed in circumstance C, God knows all of the possible decisions that Judas could make), God's middle knowledge ensures that he knows what any possible

---

26. Molina, *Concordia* 4.52.9, 168.
27. Flint, *Divine Providence*, 38.
28. Molina, *Concordia* 4.52.9, 168.

free creature *would* do if placed into any possible circumstance (e.g., God knows that if placed into circumstance C, Judas would freely choose to betray Christ). Thus, if God decides to actualize a world in which Judas is placed into circumstance C, then God is able to guarantee that Judas *will* freely choose to betray Christ. Given God's decision to actualize a world in which Judas is in C, God's knowledge that Judas *will* actually betray Christ in C is then part of God's free knowledge.

Once one recognizes that God's possession of middle knowledge would allow God to know with certainty what a free creature would freely choose to do if placed in any given circumstance, it is not hard to see how God can use this knowledge to arrange providentially an entire world. Given that God knows all possible worlds with his natural knowledge, God can use his middle knowledge to determine which of those possible worlds are feasible for him to create. Some possible worlds are not feasible for God to actualize because the free creatures in those worlds would not make the free choices that they would have to make in the circumstances in which they find themselves in those worlds in order for those worlds to be actualized. For example, if Judas is placed in the exact circumstances in which he is placed in this actual world on the night that he betrayed Christ, God cannot change the fact that Judas would freely choose to betray Christ in those circumstances. That is simply what Judas would freely choose to do in those precise circumstances. God could not actualize a world that is exactly like the actual world up to the very moment that Judas chooses to betray Christ but then Judas freely chooses not to betray Christ. Such a world is not feasible for God to make because it is simply a counterfactual truth concerning creaturely freedom that Judas would freely choose to betray Christ in those circumstances. So God understands which worlds are feasible by using his middle knowledge to comprehend which out of all of the possible worlds are actualizable. God then decrees to actualize one of these feasible worlds. God thus knows exactly and entirely what the future will be—God's free knowledge. In this way, God's middle knowledge is the means by which Molina reconciles God's sovereignty and providence with human freedom. It also provides a clear answer to theological fatalists such as Martin Luther by showing that God's foreknowledge of the choice that a creature will make is consistent with that creature having libertarian freedom.

Molina meticulously clarifies the nature of middle knowledge, emphasizing how it is distinct from natural knowledge and free knowledge even though it bears similarities to both. Middle knowledge is distinct from free knowledge "because it is prior to any free act of God's will and also because it was not within God's power to know through this type of knowledge anything other than what He in fact knew."[29] That is, God's middle knowledge resembles natural knowledge more than free knowledge in one sense—the sense that it does not depend on any act of God. God's middle knowledge is determined by what the free creatures would choose to do in various circumstances, and the free choices of free creatures are not determined or controlled by God. Natural knowledge is also that way because God simply knows all possibilities, and this knowledge does not depend upon any choice or action on God's part.[30] Nevertheless, middle knowledge is also distinct from natural knowledge in the sense that it is not "so innate to God that He could not have known the opposite of that which He knows through it. For if created free choice were going to do the opposite, as indeed it can, then God would have known that very thing through this same type of knowledge, and not what He in fact knows."[31] Thus middle knowledge is like free knowledge in the sense of not being what it is by necessity (though middle knowledge is contingent upon the creatures' free will whereas free knowledge is based upon God's will).

We have seen that Molinism arose during the period of the Catholic Counter-Reformation at a time when theologians within Protestant and Catholic circles were focused upon working out the tension between human free will and God's sovereignty, providence, and grace. We have also laid out Molina's basic position for resolving this tension. Yet an obvious question remains: Is there any reason to think that Molinism is true?

---

29. Molina, *Concordia* 4.52.10, 168.

30. It is important to recognize that it is no strike against God's omnipotence that God cannot control the truth values of counterfactuals of creaturely freedom. Omnipotence is widely understood to exclude the ability to do what is logically impossible. For example, it does not count against God's omnipotence that God cannot create a square circle, since there cannot be a square circle. A square circle is logically impossible, for by definition a shape cannot be both a square and a circle at the same time. In the same way, as MacGregor puts it, it would be "logically impossible to *determine* that a libertarian creature *freely* does something such that it cannot do otherwise or to *determine* that a stochastic (i.e., utterly random) process *contingently* turns out in a certain way such that it could not turn out otherwise." See MacGregor, *Luis de Molina*, 90.

31. Molina, *Concordia* 4.52.10, 168–69.

Evidence for Molinism

Since Alvin Plantinga brought the doctrine of Molinism back into prominence in the 1970s, much has been written concerning its biblical and philosophical viability.[32] While a full-blown critique of all the arguments for and against Molinism cannot be done here, the aim of this portion of our examination of Molinism is to offer a concise but thorough assessment of the most prominent issues surrounding this doctrine, succinctly making a case for its faithfulness to the Scriptures and its philosophical coherence. We begin with the biblical evidence in favor of Molinism.

Biblical Evidence for Molinism

Although there is no explicit proof-text for Molinism in the Bible, the sum total of the biblical evidence in its favor is impressive. Molinism is not only consistent with the biblical data, but it seems to be strongly indicated in Scripture by the combination of three key concepts that appear to be biblical: (1) God has counterfactual knowledge of how humans would act in circumstances that will never come to exist; (2) humans possess libertarian free will; and (3) God has sovereign control of the world and the ability to achieve his precise plans. I will show in the discussion that follows that there is good biblical reason for affirming all three of these points and that Molinism appears to be the only way to reconcile them.

God's Counterfactual Knowledge of Creaturely Actions

Let us begin with God's knowledge of counterfactuals concerning creaturely actions. God's having counterfactual knowledge is clearly a necessary condition for his possession of middle knowledge; however, it is not a sufficient condition because true middle knowledge requires that God's counterfactual knowledge must logically precede God's creative decree. If it turns out that God only has counterfactual knowledge of creaturely actions on the basis of (i.e., logically after) his creative decree, then God would not possess true middle knowledge; this is because God's counterfactual knowledge would simply involve his knowing how he would actively *cause* a person to act in any possible

---

32. Some notable opponents of Molinism include: Robert Adams, William Hasker, David Hunt, and Anthony Kenny.

circumstance (even ones that he does not actualize). This, for example, is the position taken by the Dominicans,[33] and it leaves no room for humans to possess genuine libertarian freedom because they could not choose to act other than the way God decrees that they must act. Thus, God only knows counterfactuals of creaturely *freedom* if God has middle knowledge. If God's counterfactual knowledge is logically subsequent to his creative decree, then it is not knowledge of choices that are made by creatures who possess libertarian freedom.

Given that God's knowledge of counterfactuals concerning creaturely actions is a necessary condition for Molinism, it would be advantageous for the Molinist to find biblical evidence that God has such knowledge. As it turns out, the Bible contains many instances in which God indicates outcomes that would result in non-actual circumstances, and a number of these involve human decisions. Molina focuses on two biblical examples in particular. First, in Matthew 11:20–24 Jesus states that the wicked people of Tyre, Sidon, and Sodom would have repented if they had seen the miracles Jesus performed in Chorazin, Bethsaida, and Capernaum. Molina sees this statement as a clear example of Jesus expressing a counterfactual truth concerning human decisions. He emphasizes that "because the hypothesis on which it was going to occur was not in fact actualized, this repentance never did and never will exist in reality—and yet it was a future contingent dependent on the free choice of human beings."[34] While William Lane Craig has put forth the possibility that this particular statement from Jesus was merely expressing hyperbole rather than a true counterfactual (Craig seems to propose this interpretation largely because, as we will later discover, interpreting this particular statement as a true counterfactual would undermine the theodicy that Craig proposes for dealing with the problem of the contingently lost), Molina's literal interpretation is widely accepted by biblical commentators for good reason. When we discuss Craig's soteriological theodicy, we will examine this passage in detail and discover why the best exegesis of the passage is to take it as a true counterfactual of creaturely freedom (i.e., Jesus is truly expressing knowledge of what free creatures would have done in non-actual circumstances).

---

33. Craig, "The Middle-Knowledge View," 121–22. Craig has a good discussion of how this difference in the logical point at which God possesses counterfactual knowledge is the issue that creates the significant rift between how the Dominicans and the Jesuits view God's foreknowledge.

34. Molina, *Concordia* 4.49.9, 117.

Molina also cites 1 Samuel 23:4–13 as an example showing God's knowledge of counterfactuals. Here, David asks God whether Saul will attack the town of Keilah in order to capture him. God affirms that Saul will attack. David then asks whether the men of Keilah will decide to turn him over to Saul. God affirms that they will. At this point, David flees Keilah, and Saul no longer has any reason to come to Keilah and attack it. Molina points out that "God knew these two future contingent events, which depend on human choice, and He revealed them to David. Yet they never have existed and never will exist in eternity."[35] In other words, God was communicating counterfactual truths concerning human decisions. Even though the events never occur (David never stayed in Keilah so Saul never attacked the city and the men of Keilah never turned David over to Saul), God revealed to David what Saul and the men of Keilah *would* have done if David remained in Keilah.

There are many other examples indicating that God has counterfactual knowledge. For example, God reveals to Zedekiah what his enemies would do to him under the condition that he surrenders and under the condition that he does not surrender (Jer 38:17–18). God reveals to Saul how he would have prospered as king and how his kingdom would have been permanently established if he had not sinned by illegitimately offering a sacrifice to God (1 Sam 13:11–14). The Apostle Paul says that if the "rulers of this age" had understood the wisdom of God then "they would not have crucified the Lord of glory" (1 Cor 2:8). Paul seems to be expressing what the rulers who condemned Jesus would have done under non-actual circumstances. God also knows numerous counterfactuals that do not directly involve human choices.[36] Thus, the biblical evidence that God knows counterfactual truths—even ones concerning human choices—is strong. Indeed, the acceptance of God's knowledge of counterfactuals is not unique to Molinism and has been held without controversy throughout church history.[37]

---

35. Molina, *Concordia* 4.49.9, 117.

36. See for example: Isa 38:1–5; Exod 32:9–14; Jon 3:1–10; Matt 17:27; 26:24; John 15:22–24; 21:6; 1 Cor 2:8.

37. Flint, *Divine Providence*, 40. See also Craig, "The Middle-Knowledge View," 120. Craig points out that God's counterfactual knowledge was not questioned until Friedrich Schleiermacher (1768–1834).

Human Libertarian Freedom

The second key piece of biblical evidence that supports Molinism is that Scripture indicates that humans have libertarian free will. We have seen that there is biblical evidence that God knows counterfactuals concerning human actions, but such counterfactual knowledge is only middle knowledge if God knows it logically prior to God's creative decree. If it is the case that God knows counterfactuals concerning human actions *and* humans possess libertarian free will, then it is the case that God's counterfactual knowledge concerning human actions is logically prior to God's creative decree. That is, God would know what any creature would do in any given circumstance on the basis of the creature's free choice, and it would *not* be the case that God knows what a free creature would do in any given circumstance merely on the basis of God's decree that the creature would be divinely determined to act in that way. So, if humans possess libertarian free will, then God's counterfactual knowledge concerning human actions is logically prior to God's creative decree and God has true middle knowledge. Because the Bible indicates that humans do, in fact, have libertarian freedom—the ability of an agent, when confronted with a choice involving multiple options, to choose an option other than the one that the agent does in fact choose—God appears to have legitimate middle knowledge. Note, however, that I do not deny that one's conscience can be seared (1 Tim 4:2) or that one can suppress the truth and be given over to a depraved mind (Rom 1:18–32) or that one can become addicted to drugs or certain sinful behaviors. I recognize that in these sorts of cases it may eventually become hugely difficult (perhaps at some point nearly impossible) to resist sin and respond to the convicting work of the Holy Spirit or to break free of one's addictions. In such cases, one has used one's free will to become enslaved to sin or to drugs, and the freedom one has to resist these things may be greatly diminished. This recognition does not detract from the fact that God has given all of us the freedom required to be moral agents and to choose to love or reject God.

Clearly, there is disagreement among Christians as to whether it is biblical that God has given humans libertarian freedom. We have already seen that Luther regarded divine foreknowledge as incompatible with human libertarian freedom and Calvin thought God's sovereignty would be threatened if we are free. According to some Reformed Christians, humans have freedom in the sense of being able to act in accordance with the desires that God has given us, but we lack the ability to generate a choice from our own wills that departs from this predetermined desire. As Reformed theologians Robert Peterson and Michael Williams put it, "We do as we please. But we are not so absolutely free as to be able to please as we please."[38] For those who hold such a view, the catalyst behind all human actions is the will of God. While not all Reformed Christians would deny that humans possess libertarian freedom at all, we have noted that it is part of Reformed soteriology to deny that anyone has the libertarian freedom to choose to be saved; only God can give a person the gift of having the ability to place faith in Christ and be saved. We have also seen, however, that there are important difficulties with certain aspects of Reformed soteriology and that these difficulties point toward humans possessing libertarian freedom with regard to the decision to accept or reject Christ.

I argued in the previous chapter that: Christ died so that all people have the opportunity to accept God's grace and be saved; God truly desires for all people to be saved; and God has provided sufficient grace to all so that no person is without excuse for rejecting God's offer of grace. However, if God does genuinely offer salvation to all people and desires for all people to be saved, then it is evident that humans do not always act in accordance with God's will since all people clearly are not saved. As we have seen, this is why the Reformed theologian David Engelsma realizes that he must bite the bullet and assert that God does not genuinely desire for all people to be saved.[39] If my arguments from the previous chapter succeed, then God's sovereignty must have a permissive component in which God allows creatures the freedom either to set their wills against God or to allow God's promptings of their heart to soften their wills; God must allow humans to make their own choices that are not determined by God—even the choice to reject every opportunity that God gives them to respond to God's drawing them toward himself and salvation. Yet, if this is true, then humans possess libertarian freedom. The fact that some people are lost despite God's provision of sufficient grace to all people and God's genuine desire for their salvation cries out for an explanation, and that explanation is found in the rebellious will of creatures who freely spurn God's grace and reject God in favor of sin.

---

38. Peterson and Williams, *Why I Am Not an Arminian*, 156.

39. Engelsma, *Hyper-Calvinism and the Call of the Gospel*, 58. Similarly, Calvinist R. C. Sproul recognizes that limited atonement must be upheld if the other points of Calvinism are to stand. See Sproul, *The Truth of the Cross*, 142.

Aside from the importance of libertarian freedom in one's choice concerning the acceptance or rejection of the gospel, libertarian freedom seems essential to the moral agency that Scripture ascribes to humans. The Bible teaches that we choose whether or not to do good or do evil, and we thus bear responsibility when we make moral choices. It is dubious that creatures who are incapable of choosing to act differently than they do in fact act bear moral responsibility for their actions. On compatibilism, an agent is causally determined to act as she does (i.e., antecedent conditions beyond her control make it impossible for her to choose otherwise), yet she is free in the sense that she would have acted differently if she had chosen to do so (even though she could not have so chosen). Even atheists who hold to determinism often admit that this compatibilistic concept of freedom does not legitimize the *praiseworthiness or blameworthiness* of an agent. David Baggett and Jerry Walls explore the interactions between three naturalists regarding moral responsibility: Bruce Waller, Daniel Dennett, and Tom Clark. While there are differences among them, all three agree that libertarian freedom is required if moral responsibility is understood in the robust sense of the agent deserving praise or blame.[40] They recognize that lauding or condemning a moral choice is not reasonable if that person was determined to act as she did. Baggett and Walls rightly disagree with their determinism but agree with them that on determinism there could be no moral responsibility. A genuine moral agent must be the source of her moral decisions and must have the ability to take alternative action.

Notably, a number of Calvinists recognize that libertarian freedom is necessary in order to escape the moral difficulty that God is the author of sin and eternally decrees that the reprobate will have no ability to avoid their fate. Within Calvinism, there are some who hold to supralapsarianism and others who adopt infralapsarianism. According to supralapsarianism, God desires to damn certain persons and elect others. On that basis, God decrees that the Fall of Adam must happen in order to ensure

---

40. Baggett and Walls, *God and Cosmos*, 98–102. The authors note how Waller thinks freedom is compatible with determinism, but moral responsibility is not. He thinks moral responsibility means the agent deserves praise or blame, and we do not have the freedom that warrants that. Dennett also thinks we are not morally responsible if "moral responsibility" is defined in terms of praise and blame—just as Waller suggests. So Dennett opts to define it differently to lower the bar. Clark thinks we must forget about responsibility and punishment altogether because he considers these to be tied to libertarian free will, which he thinks is not possible because he holds to naturalistic determinism.

An Explanation and Defense of Molinism

that humans fall under the condemnation of sin so that God can save only the elect and damn the reprobate. Supralapsarian Calvinism thus places logical priority on God's will to damn and save certain people, and the Fall is the logically subsequent means by which God achieves this double predestination. By contrast, infralapsarian Calvinists hold that God's determination to save some and leave others to be damned is logically subsequent to Adam's sin.[41] Infralapsarians make this distinction in order to claim that the reprobate are only lost due to sin and not simply because God wills for them to be reprobate. The problem is that infralapsarianism alone fails to remove God as the author of sin. God still eternally wills the damnation of the reprobate and the election of the saved, and it is hard to see how human culpability could enter the picture if it were the case that our sins are the result of God's sovereign plan and happen by necessity. In order to avoid this, certain infralapsarians such as the late R. C. Sproul attack the real difficulty: libertarian freedom and human responsibility must enter into the equation somehow.

Sproul argues that Adam possessed libertarian freedom—the "ability to sin and the ability not to sin."[42] Sproul then adopts the controversial view that Adam functions as the federal head of the human race. Thus, when Adam chose to sin, all people essentially make the libertarian choice to sin with Adam.[43] In this way, even though all of Adam's descendants lack libertarian freedom, Sproul still appeals to libertarian freedom in order to justify sin and God's decision to *permit*, rather than cause, the reprobate to be damned. While many aspects of Sproul's view are problematic (e.g., his Reformed starting points against which I have argued, his heavy emphasis on just one act of libertarian freedom, and the dubious concept of federal headship), the central point for our purposes is this: The fact that he considers it important to work libertarian freedom into his Reformed position in order to justify God morally is a testament to the theological and moral importance of libertarian freedom in Scripture.[44] Moreover, the importance of libertarian freedom is seen in the fact that those Calvinists who reject libertarian freedom and do not see a way to avoid the conclusion that this seems to entail that God

---

41. Erickson, *The Concise Dictionary of Christian Theology*, 101–93. Erickson provides a good definition of infralapsarianism (p. 101) and supralapsarianism (p. 193).

42. Sproul, *Chosen by God*, 65.

43. Sproul, *Chosen by God*, 98.

44. Walls and Dongell, *Why I Am Not a Calvinist*, 181–84. The authors provide a helpful discussion of Sproul's version of infralapsarian Calvinism.

decrees sin are often compelled to appeal to mystery in order to brush aside this problem; Robert Peterson and Michael Williams, for example, make this appeal to "mystery" when faced with the enormous challenge of how "a supremely good and holy God can sovereignly ordain the sinful acts of human beings." They wrongly deny that we have libertarian freedom and rightly affirm the complete sovereignty of God. They thus are forced to admit that "sin ought not to be. It does not fit with any conception of a good and just God. Yet it is, and he is."[45] They simply rest content to regard this as a profound mystery. But surely this is more than a mystery—it is a deep incoherence; moreover, it is an incoherence that can be avoided when one recognizes the strong indications in Scripture that humans have the ability to choose not to sin.

Since human libertarian freedom appears to be a necessary ingredient in order to give a morally justifiable account of sin and reprobation, it is not surprising that many biblical texts highlight the human ability to choose sin or reject it. When we sin, Scripture seems to teach that we have the capability to do otherwise. For example, while condemning the Jewish leaders for continually rejecting and persecuting the prophets God has sent to them, Jesus states: "Jerusalem, Jerusalem, who kills the prophets and stones those who are sent to her! How often I wanted to gather your children together, the way a hen gathers her chicks under her wings, and you were unwilling" (Matt 23:37). The painful grief Jesus shows in this passage emphasizes how it was never his will for the people of Jerusalem to reject God; rather, Jesus states that his desire for them was not actualized due to their own unwillingness. God has eternally known what choices the people of Jerusalem would ultimately make, and God permits their decisions and accounts for them in God's sovereign plan for human history; however, God still mourns their rebelliousness and prefers that they would freely accept the prophets and turn to him. Similarly, when Cain is angry because of God's unhappiness with his offering, God reminds Cain that Cain himself has the power to sin or to do the right thing. God tells Cain, "If you do well, will not your countenance be lifted up? And if you do not do well, sin is crouching at the door; and its desire is for you, but you must master it" (Gen 4:7). Scripture is clear that God "does not tempt anyone. But each one is tempted when he is carried away and enticed by his own lust" (Jas 1:13–14). Moreover, when one is tempted, God "will provide the way of escape also, so that you will be

---

45. Peterson and Williams, *Why I Am Not an Arminian*, 159.

able to endure it" (1 Cor 10:13). Even if one takes the latter verse, given its context, to be directed at believers only, the verse at least indicates that when believers sin they always have the ability to have avoided that sin. Thus, this verse indicates that there are at least millions of people in the world (at least all believers) who have libertarian freedom with regard to their moral actions. Yet, given verses such as those noted above about Jerusalem and Cain, one should not think the Bible teaches that it is only believers who have the ability to avoid sin regardless of whether 1 Corinthians 10:13 applies only to believers.

Ultimately, Scripture indicates that at the final judgment God will praise those who acted in love toward others (Matt 25:34–40) and will eternally punish the lost for their culpability in acting wrongly (Matt 25:46). If we sin and bear moral responsibility so that we are worthy of punishment, then (as Baggett and Walls rightly argue) we must have libertarian freedom. Moral agency requires that we could have done otherwise, and the Bible portrays us as moral agents who have the ability (at least prior to being completely consumed by sin or addiction) to make different choices than the ones that we make.

Libertarian freedom is thus a biblical concept; therefore, together with the fact of God's having counterfactual knowledge concerning human actions, a strong biblical basis exists for concluding that God knows counterfactuals concerning human actions logically prior to God's creative decree. This means that God truly knows counterfactuals *of creaturely freedom*, and God has middle knowledge. It seems that we can eliminate the possibility that God knows counterfactuals concerning creaturely choices on the basis of God determining all of our choices.

God's Sovereignty, Providence, and Election of Individuals

There is, however, also a third key piece of biblical evidence that supports Molinism: God is fully sovereign over all things despite our libertarian freedom. While Arminians are correct to emphasize human libertarian freedom and responsibility, Calvinists are correct in affirming a strong view of God's sovereignty. Molinism provides a bridge that supports libertarian freedom as well as God's sovereignty, providence, and even a kind of election.

The fact that God is sovereign and providentially directs human history in accordance with his unshakable will is a thoroughly biblical concept. Scripture tells us that God's plans cannot be thwarted. For example, through Isaiah, God reveals that no person or power will prevent God from achieving what he has decreed shall occur from eternity: "I am God, and there is no one like Me, declaring the end from the beginning, and from ancient times things which have not been done, saying, 'My purpose will be established, and I will accomplish all My good pleasure'" (Isa 46:9–10). Similarly, and without denying human freedom, the psalmist declares God's ability to achieve his plans, saying: "The Lord nullifies the counsel of the nations; He frustrates the plans of the peoples. The counsel of the Lord stands forever, the plans of His heart from generation to generation" (Ps 33:10–11). Jesus affirms that not even a sparrow falls to the ground apart from the will of the Father (Matt 10:29). Indeed, Solomon goes so far as to regard events that appear to be random as falling within God's sovereign control, saying: "The lot is cast into the lap, but its every decision is from the Lord" (Prov 16:33).

Most significantly, Scripture specifically claims that God accomplishes his purposes through free human decisions—even sinful ones. Molina emphasized the power of Molinism to make sense of how Scripture teaches both the sovereignty of God and the moral responsibility of humans for their sins. Molina stressed that his view allows that "all things without exception are *individually* subject to God's providence and will." Evil acts are permitted by God and are part of God's sovereign plan, but they are brought about by evil humans who have libertarian freedom and not by God. Molinism avoids God being the author of sin and yet accounts for the biblical teaching that God is sovereign over even the evil that humans bring about.[46] Consider the following biblical example: Saul opts to take his own life rather than be captured in battle (1 Chr 10:4), yet the chronicler regards Saul's death as God's doing. The chronicler explains: "Saul died because he was unfaithful to the Lord; he did not keep the word of the Lord and even consulted a medium for guidance, and did not inquire of the Lord. So the Lord put him to death and turned the kingdom over to David son of Jesse" (1 Chr 10:13–14). William Lane Craig thinks that in this passage we see "in microcosm the mystery of divine sovereignty and human freedom. On the one hand, Saul took his own life; on the other, God killed Saul."[47] Craig sees Molinism as the key to unraveling this mystery. He explains:

---

46. Craig, "God's Middle Knowledge," 167.
47. Molina, *Concordia* 4.53.3.17, 252.

God knew what Saul would freely do in those circumstances, and though he did not desire Saul to commit suicide, he permitted him to do so freely, knowing that by this means David would take the throne, which is what God wanted. (This is obviously grossly simplified; Saul's suicide has an ever-widening ripple effect down through subsequent history, which God also takes into account.) Thus, Saul freely took his own life, but the chronicler, looking at it from the perspective of God's plan, says the Lord slew Saul.[48]

Another prime example of God achieving his plans via human free choices is seen in the account of Joseph's brothers selling Joseph into slavery. In their jealous hatred of Joseph, the brothers made a plot to kill him before ultimately selling him into slavery. After enduring slavery and imprisonment for many years, Joseph became second in command of Egypt and was reunited with his brothers when they went to Egypt for food to survive the famine that God brought about. Despite the fact that Joseph came to be in Egypt as a result of his brothers' sinful actions, Joseph reassured his brothers that everything happened according to God's plan. Joseph said, "God sent me before you to preserve for you a remnant in the earth, and to keep you alive by a great deliverance" (Gen 45:7). Even though it was the brothers who sold Joseph off to Egypt, Joseph nevertheless regarded this as God's decision. When his brothers later begged him to forgive them, Joseph responded, "Do not be afraid, for am I in God's place? As for you, you meant evil against me, but God meant it for good in order to bring about this present result, to preserve many people alive" (Gen 50:19–20). How then can one make sense of the fact that the brothers' sinful actions were intended by God to accomplish his purposes? Clearly, God does not tempt anyone to sin or cause anyone to do evil (Jas 1:13). It is unbiblical to think that God *caused* the brothers to carry out the sinful actions that brought Joseph to Egypt; however, Molinism shows how God can achieve his purposes via the free choices of humans. Although God would prefer that the brothers would not make the sinful choice that they did, God knew they would make that choice if placed into those particular circumstances. God simply brought about the circumstances, knowing how he would use their free actions to ultimately accomplish his good and loving purposes.

The death of Jesus also provides another remarkable case of God achieving his predetermined plan via sinful human actions. Peter, in his

---

48. Craig, "God's Middle Knowledge," 168.

Pentecost speech, emphasizes to the people of Jerusalem the dual truths that they were responsible for the crucifixion of Jesus and that this event was part of God's intentional plan. Concerning Jesus, Peter emphasizes that "this Man, delivered over by the predetermined plan and foreknowledge of God, you nailed to a cross by the hands of godless men and put Him to death" (Acts 2:23). Although it was God's plan, the people are responsible for this sin. Peter again declares in a subsequent speech to the people of Jerusalem that "the God of Abraham, Isaac and Jacob, the God of our fathers, has glorified His servant Jesus, the one whom you delivered and disowned in the presence of Pilate, when he had decided to release Him" (Acts 3:13). Yet Peter follows up this statement concerning the responsibility of the people by again insisting that this happened so that "the things which God announced beforehand by the mouth of all the prophets, that His Christ would suffer, He has thus fulfilled" (Acts 3:18). Similarly, after Peter and John were released from prison by the Jewish authorities, the early believers lifted up a prayer to God, saying, "For truly in this city there were gathered together against Your holy servant Jesus, whom You anointed, both Herod and Pontius Pilate, along with the Gentiles and the peoples of Israel, to do whatever Your hand and Your purpose predestined to occur" (Acts 4:27–28).[49]

These biblical statements concerning the death of Jesus reveal the incredible extent of God's sovereignty over human history. That God is able to bring about the sacrificial death of Jesus in just the time and place that God has eternally planned without violating the free will of the human agents responsible for Jesus' death is nothing short of amazing. Apart from the truth of Molinism, it is inexplicable how this could be accomplished. As Craig puts it, if we allow that God possesses middle knowledge, then

> via his middle knowledge, God knew exactly which persons, if members of the Sanhedrin, would freely vote for Jesus' condemnation; which persons, if in Jerusalem, would freely demand Christ's death, favoring the release of Barabbas; what Herod, if king, would freely do in reaction to Jesus and to Pilate's plea to judge him on his own; and what Pilate himself, if holding the prefecture of Palestine in A.D. 27, would freely do under pressure from the Jewish leaders and the crowd. Knowing all the possible circumstances, persons and permutations of these

---

49. For other biblical statements indicating both the human responsibility for Jesus' death and God's foreordination of the event, see Acts 13:27 and Luke 22:22.

circumstances and persons, God decreed to create just those circumstances and just those people who would freely do what God willed to happen.[50]

Indeed, even some opponents of Molinism recognize the fact that reconciling this type of meticulous sovereignty with human libertarian freedom cannot be done apart from Molinism. For example, William Hasker, in a response to the Molinist Thomas Flint, admits: "If you are committed to a 'strong' view of providence, according to which, down to the smallest detail, 'things are as they are because God knowingly decided to create such a world,' and yet you also wish to maintain a libertarian concept of free will—if this is what you want, then Molinism is the only game in town."[51] Of course, as a proponent of open theism, Hasker argues that God must take risks without knowing what the future holds; Hasker thus opts to deny this "strong view of God's providence." As we have seen, however, the biblical data indicates that God is sovereign over a vast range of "large" and even "small" things—and, by implication, over *all* things.

We thus have strong biblical grounds for finding Molinism attractive. Molinism is supported by the biblical evidence that God has knowledge of counterfactuals concerning human actions and that humans possess the libertarian freedom to act other than the way they do act. The fact that God does not determine our actions and yet knows what we would freely choose in non-actual circumstances strongly indicates that God has middle knowledge. Furthermore, Molinism may be the only mechanism by which God can be fully sovereign over a world of free creatures. It is also worth noting that Molinism, if true, has the benefit of resolving much of the tension between Calvinism and Arminianism.[52] The Molinist can affirm with the Arminian that humans have libertarian freedom such that they are not determined to act as they do;[53] that

50. Craig, "The Middle-Knowledge View," 134.

51. Hasker, "Response to Thomas Flint," 117–18. Flint cites this quote on page 75 of his book *Divine Providence* and proceeds to explain why Hasker is correct that Molinism is the only way to reconcile libertarian freedom with a strong view of God's sovereignty.

52. Craig, "Middle Knowledge: A Calvinist-Arminian Rapprochement?," 141–64. Craig argues effectively that Molinism captures key insights of Calvinism and Arminianism, shrinking the gap between them.

53. Of course, as I have noted previously, some Calvinists (such as Plantinga) also affirm that humans have libertarian freedom. Plantinga only denies that humans have libertarian freedom with regard to accepting Christ.

unlimited atonement is true; that God genuinely desires for all to be saved; and that all people are given sufficient grace such that they can respond to God's calling and be saved if they so choose. Yet the Molinist can, like the Calvinist, make sense of substantive sovereignty; indeed, Molinism can even affirm a sense in which God elects individuals to salvation.[54] Since, according to Molinism, God knows the various circumstances under which a person would freely choose to be saved, God can elect (in a real sense) that person to salvation by creating him or her in such a circumstance. In this way, Molinism allows that "it is up to God whether we find ourselves in a world in which we are predestined, but that it is up to us whether we are predestined in the world in which we find ourselves."[55] (Of course, if anyone would freely choose to be saved in any world in which that person has libertarian freedom or if anyone would freely choose to be lost in any world in which that person has libertarian freedom, then for such persons it would not be up to God whether they find themselves in a world in which they are predestined to be saved or predestined to be lost. It would be up to God that they exist, but it would be solely up to them that they are predestined for salvation or damnation in any world in which they exist with free will because God could not actualize any world in which such a person is free and a different soteriological outcome would occur for that person. There is no way to know, however, whether such persons exist or could exist.) If God has middle knowledge, there are a variety of ways that God could choose to use it in electing individuals to salvation; indeed, although the doctrine

---

54. Some have argued that Jacobus Arminius was actually a Molinist, but there is a limit to the comparison that should be made between the views of Arminius and Molina. Eef Dekker shows that Arminius was influenced by Molina to accept that God possesses counterfactual knowledge of human free choices. See Dekker, "Was Arminius a Molinist?," 337–52. However, Kirk MacGregor points out that Arminius only believed that God has knowledge of human free choices *logically subsequent* to God's creative decree to create the world. Once God determined to create a world of certain people, Arminius thought, God then knows on that basis how those people will freely choose. It is then the people whom God knows will choose to be saved that are corporately considered the "elect." This is not true Molinism. See MacGregor, *A Molinist-Anabaptist Systematic Theology*, 69–73. MacGregor also points out that many Reformed Christians "reject Molinism out of hand on the faulty assumption that [Molinism and Arminianism] are basically the same thing." They wrongly see Molinism as merely a "slightly more philosophically sophisticated version" of Arminianism. In reality, "Molinism agrees or disagrees with Calvinism at various points and agrees or disagrees with Arminianism at various points." See MacGregor, *Luis de Molina*, 18–19.

55. Craig, "Middle Knowledge: A Calvinist-Arminian Rapprochement?," 157.

of middle knowledge in no way requires this view, Molina actually held that God uses his middle knowledge to elect unconditionally individuals to salvation. We will examine this later.

With all of these advantages, Molinism stands on solid biblical ground. Craig goes so far as to say that "middle knowledge, if coherent, is one of the most fruitful theological ideas ever conceived. For it would serve to explain not only God's knowledge of the future, but divine providence and predestination as well."[56] But is Molinism coherent? Does it hold up to philosophical scrutiny? It is to that subject that we now turn.

Philosophical Defense of Molinism

Even though Molinism seems to be the only way to resolve the difficult biblical puzzle of explaining the combination of human libertarian freedom, God's counterfactual knowledge of our actions, and God's detailed sovereignty over all things, the question remains as to whether it is a philosophically defensible concept. In order to defend Molinism, one need not offer a "proof" that it is true; rather, a defense of the coherence of Molinism is all that is necessary. If Molinism seems to be coherent and at least possibly true, then there can be no objection to its acceptance and to leveraging its significant explanatory power. While a variety of philosophical arguments have been lodged against the claim that God has middle knowledge, these attacks really only target a couple of key areas. The first—and most important—area of attack is to deny that any counterfactual of creaturely freedom (CCF) can be true. The second is to deny that God can know CCFs logically prior to God's decision to create the actual world.[57] A CCF is a counterfactual "of the form *If S were in C*,

---

56. Craig, *The Only Wise God*, 127.

57. Craig, *The Only Wise God*, 138–39. In exploring the anti-Molinist literature, I am in agreement with Craig's assessment that these are the two basic areas of philosophical objection to Molinism. The second objection, as we will see, can be broken into two separate issues: (1) Can God know counterfactuals of creaturely freedom? (2) If so, can God know counterfactuals of creaturely freedom logically prior to God's decision to create the existing world? Ken Perszyk, in surveying the current scholarly landscape concerning Molinism, agrees with Craig that the main anti-Molinist objections are the claims that: (1) "there are or can be no true counterfactuals of freedom; all are false or neither true nor false" (or at least "there are or can be no true counterfactuals of freedom *prior* to God's creative decisions"); and (2) "God cannot *know* counterfactuals of freedom prior to his decrees even if they are true prior to them." See: Perszyk, "Introduction," 7.

S *would freely do* A, where S is a created agent, A is some action, and C is a set of fully specified circumstances including the whole history of the world up until the time of S's free action."[58] Let us begin with the first major type of objection.

The Truth of Counterfactuals of Creaturely Freedom

Some philosophers argue that there is no valid basis for the truth of any CCF—either by contending that CCFs are all false or by making the case that they have no truth value at all. The most significant reason why such philosophers—most notably Robert Adams and William Hasker—reject the truth of CCFs is what is known as the "grounding objection." Ken Perszyk, who has done much work on the viability of Molinism, is correct in his assessment that the grounding objection is "the most common objection to the coherence of Molinism in recent times."[59] Besides the grounding objection, the other key argument against there being true CCFs is one that was put forward in the 1980s—and is still defended today in an updated form—by William Hasker and is known as the "bring about" argument. These two prominent objections, therefore, will be our focus in this section.[60]

Let us begin with the grounding objection. The grounding objection originated with Adams in his 1977 article "Middle Knowledge and the Problem of Evil." In this article, he argues that it is not possible for God to have middle knowledge because CCFs cannot be true apart from a metaphysical basis, or "grounds," for their truth. Since CCFs are conditionals stating what a free creature would freely do if placed in some non-actual

---

58. Craig, "Middle Knowledge, Truth-Makers," 338.

59. Perszyk, "Recent Work on Molinism," 758.

60. Perszyk offers a nice summary of the landscape of philosophical objections to the truth of CCFs in the contemporary debate and how Molinists have dealt with them. See Perszyk, "Recent Work on Molinism," 757–60. Besides the grounding type of argument and the "bring about" argument (both of which we will examine briefly), he mentions two others: "might" arguments and "tie" arguments. These arguments are not of much prominence in the literature and are widely considered to have been answered. The "might" type of argument is explained by Perszyk on p. 757, and he summarizes the Molinist response. Thomas Flint similarly gives a helpful description of how this type of argument has been handled for over two decades. See: Flint, "Whence and Whither," 38–39. The "tie" type of argument is explained by Perszyk on p. 758, and he points out how Alvin Plantinga has provided a forceful answer to it. Neither the "might" nor the "tie" arguments will be discussed here.

circumstance,⁶¹ Adams makes the case that there is nothing in reality to ground the truth of such a conditional. He contends that "the intentions or character of the agents" cannot ground the truth of CCFs because the free agents involved "may act out of character" or their intentions or desires may change.⁶² He also argues that the free will of the agent would be undermined if the truth of the CCF is grounded in "logical or causal necessitation," so he eliminates that possibility and concludes that he does "not see how these counterfactuals can be true."⁶³ Hasker similarly raises the challenge: "Who or what is it (if anything) that brings it about that these propositions are true?"⁶⁴ He argues that there can be no true CCFs because neither God nor the agent involved in the CCF causally brings about the truth of the CCF. Hasker holds that "truths about 'what *would be the case . . . if*' must be grounded in truths about what *is in fact* the case." He thinks the truth of counterfactuals must be grounded in something about "the natures, causal powers, inherent tendencies, and the like, of the natural entities described in them."⁶⁵

Craig rightly points out that the grounding objection is an application of a theory of truth known as "truth-maker theory." This theory holds that true propositions have a "truth-maker"—a basis upon which there is sufficient grounds for the proposition being true.⁶⁶ It is important to note that truth-makers, according to the standard theory, are *not* required to be concrete objects that *cause* the proposition in question to be true; rather, truth-makers are merely states of affairs that provide a logical basis for the truth of the proposition. Truth-maker theorists generally understand truth-makers in this way for good reason. As Craig points out, statements such as the following cannot have truth-makers that are currently existing concrete objects: negative statements that

---

61. Note once again that a "circumstance" here refers to what is often called a maximal world segment—a complete description of the entire history of the world up until the exact moment that the agent who is part of the CCF freely acts.

62. Adams, "Middle Knowledge and the Problem of Evil," 114. This is a reprinting of his original 1977 article.

63. Adams, "An Anti-Molinist Argument," 345. Adams regards as false CCFs having to do with "possible but non-actual creatures" and all CCFs that "have false consequents." He thinks that if CCFs "with true consequents about actual creatures are true at all, their truth arises too late in the order of explanation to play the part in divine providence that it is supposed to play according to Molina's theory."

64. Hasker, *God, Time, and Knowledge*, 39.

65. Hasker, *God, Time, and Knowledge*, 30.

66. Craig, "Middle Knowledge, Truth-Makers," 339–40.

express the non-existence of something (e.g., "Dinosaurs are extinct today"); universal statements (e.g., "All ravens are black"); and statements about people who have died (e.g., "Napoleon lost the Battle of Waterloo") or are not yet born (e.g., "The U. S. President in [the year 2300] will be a woman").[67] Even in the case where there is an agent involved in causing the state of affairs that brings a proposition into correspondence with reality, truth-maker theorists regard the state of affairs, and not the agent, as the truth-maker. William Vallicella explains:

> All are agreed that truth-making is not a causal relation, even though there is a sense in which an agent who brings about a state of affairs 'makes true' the corresponding proposition. Thus by painting the gate red, there is a sense in which I make true the proposition expressed by 'The gate is red.' But what is really going on here is that I cause a concrete state of affairs to exist, and then it [the state of affairs that the fence is red] noncausally makes true the corresponding proposition.[68]

Thus, proponents of the grounding objection, such as Adams and Hasker, are not even consistent with standard truth-maker theory because they demand that there must be some concrete thing in reality that *causes* a proposition to be true. Of course, given the nature of a CCF, there will not be a concrete object that causes the CCF to be true. This departure from truth-maker theory ought to be an initial reason to have doubts about whether the grounding objection reveals that CCFs cannot be true.

Beyond Adams and Hasker not keeping with truth-maker theory by making it a requisite condition for the truth of CCFs that some sort of concrete object causes the CCF to be true, one may further ask why CCFs must have any truth-maker at all (even a noncausal one). As Craig points out, even very few truth-maker theorists accept the idea that all true propositions must have truth-makers (a view known as "truth-maker maximalism").[69] Craig adds:

> I have yet to encounter an argument for the conclusion that counterfactuals of creaturely freedom cannot be among those types of truths lacking a truth-maker. Indeed, when one reflects on the fact that such statements are *counter*factual in nature,

---

67. Craig, "Middle Knowledge, Truth-Makers," 341–43.
68. Vallicella, *A Paradigm Theory of Existence*, 165–66.
69. Craig, "Middle Knowledge, Truth-Makers," 343–44.

then such statements might seem to be prime candidates for belonging to that diverse class of statements which are true without having any truth-makers.[70]

Yet, in any case, a number of prominent Molinists do allow that CCFs may have *noncausal* truth-makers. Alvin Plantinga asks us to consider, for example, the following CCF: "If Curley had been offered a bribe of $35,000, he would have (freely) accepted it." Plantinga claims that "what grounds the truth of the counterfactual, we may say, is just that in fact Curley is such that if he had been offered a $35,000 bribe, he would have freely taken it."[71] That is, Plantinga allows that if CCFs must be grounded, what grounds a CCF is simply the fact that if the state of affairs described in the antecedent of the CCF were to be actual, then the specified agent would freely perform the action specified in the consequent of the CCF. Curley himself thus does not make the CCF about him true; indeed the CCF would be true even if Curley never exists. Similarly, Alfred Freddoso has argued that the grounds for CCFs being true are analogous to the grounds for past-tense or future-tense statements being true. Freddoso argues that "there are now adequate metaphysical grounds for the truth of a past-tense proposition," such as "Socrates drank hemlock," just in case "there *were* at some past time adequate metaphysical grounds for the truth of its present-tense counterpart." In the same way, future-tense propositions currently have adequate metaphysical grounds if such grounds *will* exist in the future. Likewise, CCFs currently have adequate metaphysical grounds if such grounds *would* exist under the circumstances specified in the CCF.[72] So, like Plantinga, Freddoso believes a CCF is grounded by the simple fact that its consequent would be true if its antecedent condition were to be actualized. Craig[73] and Thomas

---

70. Craig, "Middle Knowledge, Truth-Makers," 344. See also Craig, "The Middle-Knowledge View," 142.

71. Plantinga, "Reply to Robert M. Adams," 374.

72. Freddoso, "Introduction," 72.

73. Craig, "Middle Knowledge, Truth-Makers," 346. Craig agrees that "what makes it true that 'If I were rich, I would buy a Mercedes,' is the fact that if I were rich I would buy a Mercedes." If the counterfactual state of affairs described in the CCF were made actual (if I were rich), it is simply true that I would buy a Mercedes. No concrete object causes this to be true. While Craig allows for such a noncausal grounding of CCFs, he strongly rejects the very notion of causal grounds for the truth of CCFs. He argues that such grounds would be incompatible with libertarian freedom. See Craig, *Divine Foreknowledge and Human Freedom*, 261–62.

Flint[74] also find such reasoning to be plausible, should one think that CCFs need to have a truth-maker at all.

Let us now turn to an examination of Hasker's "bring about" argument. This argument originated with his 1986 article "A Refutation of Middle Knowledge"[75] and his 1989 book *God, Time, and Knowledge*. Hasker helpfully makes note of the various iterations of his argument that have been published leading up to the more recent version of the argument that he defends in a chapter of the 2013 anthology *Molinism: The Contemporary Debate*.[76] I will provide the current version of Hasker's "bring about" argument before identifying why it fails to show that there can be no true CCFs.

The most recent version of Hasker's argument is somewhat complex and has two parts. The first part tries to show that if we assume for the sake of argument both that humans have libertarian freedom (which Hasker himself accepts) and that there are true CCFs (which Hasker does not accept), then this leads to the conclusion that there must be something that a free agent could do (i.e., nothing logically or causally prevents the free agent from doing it) such that, were she to do it, it would result in CCFs that are true in the actual world being false and CCFs that are false in the actual world being true. This is because libertarian freedom requires that when an agent A is in circumstance c, A could do action z or refrain from doing z. With this conclusion in place, he moves to the second part of his argument and aims to show that the idea of true CCFs leads to a second conclusion—one that conflicts with the conclusion he reached in the first part of his argument. In the second part of his argument, he contends that any true CCFs would have to be intimately connected with the history of the world (and the world's history can no longer be changed) such that there is no possible world in which we could do anything other than act in accordance with CCFs that are in fact true; thus, this second part of his argument contends that we could not do anything such that, if we were to do it, it would alter the truth value of the CCFs. So, he claims that the conclusion of the first part of his argument contradicts the conclusion of

---

74. Flint, *Divine Providence*, 137. Flint thinks Freddoso's argument gives "powerful reasons" to reject the grounding objection.

75. Hasker, "A Refutation of Middle Knowledge," 545–57.

76. Hasker, "The (Non-)Existence of Molinist Counterfactuals," 30–34. Perszyk also provides a useful history of the iterations of this argument. See Perszyk, "Recent Work on Molinism," 759–60.

the second part of his arguments, and yet both conclusions seemingly must be true if there are true CCFs. Thus, he thinks that he has offered a *reductio ad absurdum* argument that shows that it is incoherent for there to be true CCFs, so Molinism is false. With this broad overview of what Hasker is trying to accomplish in place, let us examine the details of his argument.

He first defines what he means by an agent's "bringing about" (BA) that a proposition is true: "A brings it about that Y iff: For some X, A causes it to be the case that X, and (X & H) ⇒ Y, and ∼ (H ⇒ Y), where 'H' represents the history of the world prior to its coming to be the case that X."[77] This means that for A to bring about Y, there must be some X that A has it in his power to do such that, by A doing X, that action X (together with H, which is the history of the world up to the moment of A doing X) makes it necessarily the case that Y (i.e., it entails Y); furthermore, in order for A to bring about Y it must not be the case that H would entail Y wholly apart from A doing X. In addition, it is important to understand Hasker's definition of "power." By A "having the power" to bring about something in the circumstances that A is in, Hasker means that there is nothing that *logically or causally precludes* A from bringing about that thing in the specified circumstances.[78]

Consider now the first part of his argument:

H_1. "Agent A is in circumstances c, the counterfactual of freedom 'C □→ Z' is true of her, and she freely chooses to do z. (Molinist premise)"

H_2. "A is in c, and it is in A's power to refrain from doing z. (From [H_1] and definition of libertarian freedom)"

H_3. "It is in A's power to bring it about that: A is in c, and A refrains from doing z. (From [H_2])"

H_4. "If it is in A's power to bring it about that P, and 'P' entails 'Q' and 'Q' is false, then it is in A's power to bring it about that Q. (Power Entailment Principle)"

H_5. "(A is in c and refrains from doing z) ⇒ (C □→ ∼ Z). (Molinist premise)"

---

77. Hasker, "The (Non-)Existence of Molinist Counterfactuals," 31. Note that "iff" means "if and only if."

78. Hasker makes this understanding of "power" clear in his more recent article: Hasker, "Molinism's Freedom Problem," 93–106.

H_6. "If it is in A's power to bring it about that A is in c and refrains from doing z, and '(C $\square\!\!\rightarrow$ ~ Z)' is false, then it is in A's power to bring it about that (C $\square\!\!\rightarrow$ ~ Z). (From [H_4, H_5])"

H_7. "It is in A's power to bring it about that (C $\square\!\!\rightarrow$ ~ Z). (From [H_1, H_3, H_6])"[79]

So far Hasker's argument seems to be correct, and Molinists should see no problem with the conclusion he reaches in H_7. He establishes in H_1 that A would freely do z in c, so the CCF (C $\square\!\!\rightarrow$ Z) is true. In H_2, the Molinist should agree that, given that A is in c, it must be within A's power to refrain from doing z; that is, since A has libertarian freedom, there must be no logical or causal factors that preclude A from not doing z in c even though A actually does freely do z in c. Then H_3 is correct that there must be nothing that logically or causally prevents A from being in c and doing something such that, if A were to do it, it would entail that A refrains from doing z (whereas the history of the world alone—apart from A doing that thing—does not entail that A refrains from doing z in c). Hasker gives an argument for H_4 that is not stated here and will not be disputed. Certainly, H_5 is correct that A being in c and refraining from z would entail the truth of the CCF (C $\square\!\!\rightarrow$ ~ Z). Then H_6 and H_7 seem to follow, and the Molinist ought to agree with H_7 that there must be nothing that logically or causally prevents A from doing something in c such that, if A were to do it, the CCF (C $\square\!\!\rightarrow$ ~ Z) would be true.[80]

Let us now move to the second part of Hasker's argument in which he aims to produce a conclusion from Molinist principles that contradicts H_7. Hasker points out that "according to (BA), if the agent is to bring about the truth of a counterfactual (C $\square\!\!\rightarrow$ X), it must not be the case that (H $\Rightarrow$ (C $\square\!\!\rightarrow$ X)). That is to say, the counterfactual must not be entailed by

---

79. Hasker, "The (Non-)Existence of Molinist Counterfactuals," 31–32. The CCF (C $\square\!\!\rightarrow$ Z) should be understood as: "If A were in c, A would freely do z." The CCF (C $\square\!\!\rightarrow$ ~Z) should be understood as: "If A were in c, A would freely refrain from doing z." Also note that the symbol '$\rightarrow$' represents entailment or necessitation.

80. Note that the truth of H_7 does not mean that A is a truth-maker that causes the CCF to be true. As I explained previously, what makes a CCF true (if CCFs need a truth-maker) is the fact that if the counterfactual state of affairs described in the antecedent of the CCF were made actual then the consequent accurately describes what the agent would do. H_7 only means that there is nothing that logically or causally prevents A from doing something in c such that, if A were to do it, the CCF (C $\square\!\!\rightarrow$ ~ Z) would be true. Thus, H_7 is just accepting the libertarian freedom of A to have refrained from doing z in c and allowing that if it were true that A would refrain from doing z in c then (C $\square\!\!\rightarrow$ ~ Z) would be true and (C $\square\!\!\rightarrow$ Z) would be false.

the world's past history."[81] But Hasker thinks that *all* true CCFs (again, he is granting only for the sake of argument that there are true CCFs) would necessarily be entailed by the past history of the world. This does not mean that the history of the world would make the CCF true (since the CCF would be true even if God never created anything). Rather, it means that the history of the world is the way it is because God designed it that way in virtue of the truth of the CCF. Given that the world is ordered the way it is, that entails that the antecedent of the CCF will be made actual (i.e., the agent will be in the specified circumstances). The agent will thus (since the CCF is true) act in accordance with the consequent of the CCF. So the truth of the CCF has had a causal impact on events in the past history of the world, since God was ordering the world as he did because he knew the truth of the CCF and wanted the agent to do what is specified in the CCF. Therefore, Hasker argues that if (C $\Box\!\!\rightarrow$ Z) is true, then it is impossible for A to bring it about that (C $\Box\!\!\rightarrow$ ~ Z) is true. Given that the history of the world (made up of events that have occurred and that are now unchangeable) is intimately bound up with the truth of (C $\Box\!\!\rightarrow$ Z), there is no possible world in which A is in c and freely refrains from doing z. That means there is no possible world in which (C $\Box\!\!\rightarrow$ ~ Z) can be true. So there is nothing that A can do in c such that the truth value of (C $\Box\!\!\rightarrow$ Z) or (C $\Box\!\!\rightarrow$ ~ Z) would be different. From this, he concludes that it is not within A's power to bring it about that (C $\Box\!\!\rightarrow$ ~ Z). So the premises for the second part of Hasker's argument are:

> H_8. "It is not in an agent's power to bring about the truth of the counterfactuals of freedom about her. (Argued for above)"
>
> H_9. "It is not in A's power to bring it about that (C $\Box\!\!\rightarrow$ ~ Z). (From [H_8])"[82]

So H_8 contends that the agent is logically or causally prevented from doing something in any circumstances in which she finds herself such that, if she were to do it, any CCF about her that is already true would be false or any CCF about her that is already false would be true. For example, if (C $\Box\!\!\rightarrow$ Z) is true and this CCF is causally bound up with the history of the world, then there is no possible world in which A freely does something in c such that (C $\Box\!\!\rightarrow$ ~ Z) is true. So from H_8, Hasker concludes H_9. H_9 contradicts H_7, and Hasker concludes that since both

---

81. Hasker, "The (Non-)Existence of Molinist Counterfactuals," 32.
82. Hasker, "The (Non-)Existence of Molinist Counterfactuals," 34.

H_9 and H_7 seemingly must be true if there are true CCFs and since they contradict each other, then he has offered a successful *reductio ad absurdum* argument that shows that it is incoherent for there to be true CCFs. Molinism, therefore, is false.

A crucial mistake in Hasker's argument is pointed out well by Thomas Flint, and it involves the second part of the argument. Let us grant to Hasker his contention that if there are true CCFs then the history of the world would necessarily include all true CCFs. In arriving at H_8, Hasker is assuming the following flawed assumption (FA): "If it's not possible that A brings it about that X, then it's not possible that A has the power to bring it about that X."[83] His FA comes into play in H_8 because he correctly recognizes (assuming, again, that we grant that all true CCFs are indeed included in the history of the world) that there is no world in which A *actually brings it about* that any true CCF is false or that any false CCF is true; however, he wrongly infers from this that there is no world in which A *has it in her power* to act freely so as to bring it about that any true CCF is false or that any false CCF is true. For example, Hasker is correct that there is no world in which A freely brings it about that (C $\Box\to$ ~ Z). This is because A would freely do z in c (and, in fact, did do z in c), as H_1 makes clear. So there simply is no world in which A would freely refrain from doing z in c; that is just not what A would freely do in c. But it is not legitimate to start with the fact that in no world does A "bring it about that (C $\Box\to$ ~ Z)" and then infer that there is no world in which A has "the power to bring it about that (C $\Box\to$ ~ Z)."[84] This is because, if A has libertarian freedom, there is nothing that logically or causally precludes A from doing something such that, were she to do it, she would refrain from doing z in c—even though there is no world in which she would freely refrain from z in c. An agent can have freedom to refrain from doing z in c, and yet it can still be the case that there is no world in which the agent freely refrains from doing z in c.

So even if we grant that all true CCFs are bound up in (i.e., entailed by) the history of the world, Hasker's argument does not succeed. Of course, if we do not grant that all true CCFs are bound up in the history of the world, then Flint is correct in pointing out that "Hasker has given us no reason at all to think that [H_8] is true."[85] Thus we may conclude that

83. Flint, "Whence and Whither," 41.
84. Flint, "Whence and Whither," 42.
85. Flint, "Whence and Whither," 43.

Hasker's argument is in trouble either way. Flint sums things up nicely with regard to Hasker's "bring about" argument by saying:

> Molinists think that certain counterfactuals of creaturely freedom are true. The truth of those counterfactuals, they believe, does not interfere with the relevant creatures' freedom to do otherwise. Even though (C □→ Z) is true and A is in C, A still is able to do ~ Z. Had she done ~ Z, (C □→ Z) wouldn't have been true. Instead, (C □→ ~ Z) would have been true. So A has the power to do something (~ Z), such that, had she done it, a counterfactual that is true—namely, (C □→ Z)—would have been false. Of course, God in fact believed, and acted on the belief, that (C □→ Z) was true (as were innumerably many other such counterfactuals). And those beliefs, along with the creative actions which they informed, have had causal consequences. So Molinists think that a creature such as A can have the power to do something such that, were she to do it, God never would have believed, and never would have acted on, the counterfactuals of creaturely freedom he in fact believed and acted on, but instead would have believed and acted on other counterfactuals of creaturely freedom; and had he acted on *them*, some of the causal consequences that *in fact* followed from his actual beliefs and actions might well not have occurred.
>
> That's the Molinist view. Is it reasonable? I and others have argued that it is—that the *type* of 'power over the past' that it affords us is one that, carefully considered, is extremely plausible. Hasker and others disagree. But Hasker has little new to say in opposition to this view, and I have little new to say in defense of it. What I *am* convinced of, though, is that attempts to 'refute' this view by this, that, or the other elaborate account of 'bringing about' is not going to get us very far.[86]

Beyond the above defensive measures aimed at upholding the coherence of true CCFs by responding to the "grounding" and "bring about" objections, it is important to recognize that there are positive reasons to accept the truth of CCFs. Perhaps most significantly, it is intuitively quite reasonable to think that some CCFs are true. Plantinga remarks that the claim that there are no true CCFs "seems odd" on the surface of things simply because "it seems that we often believe them to be true."[87] For example, Plantinga is convinced that "if Bob Adams were to offer to

---

86. Flint, "Whence and Whither," 43–44.
87. Plantinga, "Reply to Robert M. Adams," 374.

take me climbing at Tahquitz Rock the next time I come to California, I would gladly (and freely) accept."[88] As Craig points out, we commonly accept the truth of CCFs in everyday life, making statements such as: "If I had known you were coming, I would have baked a cake."[89] We can even see that some CCFs turn out to be true. Freddoso asks us to imagine the Apostle John, just prior to the arrest of Jesus, making the following statement: "If Peter were tempted anytime soon to deny Jesus, he would succumb." Then, after Peter does deny Christ, Freddoso contends that John could legitimately "maintain that what he asserted was true."[90] Although Peter's denial provides John with the evidence that his statement was true when he made it, Freddoso rightly points out that John's statement would still be true even if Peter was never tempted (regardless of whether we have epistemic justification for knowing it is true).

Additionally, CCFs follow the Law of Conditional Excluded Middle[91] and must, therefore, be either true or false. Craig reasons that "since the circumstances C in which the free agent is placed are fully specified in the counterfactual's antecedent, it seems that if the agent were placed in C and left free with respect to action A, then he must either do A or not do A. For what other alternative is there?"[92] There must, to offer an example, be a truth about what Mary would have done in response to Robert sending her a text message this morning at 9:50 am EDT that read, "Would you like to go to a movie with me tonight?" Robert did not send the text. If, however, he had sent it to her, then there is surely a truth about what she

---

88. Plantinga, "Reply to Robert M. Adams," 373.

89. Craig, *The Only Wise God*, 139. It is even common to believe that life-altering outcomes would have been different if circumstances had been different. For example, "If his vision had not been blocked by the parked van, he would not have run out into the road and been killed."

90. Freddoso, "Introduction," 72. Jonathan Kvanvig makes a similar point. See Kvanvig, *The Possibility of an All-Knowing God*, 138.

91. The Law of Conditional Excluded Middle holds that: $(P \rightarrow Q) \vee (P \rightarrow \sim Q)$.

92. Craig, "Middle Knowledge, Truth-Makers," 338. Suggesting as a third alternative that the agent *probably* would do A does not work, since "probably" merely reflects epistemic uncertainty that one might have about predicting the outcome and is not a genuine alternative; there is surely a truth about what the outcome would be (either A or not A) even if we cannot know what it would be. Craig comments in the footnote on this page that Peter van Inwagen's "objection that it might be the case that the agent would on one occasion do A and on a second go-around not do A actually supports the Molinist case, for there are two different turns and thus different sets of circumstances, and by Van Inwagen's own lights on each turn the agent would do something (Peter Van Inwagen, 'Against Middle Knowledge,' lecture dated April 12, 1996)."

would have freely done in response. Regardless of the fact that humans can never have certainty about what Mary would have done (indeed, Mary, if asked later about what her response would have been if Robert had sent her that exact text at 9:50 am EDT this morning, may not be sure about what precise words she would have used in her response to Robert at that time), it seems clear that she would have had to respond in some particular way (even if the response was to ignore him). It seems that the following CCF must either be true or false: If Mary received a text from Robert at 9:50 am EDT this morning that asked, "Would you like to go to a movie with me tonight?", then Mary would have sent Robert a text at 9:54 am EDT with the words "That sounds fun. Let's do it!" If this CCF is true, then the reason it is true is because the consequent accurately describes what would have resulted if the antecedent conditions had been actual. If this CCF is false, it is because the consequent does not accurately describe what would have resulted if the antecedent conditions had been actual. The CCF must either be true or false.

We have now seen that, in addition to the Bible affirming the truth of CCFs, some CCFs intuitively appear to be true. In addition, we have discovered that neither of the most prominent objections to the truth of CCFs seem to carry much force. To my knowledge, nobody has yet to offer a forceful philosophical reason to call into question the strong reasons for thinking that CCFs are true. It seems to be at least possible—if not plausible—that there are true CCFs. Apart from a compelling argument against the possibility of true CCFs, one appears to be justified in thinking that the intuition most people seem to have that there are true CCFs is reasonable. Let us now turn our attention to the remaining key philosophical challenge to Molinism: Can God know CCFs logically prior to his decision to create the existing world?

God's Knowledge of Counterfactuals of Creaturely Freedom

It might seem obvious that if CCFs can be true, then God, because he is omniscient, must know these truths. Yet some philosophers disagree. Richard Swinburne, for example, holds that even if we "suppose that there are counterfactuals of freedom with truth-value," we would be "wrong in supposing that anyone could have incorrigible knowledge of the truth-value of a counterfactual of freedom." Why does Swinburne insist that such a truth cannot be known? It is for the same reason "that no one can foreknow incorrigibly the future free actions of an agent in circumstances which *will* be realized."[93] That is, he thinks it is logically impossible to know *any* true proposition about how a creature with libertarian freedom will act unless and until the creature acts. His reasoning concerning the future actions of free creatures is as follows:

> Consider such a free agent f faced with a choice tomorrow of doing x or not doing x; and any pre-cognizer G. If G were to know today what f will do tomorrow, he will have a belief about this—for knowledge entails belief. Given that, of logical necessity, the past is unaffectable by present actions (causes cannot follow their effects), then G's belief today will be what it is before and independently of what f does tomorrow. If f is indeed free, he is free to make G's belief, whatever it is, false. He may not do so, but he has it in his power to do so, and so G's belief cannot be necessarily true, and so cannot amount to incorrigible knowledge.[94]

So, for Swinburne, the reason that God cannot know CCFs (or future free actions, for that matter) is that there is no *justification* for God knowing what a free creature *would* (or, in the case of future free actions, *will*) choose to do. Because the actions of a creature with libertarian freedom are "not necessitated by other agents or prior states of the world," Swinburne holds that it would be a "very fortunate coincidence" if God should be lucky enough to hold true beliefs about all such actions apart from them actually happening.[95] This means that true CCFs that never come to pass can never be known, and any true proposition involving future free actions cannot be known until the event occurs. It also means that Swinburne, since he still wants to hold that God is omniscient, must revise the traditional understanding of God's omniscience in order to accommodate the fact that there are numerous true propositions of which God is ignorant. Departing from the traditional definition of omniscience ("knowing all true propositions and only true propositions"), Swinburne claims that omniscience should be understood as "knowledge at every time of all that is logically possible for God to know at that time. This knowledge does not include knowledge of the true propositions about the future actions of free agents."[96] So, just as God's omnipotence is not limited

---

93. Swinburne, *Providence and the Problem of Evil*, 131.
94. Swinburne, *Providence and the Problem of Evil*, 132.
95. Swinburne, *The Coherence of Theism*, 170–71.
96. Swinburne, *Providence and the Problem of Evil*, 133–34. William Hasker

An Explanation and Defense of Molinism

by God's inability to perform logically impossible tasks such as making a square circle, Swinburne does not consider God's inability to know truths concerning the unactualized actions of free creatures to be problematic because Swinburne considers such truths logically impossible to know.[97]

In response to Swinburne's position, it should first be noted that his attempt to redefine omniscience such that God can be considered omniscient despite being ignorant of countless true propositions is problematic. Jonathan Kvanvig rightly argues that the analogy Swinburne makes between excluding logically impossible tasks from God's omnipotence and excluding truths that are (purportedly) logically impossible to know from God's omniscience is "crucially defective."[98] Kvanvig asserts: "Whereas an unknowable truth is still a truth, an unfeasible task is not a task at all."[99] God, for example, cannot make a square circle because it is not a thing at all; thus, this "limitation"[100] on God's omnipotence is "a limitation regarding the thing done: self-contradictory descriptions are not descriptions of any task at all." However, when it comes to an omniscient being's ability to know a legitimately true proposition, one cannot say that there is no proposition to be known; rather, "the apparent limitation regards the *person* in question: the knower is somehow unable to access the proposition."[101] So Swinburne's redefinition truly puts God's attribute of omniscience at stake. If Swinburne is correct that God does not know all true propositions, then God cannot be considered omniscient in any legitimate sense.

Swinburne has provided no convincing evidence that CCFs (or future free actions, for that matter) cannot possibly be known by God. As we have seen, Swinburne's contention is that it is not possible for God to

---

redefines omniscience in a similar way. See Hasker, *God, Time, and Knowledge*, 187.

97. Swinburne, *The Coherence of Theism*, 175.

98. Kvanvig, *The Possibility of an All-Knowing God*, 22.

99. Kvanvig, *The Possibility of an All-Knowing God*, 22.

100. Of course, as Kvanvig correctly clarifies, it is technically a "misnomer" to describe God's inability to perform logically impossible tasks as a "limitation" on God's omnipotence because these are not tasks to perform.

101. Kvanvig, *The Possibility of an All-Knowing God*, 23. One might say there are other "limitations" on God's omnipotence that do not involve self-contradictory tasks (e.g., God cannot act immorally). In such cases, however, it is simply impossible that God would act in opposition to his essential attributes. God cannot act immorally because God is essentially the very paradigm of goodness. God cannot give up any of his essential attributes or act in opposition to them because to do so would mean that he is not God, which is impossible.

know how a free creature would act "before and independently" of the free creature acting. God cannot perceive the action, since it has not yet occurred. Moreover, since the creature is free and is not determined to choose to act one way rather than another, there are no causal factors that allow God to deduce with certainty what the free creature would do in the specified circumstance. He thus concludes that it cannot be known how the free creature would act. Swinburne's view, however, assumes without warrant a *perceptualist model of God's knowledge*.

The perceptualist model assumes that God can only know things by directly perceiving them or inferring them based on existing causes. This, however, seems to be a highly dubious requirement to place on God's means of acquiring knowledge. Craig's point is a good one:

> How do we know that the heavy reliance which we as embodied persons have on perception and causal inference would apply to an infinite disembodied Mind? Obviously God does not have knowledge based on sense perception (since he has no organs). So could he not possess all knowledge apart from causal inferences as well?[102]

If one instead adopts a *conceptualist model* of divine knowledge by which God *innately* possesses the knowledge that he has, then Swinburne's objection is resolved. This would not be, as Swinburne fears, a case of "causes following their effects"; this is an epistemological matter rather than an ontological matter, and there is no backward causation taking place. If God eternally has an innate knowledge of all true propositions (which, as has been argued, includes CCFs), then God need not "observe" things that occur or reason to things that will (or would) occur in order to know them. Swinburne must show that it is *impossible* for God to have such innate knowledge if he hopes to reject the possibility of God knowing CCFs (or even future free actions). This seems to be a tall order. When it comes to the heart of this question concerning the possibility of God's complete omniscience, Craig seems to be on target in saying:

> Of course, someone might persist in demanding, '*How* can God have innate knowledge of all future-tense [and counterfactual] propositions?' But the purport of this question is not altogether clear. It cannot mean, 'How did God come by such knowledge?', for His knowledge is said to be innate. Nor do I think the question means, 'How is the concept of innate knowledge possible?',

---

102. Craig, *The Only Wise God*, 121.

for the concept does not appear to be incoherent. Perhaps the question really means, 'How is it the case that God has innate knowledge?' But then it appears to be just an expression of incredulity which could be posed of any of the divine attributes: how is it that God exists necessarily? How is it that God is omnipotent? How is it that God is morally perfect? This sort of 'how' question does not seem to have any answer—He just is that way... Being maximally excellent, He has that property in all worlds in which He exists and since He exists in the actual world, it is the case that God knows all true propositions. To ask how it is that God is omniscient is therefore like asking how it is that vacuums are empty.[103]

Having seen that CCFs are plausibly true and that God's omniscience would seem to require that God must know these truths, the key remaining question is whether God can know CCFs *logically prior* to his decision to create the actual world. Anthony Kenny puts forth a prominent argument that God cannot know CCFs logically prior to his creative decree:

> The difficulty is simply that if it is to be possible for God to know which world he is actualizing, then his middle knowledge must be logically prior to his decision to actualize; whereas if middle knowledge is to have an object, the actualization must already have taken place. As long as it is undetermined which action an individual human being will take, it is undetermined which world is the actual world... And as long as it is undetermined which world is actual, it is undetermined which counterfactuals about human free behaviour are true.[104]

Kenny thus contends that God cannot use his knowledge of CCFs to determine the actual world that he will create because God cannot know the truth of CCFs until the actual world exists. If an actual world must exist before CCFs can be true, then how can God know them and utilize them logically prior to creating the actual world? Robert Adams offers a similar argument.[105]

---

103. Craig, *Divine Foreknowledge and Human Freedom*, 229. Of course, God also has justification in believing everything that he believes simply by virtue of knowing that he is God and possesses the essential property of omniscience.

104. Kenny, *The God of the Philosophers*, 71.

105. Adams, "Middle Knowledge and the Problem of Evil," 118–20. Note what Adams says beginning on p. 118 about his Premise (9).

Contrary to this objection from Kenny, it is simply not true that a world must be actualized in order for middle knowledge "to have an object." Since CCFs are true or false apart from the existence of the circumstances and agents described in them, there does not need to be an actual world already in place in which the relevant agents or circumstances exist in order for God to know these truths (so long as one accepts the conceptualist model of divine knowledge and allows that God can somehow know CCFs in an innate way). The problem with Kenny's objection is that it requires that every aspect of the actual world must be fully actualized by God before there can be true CCFs, but this is not the case. Eef Dekker rightly argues that it is "not possible that no world is actual. There is a logical order in the way the world is 'built up,' and at one level the actuality is dependent on God's volition, while at another ('earlier') level it is not."[106] What Dekker is showing is that, even logically prior to God's creative decision, an actual world exists because numerous truths exist that do not depend upon God's creative decision-making for their truth.

Craig, in agreement with Dekker, points out that Kenny overlooks the fact that "corresponding to the logical sequence in God's knowledge there is a logical sequence in the instantiation of the actual world as well."[107] That is, the way the actual world is logically "built up" mirrors the three logical moments that Molina describes concerning God's knowledge. First of all, in correspondence with God's natural knowledge, there are clearly many necessary truths that are already actual prior to any creative decision by God. As Plantinga says, God does not "actualize his own existence; that is to say, he does not create himself. Nor does he create his own properties . . . Again, since God did not create numbers, propositions, pure sets, and the like, he did not actualize the states of affairs consisting in these things."[108] Next, in correspondence with the second logical moment of God's knowledge (i.e., middle knowledge), which is still logically prior to God's decree to create the world, there are additional truths about the world. In this way, Craig notes that the "actual world is even more instantiated than at the first moment. For now all those states of affairs corresponding to true counterfactuals of freedom obtain."[109] Like necessary truths, God's knowledge of how any free crea-

---

106. Dekker, *Middle Knowledge*, 58.

107. Craig, *Divine Foreknowledge and Human Freedom*, 265. See Craig's analysis, which is much like Dekker's, on page 265–67.

108. Plantinga, *The Nature of Necessity*, 169.

109. Craig, *Divine Foreknowledge and Human Freedom*, 266.

ture that he might add to this world would freely act in whatever possible circumstances that God considers placing him or her does not depend on God choosing to actualize anything. Thus, although at this logical point God has not yet issued a decree to actualize anything, Craig agrees with Dekker that God is able to build up all of the feasible worlds via God's middle knowledge. Once the divine mind then freely "actualizes all remaining states of affairs" (those that depend on the divine creative decree), the actual world fully obtains. Craig rightly concludes that, "Once it is appreciated that there is a logical sequence in the exemplification of the actual world just as much as there is in God's knowledge, then objections to middle knowledge based on counterfactuals' being true 'too late' to facilitate such knowledge disappear."[110] Kenny's objection thus appears to be resolved.

Beyond the fact that arguments such as Kenny's do not succeed, there is good reason for thinking that God knows CCFs logically prior to God's creative decree. If, as I have argued, it is correct that CCFs can be true and that God, in his omniscience, knows them, then it follows that God *must* know them logically prior to God's creative decree. As Craig notes, "If God knows counterfactual truths about us only logically posterior to his decree, then there really are no counterfactuals of freedom."[111] In this case we would not possess libertarian freedom because our actions would be determined by God's decree. Craig gives a forceful argument to this effect that runs as follows:

> WC_1. "If there are true counterfactuals of creaturely freedom, then God knows these truths." (I have argued for this above.)
>
> WC_2. "There are true counterfactuals of creaturely freedom." (I have also argued for this above.)
>
> WC_3. "If God knows true counterfactuals of creaturely freedom, God knows them either logically prior to the divine creative decree or only logically posterior to the divine creative decree." (These are the only alternatives.)
>
> WC_4. "Counterfactuals of creaturely freedom cannot be known only logically posterior to the divine creative decree." (A counterfactual truth known only subsequent to the divine creative decree would not be a counterfactual of creaturely *freedom*. It would mean that God knows what creatures would do in all

110. Craig, *Divine Foreknowledge and Human Freedom*, 267.
111. Craig, "The Middle-Knowledge View," 143.

possible circumstances because He decrees what they will do in all possible circumstances and then only on that basis knows these truths.)

WC_5. "Therefore, God knows true counterfactuals of creaturely freedom." (This follows from WC_1 and WC_2 by *modus ponens*.)

WC_6. "Therefore, God knows true counterfactuals of creaturely freedom either logically prior to the divine creative decree or only logically posterior to the divine creative decree." (This follows from WC_3 and WC_5 by *modus ponens*.)

WC_7. "Therefore, God knows true counterfactuals of creaturely freedom logically prior to the divine creative decree." (This follows by disjunctive syllogism from WC_4 and WC_6.)[112]

So WC_1 and WC_2 are the crucial premises in this argument, as WC_3 and WC_4 should be uncontroversial and the remaining premises follow logically from the first four. I have already argued that WC_1 and WC_2 are true (i.e., that there are true CCFs and that God would know any true CCFs). If these two premises are true, then this argument gives us good reason to think that God must know true CCFs logically prior to God's creative decree. And if God knows true CCFs logically prior to God's creative decree, then God possesses middle knowledge. Molinism is true.

We have now seen that the truth of Molinism is well supported. Molinism is in agreement with the biblical data. It has the powerful theological advantage of being the only system that reconciles human libertarian freedom with God's sovereignty, providence, and election of individuals to salvation. Moreover, when it comes to the philosophical coherence of Molinism, there is also good reason to agree with Plantinga's statement: "I don't believe there *are* any good arguments against counterfactuals of freedom, or middle knowledge, or the claim that some of God's actions are to be explained in terms of middle knowledge."[113]

With this brief case for the viability of Molinism in place, we are now in position to return to the soteriological difficulty that is described in the first chapter: How can an omnibenevolent, omnipotent, omniscient God allow some persons to be lost who would have freely chosen to be saved if placed into different circumstances? In the next chapter, we will explore how some thinkers—particularly William Lane Craig—utilize Molinism in an attempt to resolve this problem. I will identify theological

---

112. Craig, "The Middle-Knowledge View," 136–37.
113. Plantinga, "Reply to Robert M. Adams," 378–79.

and philosophical difficulties with these Molinist solutions, and this will reveal the value of offering a different theodicy that draws upon the explanatory power of Molinism.

3

Assessment of Existing Molinist Theodicies

MOLINISM'S UNIQUE ABILITY TO reconcile human libertarian freedom with God's sovereignty and providence has inspired many contemporary Molinists to attempt to harness the power of Molinism in a variety of creative ways. As Craig puts it, even though divine middle knowledge is consistent with Scripture and philosophically defensible, "the strongest arguments for the Molinist perspective are theological. Once one grasps the concept of middle knowledge, one will find it astonishing in its subtlety and power."[1] Besides its relevance to reconciling God's providence and election with human libertarian freedom (which was Molina's aim), the doctrine of divine middle knowledge has been leveraged in contemporary scholarship in an attempt to make sense of theological issues as diverse as: showing how perseverance of the saints might work; justifying God's ability to inspire the biblical authors to write in their own words exactly what God wants them to write; attempting to show the reasonableness of the Roman Catholic doctrine of papal infallibility; endeavoring to show how evolutionary theory is not incompatible with intelligent design; suggesting how the consistency of quantum indeterminacy and divine sovereignty might be upheld; offering a theodicy against the problem of the gratuitousness of evil; and reconciling intelligent design with certain alleged biological design flaws.[2] Of course, a Molinist is *not committed to*

---

1. Craig, "The Middle-Knowledge View," 125.

2. William Lane Craig and Kirk MacGregor offer helpful lists of scholarly works that apply Molinism to these areas. See Craig, "The Middle-Knowledge View," 125;

accepting every theory that makes use of divine middle knowledge, for the truth of divine middle knowledge (a doctrine that I have argued is consistent with the Bible and philosophically coherent) obviously does not require that God *utilizes* this knowledge to accomplish the particular objectives that all such theories suppose. What is clear, however, is that middle knowledge is a powerful theological doctrine that opens up many possibilities for how God *may* choose to exert his sovereignty and achieve his desired ends. This chapter will examine how Molinism has been applied to answering the residual difficulty concerning the soteriological POE that was introduced at the end of the first chapter. I will contend that the Molinist soteriological theodicies that have been proposed to date are inadequate and that it is possible to offer an even better Molinist theodicy.

As we have seen, the residual difficulty identified in the concluding pages of the first chapter—referred to hereafter as the "problem of the contingently lost" (PCL)—seeks to demonstrate that P_1 and P_2 are inconsistent by adding P_8 and P_9. Recall that these premises have been stated as follows:

> P_1. God possesses the attributes of omniscience, omnipotence, and omnibenevolence.
>
> P_2. Some persons do not accept the forgiveness that is available via receiving Christ and are thus damned.
>
> P_8. God will necessarily not allow persons to exist who are lost in their actual circumstances but who would have been saved if placed into different circumstances.
>
> P_9. Some persons who freely reject the grace that God offers them in their actual circumstances and are lost would have freely accepted God's grace and been saved in different circumstances.[3]

MacGregor, *Luis de Molina*, 248–70.

3. Refer to Table 1.1 at the end of chapter 1 for a summary of all of these premises. P_1 and P_2 are the two basic premises that proponents of the soteriological POE claim are in conflict, as Craig rightly identifies in Craig, "No Other Name," 180. Since there is no explicit contradiction between P_1 and P_2, we have considered various arguments that conjoin additional premises to these two basic premises in order to make the contradiction explicit. The PCL involves adding P_8 and P_9. As previously explained, if one denies that God has middle knowledge so that God cannot know for sure whether any of the lost would have been saved if placed into different circumstances, then P_8 could instead be stated as: "God will necessarily not allow persons to exist who are lost in their actual circumstances but who would have had a *significantly better opportunity* to be saved if placed into different circumstances."

Recall that the PCL argues that God's possessing the attributes of omniscience, omnipotence, and omnibenevolence (P_1) entail that God would not create persons who are lost in their actual circumstances but who would have been saved if placed into different circumstances (P_8). The PCL further makes the claim that P_2's recognition that those who never place faith in Christ are lost plausibly makes it unavoidable—given the lack of access to hearing the Christian gospel and other difficult life circumstances that many non-Christians face—that some of the lost are only contingently lost (P_9); that is, it appears quite likely that some of the lost (e.g., at least a portion of the lost who are unevangelized) would have freely accepted God's grace and been saved if only God had placed them into different circumstances (e.g., being born in a strong Christian home where they hear the gospel faithfully presented). Thus, if P_8 and P_9 are both true, then we seem to have a contradiction. God's attributes would then be incompatible with the purported reality that some of the lost are contingently lost. Thus, if the PCL is to be refuted, one must show that either P_8 or P_9 (or both) should be rejected. One must show that at least one of these two premises is neither necessarily true nor required by Christian doctrine.

There seem to be three general categories of strategies that have been utilized in an attempt to provide a Molinist soteriological theodicy that resolves the PCL. The similar theodicies proposed by Donald Lake and Jerry Walls as well as the quite different proposal offered by Jason Marsh are representative of the first broad category. In all of the theodicies within this first category, Molinism is combined with postmortem opportunities for salvation. We will see that Marsh utilizes Molinism and postmortem opportunities for salvation in a different way than Lake and Walls, but they may be fairly regarded as falling under the same umbrella. After exploring and rejecting these sorts of Molinist theodicies, we will examine an interesting proposal by David Hunt that falls into a second category. Hunt, who is not himself a Molinist and thus does not endorse his own Molinist proposal, has suggested a means by which he thinks God could achieve both a resolution of the PCL and universal salvation if God were to possess middle knowledge. We will see that Hunt suggests that God could create soulless automata to fill the role of all lost persons so that universalism could be achieved on Molinism. After quickly examining this sort of view and finding it inadequate, we will turn to a third category of Molinist theodicies (those involving God's optimization of the soteriological balance) and focus on the theodicy that has famously been put forth by William Lane Craig. We will examine and assess Craig's view carefully before briefly surveying a view that has recently been given by Kirk MacGregor and is derived from Craig's view. MacGregor actually attempts to merge Molina's soteriological view with Craig's Molinist theodicy. Craig's position is by far the most prominent Molinist theodicy concerning the contingently lost, and it will be the primary focus of this chapter. We will see that Craig claims that God providentially uses his middle knowledge to arrange the world in such a way that nobody is contingently lost. Moreover, Craig attempts to show that God's middle knowledge enables him to minimize the number of those who are lost relative to the number of those who are saved. This chapter will critique Craig's position, identifying both its strengths and weaknesses. However, before arguing for the inadequacy of these Molinist theodicies, let us begin by examining why the adoption of Molinism does not commit one to a particular view of election and predestination. This fact will highlight why it is possible to incorporate Molinism into a variety of quite different soteriological theodicies and why it is critical to scrutinize the biblical and philosophical viability of such theodicies.

Molinism's Relationship to Theories of Election and Predestination

Before exploring the ways in which contemporary theodicies have utilized Molina's basic concept in their rejection of the PCL, it is critical to recognize that Molinism does not entail a certain theology of election and predestination. The mere fact that God possesses middle knowledge does not, by itself, say anything about what soteriological objectives God might have; moreover, it says nothing about how God might make use of his middle knowledge to accomplish his objectives. Examining the divergent perspectives held by the two most prominent early Molinists—Molina himself and Francisco Suarez—illustrates this well.

Molina's reconciliation of libertarian freedom with God's sovereignty runs him directly into deep questions concerning the nature of divine predestination. Given that, logically prior to actualizing a world, God knows what every human in that world would freely do in the circumstances in which God creates him or her, it is true that God has always known the eternal destiny of every human that will exist in the actual world and that God could have brought about a different world that results in different soteriological outcomes. By actualizing one particular world of free creatures rather than other worlds of free creatures that God could have actualized, God guarantees the eternal fate of each person that will exist in the actual world—despite the fact that each person has genuine libertarian freedom. This is an unavoidable conclusion on Molinism. So the question arises as to what aims God might have in terms of why God opted to create the world of free creatures that he did (in which certain people exist and are saved or lost) rather than a different world of free creatures (in which other people exist and are saved or lost). Why this world? What soteriological goals might God have wanted to achieve via his middle knowledge by actualizing the particular world of free creatures that he did? Molinists can and do adopt all sorts of positions on this question.

Molina took a particular position on the issue of predestination, but his position clearly is not demanded by the truth of divine middle knowledge. Based on his understanding of Scripture (in particular, Romans 9), Molina held firmly that God unconditionally elects individuals to salvation.[4] Contrary to Arminius, who saw election as corporate and held that the "elect" is merely the group of people who ultimately freely choose to accept Christ, Molina took Romans 9 to be teaching that God is sovereign over which individuals are saved and lost and that no quality of any individual can compel God to save or damn that individual. If one were to allow that the characteristics of a person could determine whether that person is saved or lost, Molina thought it would detract from God's sovereign choice over the eternal destiny of each person.[5] Yet Molina insisted that God offers prevenient grace to all people in such a way that nobody receives grace that is irresistible but all people receive sufficient prevenient grace so that they are able to choose to accept or

---

4. MacGregor, *Luis de Molina*, 25–28, 135–40. MacGregor has a helpful discussion of Molina's interpretation of Romans 9, citing the relevant portions of the *Concordia* (especially the—as of yet—untranslated Part VII). To date, the only published English translation of Molina's *Concordia* is Alfred Freddoso's translation of Part IV of the *Concordia* (the part that discusses middle knowledge), which I have previously cited. There is no published English translation of the rest of the *Concordia*. It is in Part VII that Molina expounds his view on predestination, and the key points related to Romans 9 are especially found in 7.23.4.

5. Molina especially emphasizes these points in 7.23.1/2.2; 7.23.4/5.1; and 7.23.4/5.4 of his *Concordia*. Note the footnotes on the following page for the relevant parts of the *Concordia* and MacGregor's translations of the key passages: MacGregor, *Luis de Molina*, 26–27, 135–40.

reject it.[6] Molina also thought that God uses his middle knowledge to uphold human libertarian freedom while achieving unconditional election of individuals in the following way. God decides that he will create a world of free creatures. God determines that he will create a world without regard for which persons would exist in this world and without regard for who would be saved and lost in this world. That is, the world that God creates is based upon his sovereign choice, and God does not save or damn anyone because of some quality or characteristic of that person that requires God to save or damn that person. Molina speculated that every human that God creates would freely choose to be saved in some world that God could actualize and would also freely choose to be lost in some world that God could actualize. Moreover, every human that God creates would also not exist in some world of free creatures that God could actualize. Molina considered it unlikely that (given our fallen nature) any human would freely choose to be saved in all feasible (i.e., actualizable) worlds in which he or she exists, and he similarly doubted that any human is so bent against God that he or she would be lost in all feasible worlds in which he or she exists. If this is the case, then God did not have to save any particular person who is saved in the actual world or damn any particular person who is lost in the actual world. The existence and eternal destiny of every person is entirely up to God despite humans having libertarian freedom with regard to their decision about whether or not to accept God's salvation.[7] Therefore, on Molina's soteriological view, everyone who is saved is contingently saved, and everyone who is lost is contingently lost. Thus, every person who exists in the actual world could have been freely saved, freely damned, or nonexistent—it was all

---

6. Molina emphasizes this in 3.14.13.40.2–17; 3.14.13.40.18–27; and 7.23.1/2.1.5, 8 of his *Concordia*. Note the comments MacGregor makes about these key passages in MacGregor, *Luis de Molina*, 142.

7. Molina especially expounds these points beginning in 7.23.4/5.1. See MacGregor's comments and helpful translations of Molina in MacGregor, *Luis de Molina*, 27–28, 145–57. For example, MacGregor (p. 27) translates a key passage from the *Concordia* (Molina's direct words are in quotes) that indicates the following: Despite affirming human libertarian freedom with regard to accepting or rejecting Christ, Molina held that "the total effect of predestination . . . depends only on the will of God." It was thus within God's power to have predestined "any of the elect to have been truly reprobate" and any "of the reprobate to be truly elect" (*Concordia* 7.23.4/5.1.2). MacGregor also highlights (p. 147) how Molina held that every person who exists in the actual world would have freely chosen the opposite soteriological outcome (i.e., the opposite of what he or she chooses in the actual world) in at least one other world that God could have actualized (*Concordia* 7.23.4/5.7.1.1).

dependent upon God's sovereign choice about which world to actualize. Given this view of predestination, it is notable that Molina would have no objection to P_9.

Despite the fact that God's decree to actualize a certain world ensures the fate that all people in that world will freely choose for themselves, it is not clear that Molina ever speculated about what specific soteriological purposes God might have behind actualizing the particular world that he did. God's decree to create the actual world is simply an act of God's sovereign will. Molina does, however, depart strongly from the Dominican position that God's decision to create the world that he did is based upon the prior goal of ensuring the election of certain individuals and the reprobation of others.[8] Whatever God's soteriological motivations may have been for creating the actual world, Molina held that God did not have the goal of damning and saving certain people logically prior to his determination to create the world. Craig nicely summarizes Molina's position on predestination as follows:

> Molina held that God's choosing to create certain persons has nothing to do with how they would respond to His grace; He simply chooses to create the world order He wants to, and no rationale for this choice is to be sought other than the divine will itself. In this sense, predestination is for Molina wholly gratuitous, the result of the divine will, and in no way based on the merits or demerits of creatures.[9]

---

8. Molina, *Concordia* 4.53.1.3, 199. Note the translator Freddoso's comments in footnote 6 of that page.

9. Craig, *The Problem of Divine Foreknowledge*, 204. MacGregor, as we will discover in more detail later, does suggest that Molina *implicitly* held that God would only actualize a world that is as soteriologically optimal (and overall good) as any other world; however, MacGregor thinks Molina held that there were an infinite number of soteriologically optimal worlds (i.e., they are all "tied" in terms of having an optimal balance of saved versus lost and in terms of the overall goodness of the world) so that God could gratuitously select a world from within that range of optimal worlds (since everyone in the actual world who is saved is lost in one of the worlds in that range and everyone in the actual world who is lost is saved in one of the worlds in that range). MacGregor acknowledges that Molina never specifically states that God would only actualize a world that has a balance of saved versus lost that is as good as any other world of free creatures that is feasible for God to actualize, but he thinks that Molina would have held to this because of the goodness of God and his genuine desire for all to be saved. See MacGregor, *Luis de Molina*, 145–46 (especially footnote 53). We will examine this in more detail when we get to MacGregor's theodicy later in this chapter.

So, for Molina, God simply creates the world that he does for (presumably morally acceptable) reasons known only to him. God gives sufficient grace for all to choose to be saved, but God knows which people will freely accept salvation in the world he creates. Molina does not appear to find any theological or moral problem with God opting to create people who are contingently lost, and Molina gives no theodicy to suggest why God might have a good reason for creating them. Indeed, as we have seen, Molina thinks it is theologically important (in order to uphold his understanding of unconditional election) that all people who are lost are contingently lost and all people who are saved are contingently saved. Given the more limited knowledge of the religious diversity of the world at Molina's time as compared to today, it is likely that the PCL was simply not a matter of great concern to Molina or his contemporaries.

Francisco Suarez, in contrast to Molina, held a Molinist view that—aside from recognizing that human libertarian freedom is involved in the acceptance or rejection of Christ—is almost identical to Calvinism with regard to election and predestination. Suarez, a Spanish Jesuit theologian and a contemporary of Molina who picked up on Molina's ideas, advanced the position that God *did* intend to damn and save certain people logically prior to his determination to create the world. Suarez contends that God first desires the salvation of the elect, and then God ensures their salvation by placing them into circumstances in which God knows they will freely choose to be saved. Similarly, God ensures the damnation of the reprobate by placing them into circumstances in which God knows they will freely choose to reject him and be lost. Suarez's view is called Congruism because he held that God provides "congruent grace" to the elect and withholds such grace from the reprobate. Congruent grace includes the circumstances and aids that God places into the life of an elect person to ensure that he or she freely chooses to be saved. This grace is perfectly suited to each person; that is, the grace is "congruent" with the person's freely willing to be saved.[10] Because Suarez contended that God can give congruent grace to any person God wishes, every lost person is contingently lost (so Suarez would accept P_9).

---

10. Craig, *The Problem of Divine Foreknowledge*, 226–29. Craig provides a useful comparison of Suarez's view of predestination with that of Molina. Craig also offers useful quotations from Suarez's writings that unpack his Congruism, especially *De concursu et auxilio Dei* 3.14.9 as well as *De scientia Dei* 2.6.7.

It is evident that neither Molina nor Suarez have it as their aim to utilize Molinism in a way that would resolve the PCL.[11] Moreover, the difference between their views highlights the fact that Molinism leaves plenty of room for soteriological speculation. Any Molinist theodicy that is applied to the Christian God must, therefore, be assessed to determine whether it is biblically faithful and philosophically reasonable. We now turn to such an assessment of the primary ways Molinism has been used in theodicies against the PCL.

Category #1 of Molinist Theodicies Against the PCL: Appeals to Postmortem Salvation

The Theodicies of Donald Lake and Jerry Walls

The first of the three broad categories of Molinist strategies that have been suggested for formulating a theodicy against the PCL involves combining Molinism with postmortem opportunities for salvation. Within this category, at least two sorts of strategies have been put forth. We begin with the first of these two varieties, which is exemplified by Donald Lake and Jerry Walls. Lake and Walls propose very similar theodicies, which attack P_9 by appealing to God's middle knowledge of the circumstances in which those who are never saved within this present earthly life would have freely chosen to be saved. Let us begin with Lake's position.

Lake agrees with P_8 that God would not allow a person to be lost as a consequence of being placed into circumstances that are not conducive to that person accepting the gospel. However, Lake finds it is hard to deny that P_9 also appears to be true; it seems that many who are lost would have been saved if placed into better circumstances. Backed into this corner, Lake asserts the following claim: "God knows who would, under ideal circumstances, believe the gospel, and on the basis of his foreknowledge, applies that gospel even if the person never hears the gospel during his lifetime."[12] When Lake uses the term "foreknowledge" here, he is really speaking of God's middle knowledge. Lake acknowledges that

---

11. Both Molina and Suarez would accept P_9, and they do not seem concerned that this might be seen as conflicting with the divine attributes (as P_8 suggests). There is little doubt that they would reject P_8 and uphold God's goodness despite God permitting some to be contingently lost; however, addressing the issue of how God's omnibenevolence fits with God allowing some to be contingently lost is not their concern.

12. Lake, "He Died for All," 43.

Assessment of Existing Molinist Theodicies

some people go through life without accepting the gospel, even though they would have accepted it under other circumstances. However, he still rejects P_9 by arguing that God will grant at the time of judgment that such people (who otherwise would be contingently lost) will automatically receive the saving benefits of Christ's atonement. This is because God will judge people on the basis of what God knows (via his middle knowledge) they *would* have done if God were to have placed them into "ideal circumstances" for accepting the gospel. Lake's proposal, therefore, is that nobody will be contingently lost.[13]

Walls puts forth a view that is very similar to Lake's. Walls is an Arminian who thinks that Molinism is possibly true, though he is unsure of its philosophical viability.[14] Despite his reservations, Walls proposes what he believes is the best way to make use of Molinism against the PCL. Like Lake, Walls accepts P_8, affirming that "it does not seem God would allow anyone to be damned through unfavorable circumstances."[15] Walls then makes use of God's middle knowledge to attack P_9 by proposing that God gives an "optimal measure of grace" to all people. If a person rejects God in this life, then God knows via his middle knowledge whether this negative response is "decisive" or not. Walls clarifies that "a negative response to God is decisive only if one persists in rejecting God in the most favorable circumstances."[16] God will not allow anyone to be contingently lost; instead, "God will give [the otherwise contingently lost person] the grace at the moment of death to begin to become what he would have become" under the ideal circumstances—circumstances in which the

---

13. Lake's comments are made in the context of discussing the problem of the unevangelized, but his theory seems to extend to all of the contingently lost—those who would have believed the gospel and been saved under "ideal circumstances." That is how I interpret him. If he does intend to limit his theory only to the unevangelized who would be contingently lost (or some other subgroup), such a limitation seems arbitrary and unjustified. Many of the evangelized live in circumstances that are far from optimal for believing the gospel.

14. Walls, "Is Molinism as Bad as Calvinism?," 89. Walls' concern is that the "manner in which" God can have middle knowledge is "quite mysterious" (alluding to the grounding objection). For more on Walls' perspective on the viability of Molinism, see Walls and Dongell, *Why I Am Not a Calvinist*, 134–41.

15. Walls, "Is Molinism as Bad as Calvinism?," 92.

16. Walls, "Is Molinism as Bad as Calvinism?," 93. See also Walls, *Hell*, 89. Walls says that God will tailor the grace that God offers to each person so that everyone has the opportunity to receive "the *maximal* amount of grace which [God] can give without abrogating freedom."

person chooses to be saved.[17] Given that so many seem to lack optimal grace in this life, Walls contends, "If there can be no opportunity to receive grace at or beyond the point of death, then it seems most likely that grace is not, and perhaps cannot be, optimally bestowed on all persons."[18]

The proposal that Walls puts forth is effectively the same as Lake's in that (1) the only persons who are lost are those who would choose to be lost in every possible set of circumstances (even the "most favorable"),[19] and (2) everyone who either accepts God's grace through faith in Christ or *would have* accepted God's grace through faith in Christ in some set of circumstances will be saved. There is, however, one notable difference: Walls claims that God will allow persons whom God knows would have accepted his grace in some set of circumstances to place saving faith in Christ while in a postmortem condition. In this way, Walls allows that "further spiritual growth could occur after death." God will "bring about the appropriate favorable circumstances during the passage of death" so that the person is able to make the "fully deliberate response to God" that his circumstances did not allow during his lifetime.[20] By contrast, Lake proposes that God simply applies his saving grace to the contingently lost after they have died based on his mere knowledge that they are contingently lost.

Difficulties with the Theodicies of Lake and Walls

Unfortunately, although these theodicies would certainly succeed in undermining P_9 and resolving the PCL, they suffer from a fatal weakness: They do not seem to be supported by the biblical data. First, these views interestingly deny both exclusivism and inclusivism. They are in opposition to exclusivism because they hold that God will save some people without them having explicit knowledge of the gospel during their lifetime. As we have seen, this is a dubious proposition in light of the biblical evidence for exclusivism. Yet they go even further and transgress inclusivism by allowing that one may be saved without even responding to general revelation or having implicit faith in Christ in this life. Lake and Walls both allow that one who is unevangelized could entirely ignore

17. Walls, "Is Molinism as Bad as Calvinism?," 93.
18. Walls, *Hell*, 92.
19. Such people would be, to use Craig's term, transcircumstantially damned.
20. Walls, "Is Molinism as Bad as Calvinism?," 93.

God's general revelation in nature and conscience in this life and still be saved (though Walls at least requires a postmortem faith response). Inclusivist Clark Pinnock finds this unacceptable, correctly pointing out that the idea of "allowing certain persons salvation without exercising any faith at all" is problematic from a biblical perspective.[21] The biblical authors unanimously and consistently preach the message that God's grace is given only to those who accept this gift by faith (e.g., John 3:16; Acts 15:9; Rom 1:5, 17; 3:21—5:1; 10; Gal 3; Eph 2:8–9; Heb 11). Even if one adopts inclusivism, one recognizes that there must be faith of some kind (even if it is merely expressed via an appropriate response to God's general revelation) *in this lifetime* if one is to be saved. This is a key tenet of Scripture.

Second, there is absolutely no indication in Scripture that anyone will be judged according to faith that he or she *would have* had in Christ in other circumstances; rather, quite the opposite is taught in the Bible. Jesus claims that the wicked and godless people of Tyre, Sidon, and Sodom would have repented and turned to God if they had been given the opportunity to see Jesus' miracles, yet that does not stop Jesus from declaring that these people will be condemned (albeit less severely than the towns to which Jesus preached) for their rejection of God (Matt 11:20–24). If Lake and Walls were correct, then these people who were wicked and godless in this lifetime would ultimately be saved and not punished at all, since they are only contingently lost. Also, Jesus repeatedly makes clear the importance of always being prepared for his return and being ready to face the judgment. Jesus warns us to "be on the alert, for you do not know which day your Lord is coming" (Matt 24:42). The person who remains unfaithful to the Lord until his return will have no last-minute (or postmortem) opportunity to repent, for the Lord will come suddenly and will condemn that person (Matt 24:45–51). This is also the point of Jesus' parable about the unwise virgins who were not prepared when the bridegroom arrived (Matt 25:1–13). From these teachings of Jesus, it is evident that one's choices in this life determine whether one accepts or rejects God's grace. As the author of Hebrews says, "It is appointed for men to die once and after this comes judgment." When Christ returns, it will be to save "those who eagerly await Him" (Heb 9:27–28). No hope is ever promised to those who merely *would have* been awaiting Christ in other circumstances.

---

21. Pinnock, *A Wideness in God's Mercy*, 161.

Third, Lake and Walls allow that one who is actually evangelized can reject Christ and still be saved so long as that person is not placed into the most "ideal circumstances" for accepting the gospel. For example, consider a person who knows all about the gospel, believes that it is true, and still chooses to reject it. This person despises God's truth and ignores the many opportunities for salvation that God offers him. Nevertheless, it turns out that there is some set of circumstances in which this person would have freely chosen to be saved. Even though this person is contingently lost, it does not seem correct that he lacked the opportunity to make a decisive decision to accept the gospel during his lifetime.

A final difficulty is that these theodicies do not address the question of why God would create persons who reject God's grace even under the most optimal circumstances and are lost (the transcircumstantially damned). Why would a loving God create such people at all? God, according to this view, could certainly save all of the contingently lost without creating any who are transcircumstantially damned; it is not as though God would need to create people who are transcircumstantially lost in order for them to serve a role that aids in bringing about a better balance of saved versus lost. Walls himself acknowledges that this is a mystery his view does not solve.[22] Given God's universal salvific will and the fact that universalism could easily have been achieved by God on the views of Lake and Walls, the fact that the Bible does not teach universalism (e.g., Matt 7:13–14; 13:40–43, 49–50; 25:30–46; Rev 20:11—21:27) counts strongly against the truth of their views.

The theodicies of Lake and Walls must, therefore, be rejected. Lake illegitimately regards counterfactuals concerning a person's choices as more important than the person's actual choices, and they both run into troubling theological difficulties. We must never minimize the significance of the choice that we have to accept or reject Christ in this life, for Scripture portrays eternal life or death as hinging upon this decision.

---

22. Walls, "Is Molinism as Bad as Calvinism?," 96. If nobody is transcircumstantially damned, then Walls would have to hold to universalism because his view requires that nobody is ultimately contingently lost. Since he knows that universalism is unbiblical, he is puzzled as to why God would create anyone who will be lost (i.e., those who are transcircumstantially damned).

The Theodicy of Jason Marsh

Jason Marsh's theodicy also falls within the first of the three broad categories of Molinist strategies for formulating a theodicy against the PCL, as it involves combining Molinism with postmortem opportunities for salvation. Unlike Lake and Walls, however, Marsh does not suggest that God uses his middle knowledge to take into account whether those who were never saved in this life would have accepted Christ under ideal circumstances; rather, Marsh proposes that God uses his middle knowledge to keep as many people as possible who are not saved during this present earthly lifetime from being hardened against God so that these people can be saved in the afterlife. Marsh's theodicy arises in response to an article by Stephen Maitzen in which Maitzen argues that the geographical distribution of theists and non-theists is unlikely if theism were true. Maitzen points out that Saudi Arabia, for example, is almost entirely made up of theists (Muslims) whereas Thailand is almost entirely composed of non-theists (Buddhists). Maitzen argues that such a distribution would be odd on theism but unsurprising on naturalism. He finds it difficult to account for why the hiddenness of God would be so unevenly distributed if a loving God were to exist, since the eternal implications that such a distribution would seem to have on the people of certain regions of the world are severe.[23] (Note that I will address Maitzen's concern later when I discuss the plausibility of Craig's proposal that God may be optimizing the balance of saved versus lost over the course of human history.)

Marsh responds to Maitzen's argument by suggesting that this clumping—what Marsh calls a "grouping strategy"—of unbelievers into certain geographical areas may actually be the means by which God protects certain people from becoming hardened to the love of God so that they will ultimately be saved. Marsh points out that God may be concerned with much more than mere theistic belief. God may want people to respond to him properly and enter into a love relationship with him.[24] It may be that God has middle knowledge and knows that some persons would refuse to love God under any circumstances in this life. Marsh suggests that God may have, in his providence, used his middle knowledge to arrange the world such that any person who is sequestered into an area in which people lack belief in a personal deity and never has

---

23. Maitzen, "Divine Hiddenness," 177–91.
24. Marsh, "Do the Demographics of Theistic Belief Disconfirm Theism?," 466–67.

a good opportunity to believe in God in this life is a person who would freely refuse to love God under any circumstances in this life.[25] Marsh proposes, however, that these people who would refuse to love God under any circumstances in this lifetime would freely choose to love God in the afterlife if they were kept from being hardened against the love of God in this present life and if they were presented with "something like a beatific vision" in the afterlife. So, God groups these people together in this present earthly life as a means of keeping "these individuals innocent for a later time, when they will be in a position truly to love God." Marsh is open to universal salvation and views this theodicy as a way for God to bring about universal salvation in the afterlife.[26] In defending his theodicy, he notes that some large groups of people who had previously been geographically separated from hearing about God have converted in large numbers once missionaries reached that location. In response to this fact, Marsh contends that it just shows that God can have different reasons for God's grouping strategy. In some cases, the grouping strategy is intended to preserve the innocence of the people so that they will be converted in the afterlife; in other cases, God groups people so that it will result in mass conversion during this lifetime.[27] Although Marsh is attempting to respond to Maitzen's particular challenge to theism rather than responding to the PCL, it is not hard to see that this theodicy—if true—would also resolve the PCL.

Difficulties with the Theodicy of Marsh

Like the theodicies of Lake and Walls, even if Marsh's theodicy may be philosophically coherent, it comes into conflict with biblically teaching. For this reason, it cannot serve as an effective theodicy that can be applied to the Christian God. It is not enough for a theodicy to defend a generic sort of theism. Any theodicy that appeals to unbiblical concepts is inadequate for defending Christian theism against the PCL.

Two of the same criticisms that apply to the theodicies of Lake and Walls apply to Marsh's proposal as well. First, Marsh's view goes beyond inclusivism and allows that one need not place any sort of faith in God—even the implicit sort of faith that inclusivism requires—in this life in

25. Marsh, "Do the Demographics of Theistic Belief Disconfirm Theism?," 467.
26. Marsh, "Do the Demographics of Theistic Belief Disconfirm Theism?," 468.
27. Marsh, "Do the Demographics of Theistic Belief Disconfirm Theism?," 469.

order ultimately to be saved. Second, Marsh's view allows that one who is actually evangelized in this life can reject Christ and still be saved so long as that person accepts Christ in the afterlife. This denies the many biblical warnings I have highlighted that stress urgency in turning to God in this life in view of the fact that one's fate is sealed when one dies and faces God's judgment. Since I have already examined the biblical problems associated with both of these points in the above critique of Lake and Walls, I need not repeat those here. There simply is no explicit teaching in the Bible that there will be postmortem opportunities for salvation, and it appears that the Bible explicitly teaches the opposite.

The universalism that Marsh espouses is also unbiblical. Clearly, Scripture teaches that there will be a judgment of all humanity and that some will be lost (e.g., a few of these passages include Matt 7:13–14; 13:40–43, 49–50; 25:30–46; Rev 20:11—21:27). While Marsh's appeal to universalism is problematic from a biblical perspective, it is not necessary to examine this point closely for two reasons. First, the concerns noted in the previous paragraph are enough to show that this theodicy is not an adequate Christian response to the PCL. Second, it seems that this universalist aspect of his theodicy could be excised entirely and is not central to his theodicy—at least it is not central in terms of applying it as a theodicy against the PCL. One could simply make the following sort of proposal: God uses his middle knowledge to arrange the world so that as many people as possible either come to accept Christ in this life or are kept from being hardened against God in this life so that they will accept him in a postmortem state. One could make such an appeal without also adding, as Marsh does, that nobody will be lost in the end. The PCL would be overcome if nobody is contingently lost, and that would be the case even if some continue to reject God in the afterlife. So long as nobody who rejects God in the afterlife would have repented and turned to God (either in the present life or in the afterlife) if only God had placed them into different circumstances, then nobody is contingently lost.

Category #2 of Molinist Theodicies Against the PCL: The Lost Lack a Soul

The Theodicy of David Hunt

The second of the three broad categories of Molinist theodicies against the PCL that have been proposed involves God leveraging his middle knowledge to ensure that all humans that he creates (i.e., all those with a human mind or soul) are saved and that everyone else who appears to be a human is actually a human-looking automaton that lacks a human mind or soul. This intriguing proposal has been put forth by David Hunt, who is not himself a Molinist and thus does not endorse his own Molinist proposal. His claim, however, is that if God did have middle knowledge then God ought to be able to ensure universal salvation by employing this sort of strategy. God could create soulless simulacra to fill the role of all lost persons so that universalism could be achieved on Molinism.

Here is how Hunt lays out this Molinist theodicy. Hunt first suggests that one may assume that God desires that people would enjoy "eternal felicity and communion with Him" and that, in order to allow for this postmortem condition, it may have been necessary for these people to have "a pre-mortem history" (i.e., this present life) in which they have the opportunity to decide whether or not they want to spend eternity with God. Hunt also suggests that God surely does not desire that anyone should eternally suffer in separation from him and that God would not bring about the pre-mortem existence of the lost for the purpose of ensuring that the lost eternally suffer in their postmortem state; rather, the "eternal suffering of the damned is held to be an unfortunate concomitant of the eternal felicity of the blessed."[28] That is, God would only create the lost because the impact that the lost have on the world in their pre-mortem existence is plausibly crucial to the saved being in pre-mortem circumstances in which they freely choose to be saved. So the postmortem condition of the lost is just the unfortunate outcome that results from God needing to create the lost in their pre-mortem circumstances in order to bring about a world in which God knew that the saved would freely choose to be saved. So the only thing (in terms of pre-mortem conditions) that leads God to bring about a pre-mortem state at all is that God wants to ensure that the saved are placed into an environment in which they are able to choose freely that they want to love God and accept his salvation. But if God were to have middle knowledge, Hunt suggests, then there is no reason why God could not bring about a world in which all of the saved have a pre-mortem existence in which they all freely choose to be saved *without God creating any human who is lost*. Hunt argues that the saved could still be placed in an environment in which they "have actual experiences of trials and temptations" without

---

28. Hunt, "Middle Knowledge" 21.

Assessment of Existing Molinist Theodicies

there being any "pre-mortem instantiation of the damned." Even if the lost play an essential role in affecting the circumstances of the saved so that all of the latter freely choose to be saved, this could be accomplished by God creating "soulless simulacra" to play the roles that would otherwise be played by actual humans (with a soul) who would be eternally lost if they existed in this world. Hunt thinks that "each of us [real humans with a soul] could have exactly the experiences we actually have even though (unbeknown to us) none of the other bodies in our experience is itself a centre of experiences." So Hunt avers that a God who possesses middle knowledge ought to create only the elect with "a mind or soul," and everyone else should be merely simulacra playing the roles that God knows is conducive to bringing about the salvation of the elect.[29] Hunt realizes that some may object to his proposal on the grounds that it involves deception and is contrary to the nature of God. Hunt responds that "it is far from obvious" that his proposal would involve deception (though he opts not to make a case to support this claim); moreover, Hunt stresses that even if this theodicy does involve some level of deception, it is a morally better approach for God to take than the alternative of creating actual people who are lost to an eternity in hell. It is often thought that God's permitting evil is morally permissible because of the various benefits that it allows (character building, free will, etc.). How much more, argues Hunt, does the avoidance of eternal suffering in hell justify God engaging in a bit of deception?[30] So, if God has middle knowledge, Hunt thinks God should providentially arrange the world so that all genuine humans (who have a soul) are placed into circumstances in which they are saved and nobody is lost. It is only if God lacks middle knowledge (which Hunt believes is the case) that Hunt thinks God would be justified in creating humans who end up freely choosing to be lost.[31]

Difficulties with the Theodicy of Hunt

Hunt's proposal is intriguing. There are, however, two major moral problems with it, and these alone undermine it as a viable soteriological theodicy. The first problem is that it certainly does appear that this theodicy would involve massive deception on the part of God—deception that is

---

29. Hunt, "Middle Knowledge," 22.
30. Hunt, "Middle Knowledge," 23.
31. Hunt, "Middle Knowledge," 24.

surely beneath God. The second problem is that on this view God would be the initiator of the evil acts performed by the simulacra (since they lack a mind and are not free agents). Although Hunt is correct that, in responding to the problem of evil, theists have rightly suggested that God may permit certain evils in order to bring about greater goods, what Hunt is suggesting is not a case of God permitting evil; rather, God would be carrying out evil. God would be engaging in the evil of massive deception, and God would be responsible for initiating the evil acts carried out by the simulacra. Both of these problems are simply unacceptable—even if engaging in them would allow God to achieve universal salvation. Let us examine each of these problems in turn.

The first problem—that God would be carrying out massive deception if Hunt's proposal were true—has been identified and stated well by William Lane Craig. It is worth quoting him at length. Craig says:

> But to my mind, Hunt's proposal is so morally abhorrent and unworthy of God that He could not entertain it. After all, we are not talking here of the sort of mild deception involved by, say, Berkeleian idealism. We are talking about a world filled with automata with which the elect enter into significant human relations, a scenario which constitutes a moral offence to the elect of unspeakable proportions. Can one imagine being married to an automaton, giving oneself to that thing in love, trust, and sexual surrender? Or giving birth to and loving an automaton? Or having a mother and father or trusted friends who are automata? I cannot convince myself that God would create such a world. And though the fate of the lost is tragic, their creation involves no moral failure on God's part as does Hunt's proposal. It must always be remembered that God loves the lost, desires their salvation, and provides sufficient grace for them to be saved; their ability to reject God's love is testimony to their status as morally significant persons whom God treats with due respect. By contrast Hunt's proposal involves God's treating real persons without the moral respect they deserve.[32]

It would be misleading for God to intermingle simulacra that appear to be freely acting persons with true persons who possess a mind and freedom of the will. As Craig says, God would be giving us good reason to believe that we are interacting in deep and meaningful personal relationships with other persons like ourselves when this is actually not the

---

32. Craig, "Middle Knowledge and Christian Exclusivism," 133–34.

case. Now Hunt is arguing that we ought not hold to Molinism because, were God to possess middle knowledge, God should be able to bring about universalism using this simulacra strategy; since Hunt recognizes that there is a "paucity of scriptural support for universalism," he argues that we ought to think that God must not have middle knowledge.[33] But surely Hunt underestimates how serious God's deception would be if God were to lead us to believe that we have personal relationships with things that are not persons. Any such proposal (including the similar proposal that each real person undergoes his or her pre-mortem existence in a virtual reality in which everyone around him or her is not a real person) is morally beneath God. For this reason alone, Hunt's theodicy is simply not adequate for Christian theists to adopt.

A second crucial problem with what Hunt proposes is that it makes God the initiator of the evil acts performed by the simulacra. The soulless simulacra would have to lack free agency. They are not creatures who have a will of their own, as they have no mind that stands apart from their actions and is the source and initiator of their actions. Indeed, it is for this very reason that they are not condemned to hell (which is the key benefit that Hunt emphasizes in proposing this theodicy). As I have argued previously, in order to be a moral agent who is worthy of punishment for wrongdoing, a creature must be capable of making libertarian free choices. A creature has to have a mind that initiates choices, and that mind must be capable of choosing to act other than how it does act. Hunt is correct that simulacra would not be worthy of eternal punishment because they lack a mind and lack moral agency; however, this advantage gets turned on its head as soon as one asks who is responsible for the actions of these simulacra. Clearly, it would have to be God. God would be the creator of these things and would be using his middle knowledge to cause them to act in precisely the ways that he knows will lead to the world playing out in such a way that no human freely chooses to reject God. This means that when a simulacrum engages in sin (whether it be a "white lie" or whether it be murder or rape or child molestation), it is God who is causing the simulacrum to take this action. That means God would not merely be responsible for permitting evil; God would undeniably be responsible for causing evil as well.

So this soteriological theodicy is clearly unacceptable for the Christian theist, as it produces problems far greater than it solves. Although

---

33. Hunt, "Middle Knowledge," 24.

God may permit certain evils in order to bring about greater goods, we have seen that Hunt's theodicy entails that God himself carries out all sorts of evils. Regardless of the advantages that Hunt's proposal may offer as a soteriological theodicy, it is contrary to the character of God and only amplifies the broader problem of evil. Even if, as I have argued, God does possess middle knowledge, it is not hard to see why God did not opt to carry out Hunt's simulacrum strategy. Hunt's view must be rejected.

We now turn to the final category of currently existing Molinist theodicies against the PCL—a category that, most notably, includes Craig's famous theodicy. Craig's view utilizes Molinism in an entirely different way than the proposals that we have considered above. While his theodicy is insightful and has many positive aspects, we will see that it also has its own difficulties.

Category #3 of Molinist Theodicies Against the PCL: Optimizing the Soteriological Balance

The third and final category of Molinist theodicies against the PCL that we will examine includes theodicies that have the common feature of proposing that God actualizes a world in which some people freely choose to be saved and others freely choose to be lost but God ensures an optimal soteriological balance such that the ratio of saved to lost is as good as possible (given human freedom). I will first examine and critique Craig's soteriological theodicy in significant detail. After that I will give brief attention to Kirk MacGregor's recent modification to Craig's theodicy.

The Theodicy of William Lane Craig

Craig's theodicy requires significant attention because my own theodicy draws upon—and departs from—key concepts in his theodicy and because Craig's theodicy against the PCL is by far the most prominent of all the Molinist theodicies that deal with the PCL. Like all of the above Molinist proposals, Craig's theodicy accepts P_8 while attacking P_9. This, however, is where the similarities between these theodicies end. Craig does not appeal to postmortem opportunities for salvation or to a soulless simulacra strategy or to the idea that anyone will be saved on the basis of what God middle-knows the person would have done in non-actual circumstances. Instead, Craig argues that God uses his middle knowledge

Assessment of Existing Molinist Theodicies

to arrange the world such that none of the lost are contingently lost and that God ensures that as many people as possible are saved and as few as possible are lost. Let us now explore Craig's theodicy, a position that can be boiled down to three key claims.

Craig's first claim is that it may be the case that nobody is contingently lost because God is able to arrange the world such that all of the lost are transcircumstantially damned (TD). This term, coined by Craig, was introduced in the first chapter. We have seen that Craig defines TD as "a contingent property possessed by an individual essence if the exemplification of that essence would, if offered salvation, freely reject God's grace and be lost no matter what freedom-permitting circumstances God should create him in." A transcircumstantially damned person is also "transworldly damned." He or she would freely choose to reject God and be lost in any world that God could actualize.[34] So, in order to reject P_9, Craig argues that God could ensure that "anyone who actually is lost would have been lost in any world in which God had created him."[35] Craig describes his position as follows:

> With respect to persons who do not respond to His grace under especially disadvantageous circumstances, God can so order the world that such persons are exclusively people who would still not have believed even had they been created under more advantageous circumstances. Far from being cruel, God is so loving that He arranges the world such that anyone who would respond to His saving grace under certain sets of circumstances is created precisely in one such set of circumstances, and He even provides sufficient grace for salvation to those who He knows would spurn it under any circumstances.[36]

Craig's claim is quite remarkable. Since God has middle knowledge, God knows what any person whom he might create would do in any possible set of circumstances. God, therefore, knows if a person is TD or not. Craig thinks that God uses his middle knowledge to actualize a world in which every person who is not TD is placed into a circumstance in which God knows that he or she will freely choose to be saved. Moreover, everyone who is lost would have been lost under any freedom-permitting

---

34. Craig, "Middle Knowledge and Christian Exclusivism," 128. Henceforth, "TD" will stand in place of "transcircumstantial damnation" and "transcircumstantially damned."

35. Craig, "No Other Name," 184.

36. Craig, "Politically Incorrect Salvation," 94.

circumstances and in any world in which that person has free will; these people are TD and would reject God no matter what graces God generously places into their lives. The fact that many of the lost are unevangelized or face other circumstances that are not conducive to accepting the gospel could not count against God's omnibenevolence. As Craig points out, those who fail to hear the gospel and are lost "would also not have responded to the gospel had they heard it. Hence, no one is lost because of lack of information due to historical or geographical accident. All who want or would want to be saved will be saved."[37] This first component of Craig's proposal that raises the possibility of all of the lost being TD, if consistent with Scripture, would be enough to undercut the PCL.

Craig's second key point is that all persons—even the unevangelized and all of the TD—receive sufficient grace to be saved in this life. Craig rightly wants to show that all of the lost do have a genuine opportunity to take advantage of the grace that God offers through Christ—even if they would never choose to take advantage of it. To accomplish this, Craig suggests that Scripture teaches Christian inclusivism in Romans 2:7, a passage which indicates that God will give eternal life to "those who by perseverance in doing good seek for glory and honor and immortality." Craig thinks this shows that "God doesn't judge people on the basis of whether they've placed their faith in Christ. Rather God judges them on the basis of the light of God's general revelation in nature and conscience that they do have." So long as one who has never heard of Christ senses her own moral guilt and seeks forgiveness from God, God will save her through Christ even though she has no conscious knowledge of Christ.[38] This, Craig suggests, means that everyone at least has an opportunity to be saved because all people are offered general revelation and have the opportunity to be saved by responding to it; nevertheless, he thinks the New Testament indicates that few actually do come to be saved in this way.[39] Regardless of whether or not many unevangelized persons access salvation in this way, Craig holds that all of them at least have the opportunity to access salvation by responding properly to general revelation.

Craig's third claim supplements his first claim, and it is intended to bolster his case for God's omnibenevolence. In considering Craig's first claim, one might wonder why God creates the TD. If God knows that

---

37. Craig, "No Other Name," 185.
38. Craig, *On Guard*, 274.
39. Craig, *On Guard*, 275.

these people will choose to be lost in any circumstances into which they are placed, why create them at all? In agreement with Craig, recall that I argued in the first chapter that God may not be able to create a well-populated world in which there is universal salvation. Although God would ideally prefer a well-populated world in which everyone is freely saved, the truth of certain counterfactuals concerning human freedom may render such a world infeasible for God. So, given that it may not be feasible for God to avoid some persons freely choosing to be lost in any well-populated world of free creatures, Craig's third key claim is that God plausibly does the best thing that he can do by optimizing the balance of saved versus lost:

> God wants to maximize the number of the saved: He wants heaven to be as full as possible. Moreover, as a loving God, He wants to minimize the number of the lost: He wants hell to be as empty as possible. His goal, then, is to achieve an optimal balance between these, to create no more lost than is necessary to achieve a certain number of the saved.[40]

So, along with his contention that all of the lost are TD and his appeal to inclusivism, Craig proposes that God brings about an "optimal balance" (i.e., an optimal ratio) of saved versus lost. God does this by using his middle knowledge to create a world in which each person—whether one who will be saved or one who is TD—is born into the precise time and place in history that will ultimately result in the most soteriologically-optimal world. The existence of a single person and the events that take place in that person's life can have an enormous impact upon the lives of many other people down through history. God providentially orders the world to ensure that just the right people come into existence in just the right circumstances so that (1) the only people who are ever lost are TD and (2) there is an optimal balance of saved versus lost over the course of human history. An "optimal balance" means that the only feasible worlds of free creatures in which there is a better ratio of saved to lost are worlds in which God must "so drastically reduce the number of the saved as to leave heaven deficient in population (say, by creating a world of only four people, three of whom go to heaven and one to hell)."[41] So the actual world is soteriologically optimal in the sense that, out of all the feasible worlds containing a sufficiently large number of people, none

---

40. Craig, "No Other Name," 183.
41. Craig, "No Other Name," 183.

of those worlds has a better ratio of saved to lost than the actual world. This third point is a useful supplement to Craig's first point. Although his first point alone would undermine P_9, without this third point one could question whether God had to make so many TD individuals. Adding this third point removes the sting of that concern.

Advantages of Craig's Theodicy

Craig's proposal certainly appears to be a philosophically viable solution to the PCL so long as God does possess middle knowledge. Drawing upon Alvin Plantinga's concept of transworld depravity, Craig's concept of TD[42] is an insightful recognition of the central issue surrounding P_9. The truth of the assertion that nobody is contingently lost (the negation of P_9) would require that anyone who actually is lost must be TD. It seems entirely possible that certain individuals could be TD, and there is no philosophical argument one can give—so far as I can see—to show that it is impossible for a God who has middle knowledge to ensure that all of the lost are TD. Certainly, if the people of the world were randomly distributed geographically, then it would be overwhelmingly unlikely that all of the lost are TD and that none of the numerous individuals who never hear the gospel would have accepted it if they had heard it. One must remember, however, that Craig's proposal is that God has providentially ordered the world using his middle knowledge to ensure that none of the lost are TD. If God has middle knowledge, then there is no apparent philosophical reason why God could not arrange the world in the way that Craig proposes. Although it would require an incredibly complex providential plan in order to ensure that all of the lost are TD and that there is an optimal balance of saved versus lost, a God who is omnipotent and whose omniscience includes middle knowledge surely could carry this out. If God did, then there is no way for humans to know that God did this simply by examining the world. Just because many unevangelized persons respond to the gospel when they first hear it,

---

42. Craig, "Middle Knowledge and Christian Exclusivism," 128. In this 1995 article, Craig expands his idea of "transworld damnation" (his original concept) to the broader idea of "transcircumstantial damnation." Both terms were defined in the first chapter. Plantinga's concept of "transworld depravity" was used in his Free Will Defense against the POE and inspired Craig's TD concept. One who has the property of transworld depravity will do evil in every world in which he is a morally free agent. See Plantinga, *God, Freedom, and Evil*, 48.

that says nothing about whether God has arranged the world so that all persons who *never* accept the gospel—including all persons who remain unevangelized throughout their lives—are TD.[43]

There also does not seem to be any way to show that God is not optimizing the balance of saved versus lost over the course of human history. We saw that Stephen Maitzen has argued that the geographical distribution of religious adherents in the world is unlikely if theism were true,[44] and one may similarly think that this distribution makes soteriological optimization unlikely; however, there is simply no way for us to have any confidence that the geographical distribution of the adherents of various religions and worldviews that we observe in the world at present is incompatible with soteriological optimality over the course of human history. We do not know how many centuries or millennia may remain in human history, and it is beyond our ken to have any level of confidence that there is incompatibility between the religious demographics of the world at present and the likelihood that a God who possesses middle knowledge is providentially carrying out a plan in which soteriological optimality is achieved by the end of human history. Even if one thinks that God likely could have achieved a better balance of saved versus lost up to this point in history if God were to have arranged certain things differently, there is absolutely no way to know whether or not the present state of the world is conducive to God achieving an optimal soteriological balance over the entirety of human history. It may be that it is only in a world with the particular false religions and the specific geographical distribution of religions and worldviews found in the world today that the optimal soteriological balance will ultimately be achieved. It may be that there will be an explosion of evangelism in the world in two centuries that is only made possible because the world is the way it is at present. The complexity of such things ought to give anyone pause who would suggest that we can be confident that God is not bringing about an optimal ratio of saved to lost over the whole of human history.

In addition, if inclusivism were true, Craig is right that this would provide a philosophical basis for thinking that everyone—even those who never hear the gospel and are lost—could receive sufficient grace from God to be saved; all people could have a genuine opportunity to be saved. There would be something that every person could have done such

---

43. Craig, *On Guard*, 281–82.
44. Maitzen, "Divine Hiddenness and the Demographics of Theism," 177–91.

that, if he or she had done it, he or she would have been saved. So Craig's view, if true, would ensure that: nobody who is lost is contingently lost; God has actualized a world that has a soteriological balance that is as favorable as any feasible world of free creatures; and everyone has sufficient grace to be saved. There seems to be no evident philosophical reason (so long as divine middle knowledge is accepted) to think that his proposal fails. It seems to undermine the claim of P_9 that some are contingently lost and resolve the PCL.

Besides the philosophical attractiveness of Craig's theodicy, it is also beneficial in several other ways. First, Craig's view sees God's election as purposeful and consistent with God's perfect love. Unlike Suarez—who, we have seen, held that God utilizes middle knowledge in his predestination of individuals for the specific purpose of ensuring the salvation and damnation of particular people—Craig proposes that God uses his middle knowledge to create a world in which there is an optimal balance of saved versus lost. This idea of an optimal soteriological balance is appealing and theologically reasonable (though we will see that certain divine goals may limit this optimality). Why would an omnibenevolent, omnipotent God who possesses middle knowledge *not* want to save as many people as possible and damn as few as possible? As I argued in the first chapter, Scripture indicates that God has a universal salvific will (1 Tim 2:4; 2 Pet 3:9; Ezek 18:23). Moreover, there is biblical support for the idea that God providentially places each person in a specific time and place with the goal of causing people to reach out and find him for salvation. The apostle Paul, speaking to an audience of philosophers in Athens, says

> The God who made the world and all things in it . . . gives to all people life and breath and all things; and He made from one man every nation of mankind to live on all the face of the earth, having determined their appointed times and the boundaries of their habitation, that they would seek God, if perhaps they might grope for Him and find Him, though He is not far from each one of us; for in Him we live and move and exist (Acts 17:24–28a).

So the proposal that God's creative effort is oriented toward the goal of bringing about a soteriologically-optimal world is more than philosophically reasonable; it is biblically supported (though not explicitly stated in Scripture), and it seems to me that it is quite plausible.

Second, Craig takes seriously God's sovereignty and providence within this present earthly existence. One might think that any Molinist theory would take a high view of God's sovereignty because, as seen in chapter 2, the truth of Molinism entails that God has the ability to exercise an incredible amount of providential control—even over worlds of free creatures. Nevertheless, we saw that the Molinist theodicies of Lake and Walls (and, to a large degree, Marsh) propose that God makes use of his middle knowledge merely to clean up the PCL after this present life is over. Craig, on the other hand, attempts to explain how God in his providence uses his middle knowledge to order this world of free creatures so that nobody is contingently lost to begin with. While I will (for biblical reasons) disagree with Craig's position that God has sovereignly arranged the world so that all of the lost are TD, Craig's strong view of God's sovereignty is a positive feature of his theodicy.

Finally, Craig's theodicy is also to be commended for affirming that God grants sufficient grace to all—even the lost—and for being consistent with the truths that God genuinely wants all to be saved and that Jesus died for all. I have already argued for these positions, though I will have more to say about the way in which God offers sufficient grace to all persons when I unpack my own theodicy. While I think it is wrongheaded for biblical reasons to appeal to inclusivism in order to uphold the sufficient grace and opportunity for salvation that God provides to all people, Craig correctly sees the importance of accounting for this in some way.

Difficulties with Craig's Theodicy

It is not enough for a theodicy against the PCL—at least a theodicy that applies to the Christian God—to be philosophically sound; it must also be consistent with Scripture. It need not be explicitly stated in Scripture, but it must not contradict biblical teaching. Craig's theodicy does not adopt such biblically problematic concepts as postmortem salvation or universalism or divine deception; however, crucial aspects of his theodicy do appear to come into conflict with biblical teaching, and this points toward the need for Christian theists to adopt a different theodicy against the PCL. Most significantly, there are two strong biblical indications that some people are contingently lost, and this is incompatible with Craig's key proposal that all of the lost are TD. First, Jesus asserts that Sodom,

Tyre, and Sidon would have repented if they had been exposed to different revelation (Matt 11:20–24; Luke 10:13–15). If Jesus means this literally (and we will see why biblical commentators widely interpret it literally), then these people would be contingently lost. Second, the Bible seems to affirm in a number of places that a person can genuinely accept the gospel through faith in Christ and then later reject God and his salvation by abandoning his or her faith. Since anyone who apostatizes cannot be TD, this is another problem for Craig's theodicy. I will first unpack both of these difficulties for Craig's suggestion that all of the lost are TD. His proposal that all people who will be lost may be TD is the critical claim in his theodicy that must be plausible if it is to have force in undercutting the PCL. Anyone who thinks that Craig's suggestion that all of the lost are TD rests uncomfortably with Scripture will not be convinced that his theodicy succeeds in undermining P_9 and resolving the PCL for Christian theism. After that, I will examine briefly the difficulty with the way Craig tries to justify that his appeal to inclusivism is biblical—an appeal that, as we have seen, Craig makes in order to try to show how all people (even the unevangelized) receive grace that is sufficient for them to have an opportunity to be saved. If his particular appeal to Scripture to justify inclusivism fails, then this reinforces my earlier claim that one ought not assume the truth of inclusivism. It reaffirms why it is valuable to remain consistent with exclusivism when offering a way of justifying that all of the lost receive sufficient grace and have an opportunity to be saved.

Jesus' Statement Concerning Sodom, Tyre, and Sidon

The first biblical strike against Craig's proposal that all of the lost may be TD arises from the comments that Jesus makes about the wicked people of Sodom, Tyre, and Sidon. Despite Jesus' incredible teachings and miracles, he faced widespread rejection from the people living in Capernaum (his base of operations during his ministry) and other towns that he visited. Faced with this direct rejection, Jesus began to denounce the many people who had seen his miracles and yet still hardened their hearts against him and his message:

> Woe to you, Chorazin! Woe to you, Bethsaida! For if the miracles had occurred in Tyre and Sidon which occurred in you, they would have repented long ago in sackcloth and ashes. Nevertheless I say to you, it will be more tolerable for Tyre and Sidon

in the day of judgment than for you. And you, Capernaum, will not be exalted to heaven, will you? You will descend to Hades; for if the miracles had occurred in Sodom which occurred in you, it would have remained to this day. Nevertheless I say to you that it will be more tolerable for the land of Sodom in the day of judgment, than for you (Matt 11:21–24; see also the account in Luke 10:13–15).[45]

In this passage, Jesus explicitly says that the notoriously sinful people of Tyre, Sidon, and Sodom would have chosen to repent if they had witnessed Jesus' miracles. Even the people of Sodom, a city that is infamous for being destroyed by God for its wickedness (Gen 18—19), would have repented and turned to God if they had seen the miracles that Jesus performed.

If this statement by Jesus is taken at face value, then there is an obvious difficulty with the proposal that all of the lost are TD. If Jesus is revealing God's middle knowledge that the sinful people in these towns literally would have repented and turned to God (presumably finding salvation) if placed into different circumstances, then Jesus is claiming that this is a case of people who are contingently lost. Had Jesus appeared in Sodom and performed miracles there prior to the destruction of the city, they would have repented. If Jesus meant his statement literally, then we ought not think that the people of these wicked cities are TD. Contrary to Craig's position, these would be people who are actually lost but who would have freely chosen to change their ways and turn to God if only they had been placed into different circumstances. Although they were wicked and freely chose to reject what revelation they did have, they would have responded to the miracles of Jesus had they been given the opportunity to see them.

Craig, of course, is aware of this passage and its implications for his view. He takes a position on the interpretation of this passage that, if true, would avoid this problem. Craig suggests that "Matthew 11 is probably religious hyperbole meant merely to underscore the depth of the depravity of the cities in which Jesus preached."[46] So Craig's stance is that Jesus, in order to make his point forcefully about the extent of the hardness of heart and rebelliousness of the people who were rejecting him and

---

45. Keathley, *Salvation and Sovereignty*, 161. See footnote 54. Keathley rightly points out that the concept of TD conflicts with Matt 11:20–28 (though he does not explain why).

46. Craig, *The Only Wise God*, 137. See the footnote on this page.

ignoring his miracles, might have only been exaggerating matters so as to shock his hearers. Craig, therefore, doubts that Jesus is revealing true middle knowledge in this particular instance about what the people of the wicked cities of Tyre, Sidon, and Sodom would have freely chosen to do in different circumstances.

Now there can be no doubt that Jesus did intend for his comments to shock his Jewish listeners; the idea that they are more deserving of punishment than notoriously evil pagan cities is supposed to be startling. However, there is strong contextual evidence that Jesus intended for his statements to be taken as literally true. If Jesus did not mean that the wicked cities literally would have repented in great remorse had they seen his miracles, then his concluding comment about how the people of those wicked cities will be judged relative to those who heard and rejected Jesus (Matt 11:22, 24) becomes quite difficult to understand.

Jesus concludes his speech by declaring that "it will be more tolerable" for the wicked cities "in the day of judgment" than for those who saw his miracles and failed to repent. This proclamation ties the counterfactual statement about what the people of the wicked cities would have done in non-actual circumstances to the real-world fact about how they will actually be judged less severely. If Jesus' statement that the wicked cities would have repented had they seen his miracles is not a true counterfactual, then it seems to undercut the basis for Jesus concluding that the people of these wicked cities will actually be judged less severely than the people who rejected Jesus' miracles. The wicked cities are guilty for failing to live up to the revelation that they had received and will thus be punished, but they will not be judged as harshly as the towns that rejected the miracles of Jesus because the wicked cities would have responded positively to that same revelation had they been given it. So Jesus indicates that there are two factors involved in the reason why God will give the wicked cities a lighter punishment than those who rejected Jesus' miracles: the different amount of revelation that the two groups received *and* the fact that those with less revelation would have responded to the greater revelation had they been given it.

One might contend that Jesus' conclusion about the differing amounts of punishment would still make sense even if his counterfactual statement concerning the wicked cities is not to be taken literally. That is, one might argue that the wicked cities will be judged less severely *merely* because they received less revelation (i.e., that is the only factor that is in play). However, it must be taken seriously that Jesus' primary point of emphasis in this passage is not merely on the disparity in the amount of revelation; rather, he emphasizes just as strongly the fact that the wicked cities would have repented if they had been given the additional revelation. Both factors are emphasized, so why would only one factor be relevant to Jesus' conclusion that there will be lighter punishment for the wicked cities? Jesus' condemning blow to those who reject his miracles seems to be based upon both factors.

Significantly, if Craig's interpretation of the above passage were correct that Jesus is merely engaging in hyperbole in his condemnation of the towns that ignored his miracles (an interpretation that we have seen is necessary if Craig is to avoid a conflict between this biblical passage and the proposal he makes in his theodicy that all of the lost are TD), then it is difficult to see why God would punish the people who rejected his miracles more severely than any other lost people. If the lost people of the wicked cities of Sodom, Tyre, and Sidon are TD, as Craig's theodicy requires, then they would have rejected Jesus' miracles even if they had been given the opportunity to see them (contrary to what Jesus actually says in this passage). So why should the people of the wicked cities be judged less severely than those who rejected Jesus' miracles when they would have done the same thing had they been placed into those circumstances? Those people who rejected Jesus' miracles merely had the misfortune of being born at a time and place in which they were given more revelation than other TD individuals, but God (via his middle knowledge) knows that they do not despise his grace more than any other TD person that God has created. If God did indeed providentially arrange the world so that all of the lost are TD in order to ensure that nobody who is lost can object that God was unloving to them by placing them into circumstances in which they are contingently lost, then surely this strategy creates another problem if (according to Craig's interpretation of Matt 11:21–24) God also punishes some lost people less severely *merely* because they received less revelation and does not take into account the fact that all of the lost are TD. The problem is that it may just as easily be argued that God would be unloving or unfair if he were to factor into the level of punishment of each lost person the amount of revelation that the lost person received when all lost persons are TD and would have rejected any revelation that God presented to them.

It should also be noted that biblical commentators widely accept a literal interpretation of Jesus' statement that the people of the wicked cities would have repented if they had seen his miracles. D. A. Carson's position is representative of such commentators. Carson says:

> Three large theological propositions are presupposed by Jesus' insistence that on the Day of Judgment (see on [Mt] 10:15; cf. [Mt] 12:36; Acts 17:31; 2 Peter 2:9; 3:7; 1 John 4:17; Jude 6), when he will judge ([Mt] 7:22; 25:34), things will go worse for the cities that have received so much light than for the pagan cities. The first is that the Judge has contingent knowledge: he knows what Tyre and Sidon would have done under such-and-such circumstances. The second is that God does not owe revelation to anyone, or else there is injustice in withholding it. The third is that punishment on the Day of Judgment takes into account opportunity. There are degrees of felicity in paradise and degrees of torment in hell (Rom 1:20—2:16). The implications for Western, English-speaking Christendom today are sobering.[47]

Molina himself actually cited Matthew 11:20–24 as a case in which Scripture supports divine middle knowledge. Molina interpreted Jesus as speaking literally about what the people of the wicked cities would have done, and Molina regarded this passage as evidence that some people who are lost in the actual world would have been saved had God placed them into different circumstances.[48] Kirk MacGregor's assessment of Craig's exegesis of this passage is correct when he states that it "falls clearly outside the mainstream of Matthean scholarship." He concludes that "Craig's interpretation of this text seems a clear case of allowing philosophical presuppositions to trump grammatico-historical exegesis."[49] While the possibility that Jesus' statement is merely hyperbolic may exist, such an understanding is not strongly warranted by the text itself. As a result, this biblical passage rests quite uncomfortably indeed with Craig's proposal that all of the lost are, in fact, TD.

---

47. Carson, *Matthew Chapters 1–12*, 273. See also Bruner, *The Christbook*, 525; Leske, "Matthew," 1292.

48. MacGregor cites where Molina indicates this in his *Concordia* (7.23.4/5.1.4.13; 7.23.4/5.1.11.41; 4.14.13.49.9). See footnote 56 in MacGregor, *Luis de Molina*, 147.

49. MacGregor, *A Molinist-Anabaptist Systematic Theology*, 69. See footnote 22.

The Possibility of Apostasy

The second biblical reason that it is best to avoid a theodicy that requires all of the lost to be TD is that Scripture seems to warn in numerous places that a believer can abandon his or her faith and reject God's grace after having previously accepted it. Although this issue of "perseverance of the saints" (the view that one who accepts God's grace by faith will never turn from that faith and reject God's gift of salvation) is an area of disagreement among Christians and cannot possibly be handled in great depth in this section, I will aim to make a brief but powerful case that the biblical data strongly supports the conclusion that one can freely choose to walk away from saving faith just as one can freely choose to accept God's grace by faith in the first place. If believers can apostatize, then this fact counts as yet another strike against Craig's position. That is because one who apostatizes and is lost would have been saved in a feasible world that is identical to the actual world up until a certain point: a world in which the one who apostatizes in the actual world had instead died subsequent to accepting God's grace by faith but prior to apostatizing. When I later unpack my own theodicy, it will be clear that the viability of my theodicy is not affected by the truth or falsity of perseverance of the saints. Craig's theodicy, however, is not compatible with the falsity of perseverance of the saints because it requires that all of the lost are TD.[50] Ultimately, even if one does hold that Scripture supports the truth of perseverance of the saints and that the arguments against it are not powerful enough to warrant its rejection, the fact that there are numerous biblical passages that—at the very least—strongly call this doctrine into question makes it attractive if a theodicy against the PCL does not *depend* on the truth of this controversial doctrine.

Since at least the time of Augustine, the idea of perseverance of the saints has been held by some Christians. This doctrine later became one of the five points of Calvinism, and it is not hard to see why. If the Calvinist conception of the other four points were true, then it seems to follow that one who is unconditionally elected and is unable to resist God's grace will necessarily persevere in his or her faith and be saved. There are also some Christians who have adopted perseverance of the saints by itself (i.e., without holding to the other points of Calvinism). Proponents of

---

50. Although we will later note the interesting fact that Craig himself has expressed that Scripture indicates that believers can apostatize, this position is not consistent with his own theodicy against the PCL.

perseverance of the saints appeal to a variety of biblical passages that they believe support this doctrine. For example, in John 10:28–29 Jesus says concerning his elect, "I give eternal life to them, and they will never perish; and no one will snatch them out of My hand. My Father, who has given them to Me, is greater than all; and no one is able to snatch them out of the Father's hand." Similarly, Paul writes to the Philippian believers that "He who began a good work in you will perfect it until the day of Christ Jesus" (Phil 1:6), and he assures the Roman believers that "neither death, nor life, nor angels, nor principalities, nor things present, nor things to come, nor powers, nor height, nor depth, nor any other created thing, will be able to separate us from the love of God, which is in Christ Jesus our Lord" (Rom 8:38–39). Paul also tells Timothy that God is "able to guard what I have entrusted to Him until that day" (2 Tim 1:12). Because there is no power that can take away a believer's salvation, the Apostle John is likewise able to tell his readers that they "may know that [they] have eternal life" (1 John 5:13).

In view of such passages, we must minimally conclude that one undeniable blessing of being a believer in Christ is the assurance of knowing that no person or thing can rob a believer of his or her salvation. Moreover, God is faithful in his promise to grant eternal life to those who are saved. There is truly nothing that can snatch a believer in Christ out of God's loving hand. A believer can and should have the blessed assurance of knowing with certainty that she is saved and that this salvation cannot be taken from her against her will and is not contingent upon her maintaining her salvation by upholding a certain standard of good works.

Nevertheless, as Jack Cottrell points out, it does not seem that any biblical text "affirms that every saved child of God will unconditionally and infallibly remain in his saved state until he dies."[51] Passages such as those cited above are not at all in conflict with "the possibility that the believer *himself* may exercise his free will and voluntarily give up his salvation" by refusing to maintain faith in Christ.[52] I have argued previously that it is both indicated in Scripture and morally important that all humans possess libertarian freedom of the will, and the Bible in no way implies that one who freely chooses to accept God's grace by faith subsequently undergoes a loss of libertarian freedom with regard to his or her ability to choose freely whether or not to reject his or her faith. Moreover,

---

51. Cottrell, *The Faith Once for All*, 376.
52. Cottrell, *The Faith Once for All*, 376. The emphasis is mine.

the Bible never affirms that a believer can lack faith in Christ and still be saved. On the contrary, there are numerous warnings against turning from the faith, and these warnings are powerful evidence that one's faith—and thus one's salvation—can be abandoned if one so chooses. It needs to be recognized at this point that, in such warnings against apostasy, a believer's choice to continue in faith (just like his or her choice to accept Christ by faith originally) ought not be viewed as a work in the sense of Ephesians 2:8–9, a passage in which Paul stresses that we are saved by God's grace through faith as a gift from God and not by our own effort. As Grant Osborne rightly puts it, faith must not be regarded as a work "because it is not an active agent by which we save ourselves." Saving faith is properly understood as "a passive surrender to the God who saves us, an opening up of ourselves to God, who works salvation in us. But it is still a free choice."[53] Humans cannot save themselves or keep themselves saved, but they can refuse to accept salvation and can refuse to continue in faith. Let us examine some of the warnings against apostasy.

The writer of Hebrews, in particular, often warns against apostasy, passionately calling his ethnically Jewish readers who are believers in Christ to resist the temptation to abandon Christianity and return to Judaism. He implores them to maintain their Christian faith despite the hardships and pressures that Jewish Christians faced. Indeed, as Ben Witherington correctly observes, one of the most prominent *themes* of the book of Hebrews appears to be warnings to Christian believers against the dangers of apostasy and the need to persist in their faith.[54] It is certainly true that a believer can fall into sin and stray from the Lord without being separated from Christ. As James 5:19 indicates, such temporary wandering from the Lord occurs when one "strays from the truth and [another] one turns him back." Nevertheless, multiple passages in Hebrews seem to warn genuine believers against engaging in a *decisive* rejection of Christ. This theme arises especially in chapters three, six, and ten of Hebrews.

In the third chapter, the author of Hebrews warns:

> Take care, brethren, that there not be in any one of you an evil, unbelieving heart that falls away from the living God. But encourage one another day after day, as long as it is still called 'Today,' so that none of you will be hardened by the deceitfulness of

---

53. Osborne, "A Classical Arminian View," 87.
54. Witherington, *Letters and Homilies for Jewish Christians*, 288.

sin. For we have become partakers of Christ, if we hold fast the beginning of our assurance firm until the end (Heb 3:12–14).

It is crucial first of all to note that the author of Hebrews is addressing this warning to "brethren" (ἀδελφοί). Indeed, the author addresses the "brethren" throughout the book of Hebrews. There is good reason to think that this is a reference to believers in Christ—a group that includes the author himself. Just a few verses earlier, in Hebrews 3:1, the author makes it clear that he is speaking to "holy brethren [again, ἀδελφοί], partakers of a heavenly calling," and he is asking them to "consider Jesus, the Apostle and High Priest of our confession." Since the brethren are "holy" (ἅγιοι) and confess Jesus as their "Apostle and High Priest" and the author himself adheres to the same confession as these brethren (note the pronoun ἡμῶν, which is genitive, plural, and first-person), this certainly seems to be a description of genuine believers. The author again (in 10:19) addresses the brethren (ἀδελφοί) and again includes himself among the brethren, noting that "we" (i.e., the author and all those who are among the "brethren") are those who: "have confidence to enter the holy place by the blood of Jesus" (10:19); "have a great priest [Jesus] over the house of God" (10:21); have "full assurance of faith, having our hearts sprinkled clean from an evil conscience" (10:22); and have reason to "hold fast the confession of our hope without wavering, for He who promised is faithful" (10:23). The author also references the ἀδελφοί in the conclusion of the book of Hebrews (13:22) by making it clear that this entire letter of exhortation is addressed to the "brethren." So, returning to the passage under consideration in Hebrews 3:12–14, when the author warns the "brethren" in 3:12 to be careful not to have "an evil, unbelieving heart that falls away from the living God,"[55] there is exceptional reason to think that he is addressing true believers in Christ. There is no reason to think that the brethren the author references in 3:12 is a different group than the brethren he addresses throughout the book of Hebrews—and certainly not different than the group to which he refers just a few verses earlier when he makes clear that he is addressing the "holy brethren" who recognize Jesus as "the Apostle and High Priest of our confession."

Given that the author seems to be addressing Christians in 3:12–14, the warning that he issues is significant. He emphasizes that the brethren

---

55. The Greek word for "falls away" is ἀποστῆναι, from which we get the English word "apostasy."

must not turn away from the "living God" to any other god. Regarding the title of "living God," Donald Guthrie notes:

> This particular title for God, which is familiar in the Old Testament, occurs several times in the New Testament, frequently, as here, without the article. The form without the article draws attention more vividly to the adjective 'living'. The Christians in pagan environments would warm to the contrast between the living God, whom they worshipped, and the dead idols of paganism (cf. Acts 14:15). The title was of equal appeal to a Jewish disciple, as in Peter's confession at Caesarea Philippi (Mt. 16:16), or to a Jewish high priest as the oath in Matthew 26:63 shows. There are other places in Hebrews where the same title is used (9:14; 10:31; 12:22). The words convey the idea of a dynamic God and are particularly significant in any comments about men falling away from him (cf. especially 10:31).[56]

Guthrie points out that if this falling away has to do with a "return to Judaism," as seems to be the case in the book of Hebrews, then the reference to the "living God" is especially significant. One must ask: "[In] what sense could this [return to Judaism] be described as a falling away from the living God, since Jews did acknowledge God?" Guthrie's conclusion is that "the answer must be that 'apostates' in this sense would not find God in Judaism, having turned their backs on the better way provided in Christ."[57] Also, the fact that the author is telling the brethren to "encourage one another" (3:13; cf. 10:25) to avoid this rejection of God indicates that he is addressing those who are within the community of Christians. It is, after all, "impossible to exhort one another unless one is part of a fellowship. In the present case a hardening of heart is linked closely with 'sin' and this must have been a tendency in the case of the Hebrews who were tempted to turn away from Christianity."[58] Ultimately, in 3:14, the author indicates that "we" (again, including himself) are only "partakers of Christ" if it is the case that "we hold fast the beginning of our assurance firm until the end."

In the sixth chapter, the author of Hebrews speaks of "those who have once been enlightened and have tasted of the heavenly gift and have been made partakers of the Holy Spirit, and have tasted the good word of God and the powers of the age to come" (Heb 6:4–5). It is difficult to

---

56. Guthrie, *The Letter to the Hebrews*, 106.
57. Guthrie, *The Letter to the Hebrews*, 106.
58. Guthrie, *The Letter to the Hebrews*, 107.

deny that such a description refers to anyone other than saved believers in Christ. The author goes on to say that if such persons later "[fall] away, it is impossible to renew them again to repentance, since they again crucify to themselves the Son of God and put Him to open shame" (Heb 6:6). There may be no passage in Scripture that stands against the doctrine of the perseverance of the saints more forcefully than this one. This warning is first of all given to those who are "enlightened." With regard to the phrase ἅπαξ φωτισθέντας ("who have once been enlightened"), Scot McKnight notes that the "only other occurrence of the verb φωτίζω in Hebrews is in 10:32 where it apparently refers to conversion ('remember the former days, the days after which you had been enlightened'), as it regularly signifies conversion in early Christian literature."[59] Those receiving the warning are also said to have "tasted of the heavenly gift and have been made partakers of the Holy Spirit." The concept of tasting the heavenly gift, as Donald Guthrie rightly recognizes, "implies experience of it. This is an Old Testament usage (cf. Ps. 34:8). In the New Testament 1 Peter 2:3 contains the same idea."[60] The fact that the gift is "heavenly" shows that what is experienced is a gift from God that "is not one of human making." Moreover, "the word used here for 'gift' (*dorea*) is exclusively used of spiritual gifts in the New Testament."[61] For example, it is the same word for "gift" (δωρεὰν) that Peter uses in his presentation of the gospel at Pentacost when, in response to his audience asking him what they must do to be saved, Peter tells them how to "receive the gift of the Holy Spirit" (Acts 2:38). Although some have suggested that the "tasting" (γευσαμένους) of this heavenly gift may carry the idea of partially tasting something to get a sense of it without fully eating (such that the author is describing those who have merely been exposed to God's truth but have not actually become Christians), there is no basis for this. William Mounce points out that the word γευσαμένους literally refers to tasting or eating, and the figurative sense of the word refers to "partaking of" something. He notes that this word is used figuratively (as it clearly is in Heb 6:4) in Hebrews 2:9 to refer to "Christ's tasting of death on the cross, through which he partook of death for everyone who believes in

---

59. McKnight, "The Warning Passages of Hebrews," 45–46. Support for McKnight's claim that this term regularly has to do with conversion in the early Christian literature can be found in Attridge, *The Epistle to the Hebrews*, 169–70 (see especially note 43 on p. 169).

60. Guthrie, *The Letter to the Hebrews*, 141.

61. Guthrie, *The Letter to the Hebrews*, 142.

him." It also is used figuratively when Jesus "refers to the disciples' not tasting death until they see the kingdom of God (Mt. 16:28; Mk. 9:1; Lk. 9:27; Jn. 8:52)."[62] Certainly, in these figurative uses of the word, it does not imply a partial experience of anything. Jesus did not receive a mere partial experience of death on the cross. So, why think that the figurative use of this word in Hebrews 6:4 is any different than the way the author uses the word in 2:9? There is nothing about the word itself that implies a partial experience as opposed to a full experience when it is used figuratively in this way, and there seems to be nothing in the context that would indicate anything less than a full experience. Scot McKnight is correct that "the degree is not the issue" that is being communicated by the use of this term in this passage.[63] In addition, being "partakers of the Holy Spirit" clearly connects this gift with that given by the Spirit (much like what Peter stated in Acts 2:38 referenced above). The subsequent statement that when such people (i.e., those who have experienced the gift of the Spirit) fall away they "again crucify to themselves the Son of God and put Him to open shame" makes it quite difficult to avoid the conclusion that apostasy is in view. In this phrase "the compound verb used (*anastaurountas*) shows that the writer is thinking of a repetition of the crucifixion. He could not have expressed the seriousness of the apostasy in stronger or more tragic terms." This is because those who fall away from Christ are acting against Christ in a way that is on par with (if not worse than) his crucifixion in terms of the contempt that is shown for him.[64] The fact that this crucifying makes it "impossible to renew them again to repentance" further indicates the seriousness of what is being discussed. This cannot be a description of the sort of temporary backsliding that James 5:19 seems to be describing. It is also significant that the author introduces this warning in chapter 6 by saying "let us press on to maturity" (6:1), again including himself as one of those who needs to persevere in the faith and continually grow in the faith.

In chapter 10 there is yet another warning that seems to implore Christian believers not to apostatize: "For if we go on sinning willfully

---

62. Mounce, *Mounce's Complete Expository Dictionary*, 707. Mounce recognizes that the use of the word in 6:4–5 is controversial because of the soteriological implications of this passage, but he clearly shows that there is nothing about this word that, when used figuratively, has to carry the idea of a partial experience of something or a minimal partaking in something.

63. McKnight, "The Warning Passages of Hebrews," 46–47.

64. Guthrie, *The Letter to the Hebrews*, 143–44.

after receiving the knowledge of the truth, there no longer remains a sacrifice for sins, but a terrifying expectation of judgment and the fury of a fire which will consume the adversaries" (Heb 10:26-29). The author emphasizes that he is here describing a person who rejects Christ as Lord and Savior after having previously been sanctified and that such a person brings guilt and punishment upon himself because he "has trampled underfoot the Son of God, and has regarded as unclean the blood of the covenant by which he was sanctified, and has insulted the Spirit of grace" (Heb 10:29). As noted already, the author's use of "we" ("if we go on sinning") in 10:26 is connected with his use of "brethren" and "we" in 10:19. The author of Hebrews is including himself (one who is, of course, saved) within the group to whom this warning is addressed. These brethren are to "hold fast the confession of our hope without wavering" (10:23). Surely the fire (a common image used to describe the final state of the lost) that will consume God's adversaries in this warning (10:27) is a reference to God's final judgment of humanity. The author again uses phrases that emphasize the contempt that one who abandons faith in Christ has for Christ and for the Spirit ("trampled under foot the Son of God" and "insulted the Spirit of grace"), and he stresses that it is a horrible thing for one who has been "sanctified" through the "blood of the covenant" to then turn from the truth.

If it were literally impossible to abandon the faith, this prominent theme of warnings in the book of Hebrews would seem to be unnecessary. The severity of these warnings and the strong evidence that they are directed toward genuine Christians[65] ought to at the very least give serious pause to those who hold to the doctrine of the perseverance of the saints (where, once again, that doctrine is understood to mean that a believer herself cannot reject her faith in Christ and refuse salvation).

---

65. McKnight gives an excellent account of the way the author of Hebrews refers to his audience throughout the book of Hebrews. See McKnight, "The Warning Passages of Hebrews," 43-44. He summarizes his findings on p. 44, highlighting why the intended audience of the author's warnings should be regarded as regenerate Christians: "In summary, the author ascribes to the audience the fullness of early Christian experience: conversion (2:3-4; 6:4-5; 10:22, 32-34), gifts and manifestations of the Holy Spirit (2:3-4; 10:29), spiritual growth, and a Christian commitment that included resistance under considerable pressure (10:32-34). In short, the author treats them as 'believers' (4:3) because he saw them as 'holy brothers' (3:1). Phenomenologically, the author believes them to be, and presents them as, believers in the fullest sense possible. If these descriptions are accurate, and we believe they are, these readers are most plausibly to be seen as regenerate."

Yet, beyond the warnings found in the book of Hebrews, there are other indications in the New Testament that it is possible to apostatize.

The Apostle Paul seems to speak of—and warn against—apostasy on many occasions.[66] Consider, for example, the following statement Paul makes to the Colossians. Paul, speaking to believers (those who were "formerly alienated and hostile in mind"), affirms that Christ has "now reconciled you in His fleshly body through death, in order to present you before Him holy and blameless and beyond reproach." However, this reconciliation is conditional; it depends upon a life lived in faith. Paul says that Christ has reconciled you "if indeed you continue in the faith firmly established and steadfast, and not moved away from the hope of the gospel that you have heard" (Col 1:21–23).

Paul even goes beyond mere warnings against apostasy and speaks directly of the fact that some have actually departed from their faith.[67] In his first letter to Timothy, Paul reminds Timothy that "the goal of our instruction is love from a pure heart and a good conscience and a sincere faith." Yet, Paul makes it clear that there are some who do not share this goal. He notes that "some men, straying from these things, have turned aside to fruitless discussion" and have become false teachers (1 Tim 1:5–6). A few verses later he stresses to Timothy the importance of "keeping faith and a good conscience, which some have rejected and suffered shipwreck in regard to their faith" (1 Tim 1:19). Paul then identifies two people who have experienced this shipwrecking of faith, saying, "Among these are Hymenaeus and Alexander, whom I have handed over to Satan, so that they will be taught not to blaspheme" (1 Tim 1:20). Let us consider this passage carefully to see why Paul seems to be speaking of apostates. Paul indicates that it is the same sort of faith that Timothy has—and that Paul encourages Timothy to keep—that some others (including Hymenaeus and Alexander) have possessed and thrown away.[68] The use of the word "shipwreck" (ἐναυάγησαν) reveals that what happened to their faith is a total catastrophe. These people have rejected,

---

66. See, for example: Rom 11:17–24; 1 Cor 9:24–27; 15:1–2; Gal 5:4; Col 1:21–23; 1 Thess 3:5; 1 Tim 1:18–20; 2 Tim 2:17–18.

67. The strong warnings in Scripture against apostasy serve as a powerful sign that apostasy is possible; however, one may still argue that nobody actually does apostatize. One could argue that the warnings are part of the means by which God keeps believers in Christ from apostatizing so that they persevere in their faith. But the first chapter of 1 Timothy indicates otherwise. Here I will show that there is evidence that some actually do apostatize.

68. Oropeza, *Jews, Gentiles, and the Opponents of Paul*, 2:268.

or—more literally—thrust away (ἀπωσάμενοι), their faith so that it is a total loss and has gone down in a wreck. Paul does not say that these people have merely stopped professing their faith; rather, he indicates that "their faith" (as the NASB rightly translates τὴν πίστιν) has been shipwrecked. Some have suggested that this phrase with the article τὴν should be translated as "the faith" and should be taken to indicate a rejection of Christian doctrine or the Christian gospel and not their own personal faith in Christ.[69] But such an interpretation is not warranted by the text. As B. J. Oropeza notes (in agreement with the translation of the NASB above), "The definite article before 'faith' probably functions as a pronoun of possession to indicate 'their faith' rather than 'the faith.'"[70] Since the concept of being shipwrecked "often seems to convey utter ruin in ancient traditions" (the idea of a "complete loss of the ship"), it seems that Paul "could hardly be talking about minor damage" when he uses this word; thus, "the term makes very little sense *if attributed to the ruin of the Christian faith.*"[71] Paul is surely not saying that the Christian faith itself is utterly destroyed; instead, it is much more likely that the utter rejection of their own personal faith is in view. Paul "handed over to Satan" Hymenaeus and Alexander, using the same phrase that he used to describe his removal of a sinful man from the church in Corinth (1 Cor 5:5). Although the latter was removed due to known sexual sin, the former were removed for blasphemy and rejecting their faith. In any case, it is clear that Hymenaeus and Alexander were removed from the church by Paul in the hopes that they would repent and cease their blasphemy.[72]

The Apostle Peter also appears to speak of those who commit apostasy when he says:

> [If], after they have escaped the defilements of the world by the knowledge of the Lord and Savior Jesus Christ, they are again entangled in them and are overcome, the last state has become worse for them than the first. For it would be better for them not to have known the way of righteousness, than having known it, to turn away from the holy commandment handed on to them. It has happened to them according to the true proverb, 'A dog

---

69. Volf, "Apostasy, Falling Away, Perseverance," 44.
70. Oropeza, *Jews, Gentiles, and the Opponents of Paul*, 2:267.
71. Oropeza, *Jews, Gentiles, and the Opponents of Paul*, 2:268.
72. For a discussion of this concept of Paul handing these two men over to Satan and a comparison with the case in 1 Corinthians 5:5, see Oropeza, *Jews, Gentiles, and the Opponents of Paul*, 2:268–72.

returns to its own vomit,' and, 'A sow, after washing, returns to wallowing in the mire' (2 Pet 2:20–22).

Peter is speaking of those whose defilement has been cleaned by the blood of Jesus through faith in him (since such people have actually "escaped" this defilement by knowing Jesus) but who then abandon the faith to return to a life that is devoted to sin and impurity. This is no mere backsliding, since Peter can say of the person who escaped defilement and then returned to it that "it would be better for them not to have known the way of righteousness" at all. A person who is saved but backslidden is certainly better off than a person who has never known God. It seems likely that in this passage Peter is speaking of those who are motivated to apostastize and abandon Christian faith entirely.

From the sampling of passages cited above, it is clear that there is at least significant biblical support for the idea that one can apostatize. Interestingly, despite his theory that all of the lost are TD, Craig himself accepts that Scripture teaches the reality of apostasy. It is unclear how Craig justifies accepting this position while at the same time putting forth his theodicy against the PCL that appeals to the possibility that all of the lost are TD; nevertheless, it is quite clear that Craig does not hesitate to affirm that there is "clear biblical teaching that the elect can fall away and be lost."[73] Moreover, Craig does not presume to think that he himself is above the possibility of abandoning his faith. He confesses:

> One of my greatest concerns as a Christian is that I might somehow fall away from the faith and so betray Christ. It would be the height of folly and presumption to think that this could not happen. Think of what happened to Judas. It's amazing that a man who was one of the original twelve disciples, who had been for years in such close proximity to Jesus, should in the end turn against him. Is it then any wonder that we can similarly fall away and betray Christ? Paul speaks of several whom he knew who had left the faith (1 Tim 1:20; 2 Tim 2:17; 4:10). He warns, 'Let anyone who thinks that he stands take heed lest he fall' (1 Cor 10.12 ESV). Paul included himself in that admonition, 'lest after preaching to others I myself should be disqualified' (1 Cor 9.27 ESV). If someone of Paul's spiritual stature and commitment took seriously this danger, how much more should we? Paul

---

73. Craig, *Divine Foreknowledge and Human Freedom*, 245.

urges us, 'Examine yourselves, to see whether you are holding to your faith' (2 Cor 13.5 RSV).[74]

While I applaud Craig for his humility and his recognition of what I also take to be biblical teaching on this subject, the inconsistency of this position with his theodicy against the PCL that all of the lost are TD is unavoidable for the reason that I explained at the beginning of this section. If one can freely choose to walk away from saving faith, then such a person who commits apostasy and is lost would have been saved in another world—a world that is clearly actualizable. Had this person died after accepting God's grace by faith but prior to apostatizing, then he or she would have been saved. Thus, any person who commits apostasy is necessarily contingently lost and not TD. Even if one is not fully convinced by the biblical case offered above that one can apostatize, the fact that a strong case can be made for the reality of apostasy (along with the strong evidence that Jesus indicates that some people are contingently lost in Matthew 11:21–24) makes it attractive if one can offer a theodicy that does not depend upon the claim that all of the lost are TD. Certainly, many Christians will find such a theodicy unhelpful.

As we conclude this section on apostasy, it is interesting to raise the following possibility in passing. Given the biblical evidence that apostasy is possible in the actual world and the likelihood (in view of God's omnibenevolence and universal salvific will) that God would want to actualize a world that is soteriologically optimal, the following question arises: Might it possibly be the case that God could only achieve the most optimal balance of saved versus lost (one key point in Craig's theodicy) by *not* providentially arranging the world such that all who are lost are TD (i.e., by not carrying out another key point in Craig's theodicy)? It is interesting that the two may actually be in conflict with each other such that it is only in a world in which certain people apostatize (and thus are contingently lost) that the best balance of saved versus lost is achieved. While it is conceivable that in many ways some TD individual that God could have created may be able to play the same role in the world as some contingently lost individual (i.e., they may freely make the same choices in a wide range of circumstances), there is at least one thing that a TD individual would never do: apostatize. If it happens to be true that it is only in a world in which certain people apostatize that the optimal balance of saved versus lost can be achieved, then Craig's proposal that God

---

74. Craig and Gorra, *A Reasonable Response*, 324–25.

optimizes the soteriological balance would conflict with his proposal that all of the lost are TD. While it is impossible to know this for sure (since it depends on the truth values of CCFs to which we do not have access), it is interesting that Craig's two key proposals possibly cannot both be achieved by God. If it is the case that they are incompatible, then it would not be surprising if God would choose to create a world in which there is an optimal soteriological balance and forego ensuring that all who are lost are TD.

Craig's Appeal to Inclusivism

We have now examined two biblical reasons why it is desirable to formulate a theodicy against the PCL that does not require Craig's appeal to the possibility that all of the lost may be TD. Let us now address in brief another aspect of his theodicy that does not rest comfortably with biblical teaching: his appeal to inclusivism to justify that all people at least have the opportunity to be saved. If inclusivism were true, then every individual—even those who are unevangelized—is given revelation to which he or she could respond and be saved.

I have already made the case in the first chapter that there is strong biblical support for exclusivism and that it is therefore valuable for a soteriological theodicy not to make any appeal to inclusivism in order to justify that all people have an opportunity to be saved. While it was not necessary for my purposes to engage in a critique of all the various arguments for inclusivism, I did make the case that—in view of the many biblical passages that underscore the elevated place of responding to the gospel in the New Testament teaching concerning soteriology and the fact that there seems to be no clear teaching in Scripture that one who lives in the New Testament era can be saved without hearing and accepting the gospel—one at least ought to find it preferable to avoid relying upon inclusivism in one's theodicy. I also offered in the first chapter a way of showing how exclusivism can be true and yet all people can have an opportunity to be saved, and I noted that I will offer an even more nuanced exclusivist justification that all people have an opportunity to be saved when I unpack my own theodicy. Nevertheless, since one aspect of Craig's theodicy appeals to inclusivism and since Craig holds that a particular passage of Scripture teaches inclusivism, I will in this section go a bit further and at least offer a brief response to this specific claim of

Craig so as to support my position that inclusivism is not taught in any clear way in Scripture and that it is better if a theodicy does not need to rely on the truth of inclusivism.

Craig holds that Scripture teaches inclusivism in Romans 2:7. He contends:

> [According] to the Bible, God doesn't judge people who have never heard of Christ on the basis of whether they've placed their faith in Christ. Rather God judges them on the basis of the light of God's general revelation in nature and conscience that they do have. The offer of Romans 2:7—'To those who by patiently doing good seek for glory and honor and immortality, he will give eternal life'—is a bona fide offer of salvation. Someone who senses his need of forgiveness through his guilty conscience and flings himself upon the mercy of the God revealed in nature may find salvation. This is not to say that people can be saved apart from Christ. Rather it's to say that the benefits of Christ's atoning death can be applied to people without their conscious knowledge of Christ.[75]

So Craig interprets Romans 2:7 (without, so far as I can see, offering any detailed exegetical argument in support of his interpretation of this passage in any of his writings) to be teaching that any person—even one who has never heard of Christ—may be saved if one senses one's own moral guilt and seeks forgiveness from the God revealed in nature. This passage in Romans appears to be the only place in Scripture that Craig cites as teaching inclusivism.

In examining this biblical passage carefully within its context, however, it is not at all plausible that it supports the truth of inclusivism. Indeed, it appears to have nothing to do with God's offer of grace through any kind of faith—and certainly not an implicit faith that involves sensing in one's conscience one's need for forgiveness from the God revealed in nature. To the contrary, in the second chapter of Romans Paul seems to be talking about "the conditions that prevail within the sphere or system of *law*, or about how a person is judged for either justification or condemnation under the provisions of God's law."[76] Paul's discussion of these conditions builds up to his point that nobody is saved by persisting in obeying the law and that this reveals the need for all people to be saved through faith in Christ.

75. Craig, *On Guard*, 274.
76. Cottrell, *Romans*, 100–1.

Assessment of Existing Molinist Theodicies 147

To understand this, let us examine Paul's thought in the second chapter of Romans and see how his thought flows into the third chapter of Romans. In 2:1–5, Paul stresses that all people—which, of course, includes both Jews and Gentiles—fall under God's judgment for failing to live a perfectly righteous life. In 2:6–11 (the key passage that Craig cites), Paul's point is that Jews and Gentiles are both going to be judged by God impartially. There will be no favoritism shown to the Jews, and God will apply the same standard of the law to all people when judging them. Paul seems to be describing the way God's judgment of people is carried out under the law and apart from God's grace. Under the law, the same conditions apply to all people: those who perfectly keep the law and persevere in doing only what is good will receive eternal life, and those who fail to persist in keeping the law perfectly will be punished by God. (Since nobody can perfectly keep the law, we will see that Paul is setting up his audience for the key point that God's grace is necessary because—when judged by the standards of the law—we all fall short.) In 2:12–16, Paul stresses that, under God's judgment of humanity according to the law, everyone has knowledge of the law (i.e., we all at least have the law that is written on our hearts), but it is obeying the law that matters and not merely possessing it. In 2:17–29, Paul warns the Jews not to put confidence in having the law or in their circumcision because they all break the law in one way or another and because, when they are judged by the law, circumcision will count for nothing. In 3:1–20 Paul emphasizes that God is right in judging all people by the law and that all people are under sin and break the law. Nobody will be saved by persevering in doing good works. Then Paul follows up this distressing news with the incredible news that "now apart from the Law the righteousness of God has been manifested" (3:21) and is found in God's grace through Christ.[77]

Douglas Moo is correct that in 2:6–11 Paul "simply sets forth the criterion of salvation apart from gospel without implying that anyone meets that criterion." Paul is not yet discussing salvation under God's grace by faith; rather he is explaining "the standard by which God judges all human beings [under the law]. That standard is works (v. 6)." According to the law (and apart from God's grace in Christ), Paul says in 2:6 that God will ἀποδώσει (render what is due) to all people. If one does evil, one is punished; if one persists in doing good, then one will be granted eternal life. It is crucial to see that "it is the criterion of judgment, not the

---

77. Cottrell, *Romans*, 101–2. He has a helpful discussion of Paul's flow of thought in this section of Romans.

people who meet that criterion, that Paul has in mind. We must remember that Paul is building a case."[78] That case builds up to the declaration that *nobody* meets the requirements of the law that he is describing and *nobody accesses salvation by persisting in doing good* (Rom 3:20, 23).

So, with the context of Paul's flow of thought in mind, we ought not think that Romans 2:7 is intended to be, as Craig describes it, "a bona fide offer of salvation" to "someone who senses his need of forgiveness through his guilty conscience and flings himself upon the mercy of the God revealed in nature."[79] God's grace and forgiveness are not in view until Paul gets to 3:21–31. The passage in 2:6–11 is instead an explanation of the way God judges all of humanity according to the criterion of the law. Ultimately, as I have noted in the first chapter, responding in faith to the gospel is central in Paul's letter to the Romans. The "word of faith" (Rom 10:8) Paul has been preaching is that "if you confess with your mouth Jesus as Lord, and believe in your heart that God raised Him from the dead, you will be saved; for with the heart a person believes, resulting in righteousness, and with the mouth he confesses, resulting in salvation" (Rom 10:9–10). It seems that one needs to hear the gospel in order to believe and confess and accept God's salvation (Rom 10:14–15). For "faith comes from hearing, and hearing by the word of Christ" (Rom 10:17).

The Theodicy of Kirk MacGregor

Recently Kirk MacGregor has proposed a modification to Craig's theodicy that, like Craig's view, fits within the third category of Molinist theodicies (i.e., it involves God creating an optimal soteriological balance in a world of people who freely choose either to be saved or lost). MacGregor's aim is to merge Molina's soteriological view with Craig's theodicy. Recall that at the beginning of this chapter we explored Molina's soteriological position and saw that Molina's interpretation of Romans 9 led him to hold that God unconditionally elects individuals to salvation. Molina affirmed that God is sovereign over which individuals are saved and lost and that no quality of any individual ensures that God will save or damn that individual. Molina thought that rejecting this doctrine would detract from God's sovereignty. Molina insisted that God offers sufficient prevenient grace so that all people are able to choose to accept or reject it and that

---

78. Moo, *Romans*, 81.
79. Craig, *On Guard*, 274.

Assessment of Existing Molinist Theodicies 149

God uses middle knowledge to uphold human libertarian freedom while achieving unconditional election of individuals. Molina speculated that every human that God might create would freely choose to be saved in some world that God could actualize and would also freely choose to be lost in some world that God could actualize. Moreover, every human that God might create would also not exist in some world of free creatures that God could actualize. Thus, God did not have to save any particular person who is saved in the actual world or damn any particular person who is lost in the actual world. The existence and the eternal destiny of every person is entirely up to God. This would mean that everyone who is saved is contingently saved, and (contra Craig's proposal that nobody is contingently lost) everyone who is lost is contingently lost. For this reason (and also because Molina held that Jesus is literally expressing middle knowledge about the wicked cities in Matt 11:20–24), MacGregor correctly points out that "Molina would have regarded as false and unbiblical the doctrine of transworld damnation, formulated by leading contemporary Molinist William Lane Craig."[80]

Even though Molina rejected the idea that anybody is TD, MacGregor points out that Molina would agree with the other two components of Craig's theodicy. Just like Craig, Molina held to inclusivism on the basis of Romans 2:7.[81] Moreover, while Molina never explicitly says this, MacGregor suspects that Molina would agree with Craig that God would likely use God's middle knowledge to optimize the balance of saved and lost.[82] So MacGregor sets about the task of showing how Molina's affirmation of unconditional election (and rejection of the idea that anyone is TD) can fit with the other two components of Craig's theodicy (inclusivism and God optimizing the soteriological balance). MacGregor wants to offer a new approach to the problem of the unevangelized that upholds unconditional election and does not need to rely upon anyone being TD.

Now it should be noted from the outset that MacGregor's proposed theodicy—even if it were successful—would only address the problem of the unevangelized (PU) and not the problem of the contingently lost

---

80. MacGregor, "Harmonizing Molina's Rejection," 347.

81. MacGregor, "Harmonizing Molina's Rejection," 347. See also MacGregor, *Luis de Molina*, 183. MacGregor points out that Molina affirms this in his untranslated *De Iustitia et Iure* 5.46.13.

82. MacGregor, "Harmonizing Molina's Rejection," 347. See also MacGregor, *Luis de Molina*, 145–46.

(PCL). The PU is merely one aspect of the PCL. The PU is the objection that some people who remain unevangelized throughout their lives and are lost would have been saved in a feasible world in which they had heard the gospel. The PCL recognizes that there are other sorts of contingently lost people who (even though they may have heard the gospel at least once in their lives) were in life circumstances that made it difficult to accept the gospel and who would have been saved if only their circumstances were better—perhaps even just marginally better. We have seen that Craig's theodicy, if it were successful, would resolve the PCL because nobody would be contingently lost. MacGregor—whether or not he realizes that Craig's theodicy addresses the PCL and not merely the PU—only aims to resolve the PU with his theodicy.

In order to accomplish the merging of Craig's theodicy (or at least Craig's components of inclusivism and divine optimization of the soteriological balance) with Molina's rejection of TD and affirmation that all people would have a predestinary status in another feasible world that is the opposite of the one that they actually have, MacGregor proposes the following. At the logical moment in which God decides which of the infinite feasible worlds to actualize, God eliminates from consideration all feasible worlds in which there is not an optimal soteriological balance. Let us call the remaining feasible worlds, which MacGregor suggests might possibly still be infinite in number, the range of optimal worlds (ROOW). God will only consider actualizing a world that is within ROOW. MacGregor then proposes the possibility that, for every person P within ROOW, there may be "at least one world [in ROOW] where P is freely saved, at least one world [in ROOW] where P is freely lost, and at least one world [in ROOW] where P does not exist."[83] MacGregor recognizes that it is likely the case that within ROOW there are worlds in which some unevangelized people who are lost would be evangelized and saved in some other feasible world.[84] In order to eliminate such worlds and resolve the PU without anyone being TD and without undermining unconditional election, MacGregor proposes that God reduces ROOW

---

83. MacGregor, "Harmonizing Molina's Rejection," 348–49. I have added "in ROOW" since MacGregor makes clear that this is what he is thinking. He makes this clear on p. 349 where he notes that "it certainly seems logically possible that there is an infinite spectrum of salvifically optimal worlds and that the spectrum contains at least the three relevant worlds." His reference here to "the spectrum" is what I am calling ROOW.

84. MacGregor, "Harmonizing Molina's Rejection," 349.

Assessment of Existing Molinist Theodicies 151

to an even more narrow range of optimal worlds (NROOW). As was the case with the ROOW, in order to uphold unconditional election and ensure that God is sovereign over the choice of whether any P is saved, lost, or nonexistent, MacGregor proposes that there are an infinite number of worlds in NROOW[85] and that every P who exists in NROOW must: exist in at least one world in NROOW in which P is freely saved; exist in at least one world in NROOW in which P is freely lost; and not exist in at least one world in NROOW. Then, in order to resolve the PU, MacGregor suggests that every P in NROOW must be one of only two types. The first type (Type I) of P is "saved in at least one [feasible] world where P receives only general revelation at the moment of salvation (although P could receive special revelation at some point thereafter) and is lost in every [feasible] world where P receives special revelation without first appropriating salvation through general revelation."[86] So God could save a P of Type I via P's free response to general revelation in at least one feasible world, but God could not bring it about that such a P is saved in any feasible world via a free response to the gospel. A P of Type I will only accept the gospel if he or she was already saved via a free response to general revelation. No P of Type I is TD because there is at least one feasible world in which such a P is saved (a feasible world in which P responds appropriately to general revelation), but no P of Type I who remains unevangelized throughout life and is lost would have responded to the gospel if he or she had heard it. The second type (Type II) of P is never "lost when receiving only general revelation" in any world in NROOW (i.e., such a person will always be saved in any world in NROOW in which he or she remains unevangelized throughout life) *and also* is "saved in at least one [feasible] world where P receives special revelation without first appropriating salvation through general revelation and is lost in at least one [feasible] world where P receives special revelation without first appropriating salvation through general revelation."[87] So God could save a P of Type II in some feasible world via a free response to the gospel, but in at least one other feasible world this person would freely reject the gospel (and general revelation) and be lost; however, in order to resolve the PU

---

85. MacGregor, "Harmonizing Molina's Rejection," 348. See footnote 3. MacGregor holds the controversial position that an actually infinite number of things is possible. He then points out that a subset of an infinite set of things can still be infinite (e.g., the set of positive integers is infinite just as the set of all integers is infinite).

86. MacGregor, "Harmonizing Molina's Rejection," 349.

87. MacGregor, "Harmonizing Molina's Rejection," 349.

a P of Type II must never be lost in any world in NROOW in which he or she remains unevangelized throughout life—for that would mean that God could actualize a world in which this unevangelized person would be lost due to historical and geographical circumstances (since a P of Type II would respond to special revelation in some feasible world). The purpose of creating Type II individuals is so that God ensures that nobody who would respond to the gospel and be saved can take credit for their salvation because "God could have just as easily created them in a different [feasible] world where they heard the gospel and yet freely chose to reject it."[88]

MacGregor thinks his proposal is at least possibly true, and he emphasizes the theological and theodical value that it offers. The world would be as soteriologically optimal as any feasible world of free creatures. Humans would have libertarian freedom—even with regard to the most crucial choice of accepting or rejecting the free gift of salvation that is offered in Christ. He thinks that unconditional election would be true in the sense that everyone in NROOW has the possibility of being saved or lost or nonexistent—it all depends upon which world in NROOW that God sovereignly chooses to actualize (and all worlds in NROOW are soteriologically comparable). In addition, every person would have an opportunity to be saved in virtue of the truth of inclusivism. The PU would also be resolved because anyone who is unevangelized and lost in the actual world would have rejected special revelation in any feasible world in which he or she receives it; moreover, nobody who is freely saved via accepting the gospel is saved merely because God allowed that person to hear the gospel (since any such person would also be freely lost in at least one world in which he or she is evangelized). Finally, all of this is accomplished without anyone being TD—an attractive feature given the theological difficulties with TD that I have already identified.

Difficulties with MacGregor's Theodicy

Although MacGregor's theodicy is clever and has a number of attractive features, it nevertheless suffers from both theological and philosophical problems. Let us begin with the theological challenges that it faces. One key difficulty is his heavy reliance upon the truth of inclusivism. It is crucial to his theodicy that one can be saved—even in the New Testament

---

88. MacGregor, "Harmonizing Molina's Rejection," 350.

era—by responding to general revelation apart from special revelation, and he appeals in his argument (in agreement with both Craig and Molina) to Romans 2:7 to justify this position biblically. In light of the argument that I have already given for rejecting this interpretation of Romans 2:7 and the biblical case that I have offered in favor of exclusivism, this feature of MacGregor's theodicy alone is problematic. Anyone who regards inclusivism as unbiblical will immediately find his proposal unhelpful as a Christian theodicy. Even if one does not consider inclusivism to be decisively unbiblical, it is preferable if one can put forth a theodicy that does not depend upon such a controversial doctrine.

Even if inclusivism were true, a second theological problem is that it seems to be contrary to Scripture that anyone would be Type I or Type II. A person who is Type I would freely reject all special revelation—including, of course, the gospel itself—and be lost in every feasible world in which he or she receives special revelation without first being saved via a response to general revelation. *Nevertheless*, someone who is Type I would freely respond to general revelation and be saved apart from (or at least prior to) hearing the gospel in at least one feasible world. Scripture teaches that the gospel is the power of God for our salvation (Rom 1:16). Is it acceptable to think that a person who would always freely reject the gospel (along with general revelation) in any world in which the person hears the gospel and has not yet been saved via a response to general revelation would freely come to saving faith in some world via general revelation alone? Such a proposal seems to entail that the gospel and general revelation together are actually less effective in drawing some people to saving faith in Christ than general revelation alone. In view of a passage like Romans 1:16, it is hard to avoid the conclusion that this is an unacceptably low view of the power of God to utilize the gospel in drawing people to himself. Likewise, a person who is Type II will always be saved via a response to general revelation in any feasible world in which he or she never receives special revelation, yet such a person is lost in some world in which he or she receives special revelation. This again implies that the Holy Spirit is less effective in drawing a person to Christ with the gospel than apart from the gospel. Adopting inclusivism and allowing that one can be saved apart from hearing the gospel is problematic enough, but it is even more troublesome to suggest that general revelation by itself may be more effective than the gospel in drawing people to saving faith.

Another theological point that should be made (though I do not consider this a problem because I do not hold that Scripture teaches unconditional election) is that it is dubious that genuine unconditional election is upheld by MacGregor's proposal. As soon as MacGregor allows that humans have libertarian freedom with regard to accepting or rejecting the gospel, the possibility of unconditional election seems to be undermined. Imagine for example, that a man named Bob is Type I and exists in the actual world and is saved. Had Bob not been Type I or Type II, then on MacGregor's theodicy God would not have actualized Bob and would not have actualized this world that includes Bob. Bob would have no chance at existing or being saved. The CCFs that are true about Bob are a necessary condition for Bob existing (and one must exist in order to be saved). Even if we grant that God could have actualized a feasible world (with just as good of a soteriological balance as the actual world) in which Bob was lost and one in which Bob does not exist, the fact that Bob exists and is saved in the actual world does partially have to do with some characteristic about himself. Bob is saved both because of God's decision to create a world in which Bob exists and freely chooses to be saved and also because of the sort of free choices that Bob would make in various worlds. The latter depends upon Bob, so he is not unconditionally elected to salvation.

In terms of philosophical difficulties, there is one problem that is especially significant:[89] the fact that MacGregor's theodicy (if true) would at most only handle the PU and not the PCL. Craig's theodicy aims to

---

89. A philosophical challenge to MacGregor's theodicy that I will not address in detail and will merely note here is that MacGregor assumes the controversial position that there can be an actually infinite number of worlds that God knows. MacGregor discusses this in MacGregor, "Harmonizing Molina's Rejection," 348. See especially footnote 3 on this page where MacGregor says that "actually infinite sets of worlds can exist in the mind of an omniscient being and that it is possible for such a being to know an actually infinite number of things." It seems to me, however, that this controversial assumption that an actually infinite number of things is possible (even in the mind of God) may not be crucial to MacGregor's argument. Perhaps he could make the same case even if the number of feasible worlds that God knows is an extremely large finite number and is not infinite. Then again, perhaps not. Perhaps if there are a finite number of feasible worlds to begin with and then this group of feasible worlds is reduced to ROOW and then further reduced to those in NROOW, then the number of worlds in NROOW may be too small to accomplish what MacGregor wants to accomplish in NROOW. Ultimately, however, since we do not know the number of worlds in NROOW, it may be that there is still an extremely large finite number of worlds in NROOW—perhaps enough that what MacGregor proposes is at least possible (which is all that his argument requires).

resolve the PCL, but MacGregor's theodicy still leaves room for troubling aspects of the PCL. The PU is just one part of the broader PCL, as some contingently lost people may be evangelized and yet face horrible circumstances for accepting the gospel. MacGregor's theodicy (even if one brushes aside its theological difficulties) leaves open the unsavory possibility that someone could be lost in the actual world who would have been saved in some other soteriologically optimal world if only God would have put that person into just slightly different circumstances. Imagine the case of an inner-city teen who has an incredibly rough life and is raised by abusive parents who are hostile to religion. This teen is presented with the gospel once in her life, but she does not accept it. She is then killed at the age of sixteen in an act of random gang violence. Imagine further that, had God allowed this teen to live just one more day and had God placed the teen into a circumstance the day after she actually died in which someone witnesses to her in a way that helps her see the gospel in a new way (assume that this circumstance was feasible for God to bring about in a world that is still soteriologically optimal), then the teen would have freely accepted the gospel and been saved.[90] There is nothing in MacGregor's theodicy that prevents such a possibility. Indeed, the teen described above would fit into MacGregor's Type II because she heard the gospel and was lost in the actual world but would have responded to the gospel and been saved in another feasible (and, in this case, soteriologically optimal) world. MacGregor's proposal allows that a person could slip through the soteriological cracks; that is, a (barely) evangelized person could be lost who would have easily responded to the gospel without undue pressure or coercion in another feasible world. It would seem that God would want to eliminate such cases—especially if God could do so without harming the soteriological balance. It is hard to see how it would be any less problematic for an omnibenevolent God to allow cases such as the one above than to allow cases in which a person is unevangelized and lost but would have been saved in another feasible world in which he or she hears the gospel. MacGregor's theodicy rules

90. I credit David Baggett with raising this sort of scenario to me and stressing the importance of my own theodicy handling such troubling cases. Jerry Walls expresses his own concern about the difficult nature of similar sorts of cases in Walls, *Hell*, 86. We will see that my theodicy does handle such cases even though it allows that some people are contingently lost (in ways that do not call God's omnibenevolence into question). Craig's theodicy (setting aside its theological difficulties) would also handle such cases because it ensures that nobody at all is contingently lost. MacGregor's theodicy, however, does not handle such cases.

out the latter but not the former. What if, however, there is a feasible world that is as soteriologically optimal as any other, but nobody in that world slips through the cracks like the (barely) evangelized inner city teen? Would it not be attractive to offer a theodicy in which nobody narrowly misses out on salvation due to such unfortunate circumstances? Is it not the case that allowing a person to be contingently lost in this sort of way is as much of a challenge to the omnibenevolence of God as allowing an unevangelized person to be lost who would have been saved if only she had heard the gospel? Surely it would be an advantage to offer a theodicy that shows how it is possible that nobody is contingently lost in these troubling ways (although a good theodicy could still allow that some may be contingently lost in ways that do not count against God's omnibenevolence). Indeed, as we will see in the next chapter, that is exactly what I aim to do.

4

A New Molinist Theodicy Against the Problem of the Contingently Lost

WE HAVE NOW EXAMINED and critiqued Craig's Molinist theodicy against the PCL as well as several other Molinist proposals that attempt to undermine the PCL (or at least the PU). All of these proposals have insights as well as various drawbacks. It is now time to propose my own theodicy for dealing with the PCL. It is important at this juncture to emphasize once again that the PCL is a theological and philosophical challenge for which the Bible does not provide a specific solution. Consequently, the theodicy offered here is humbly put forth merely as one that I consider to be philosophically plausible and biblically faithful. While I find it to be consistent with Scripture, it certainly is not an explicit teaching of Scripture.

Recall once again the nature of the PCL as laid out in the first chapter. The PCL seeks to demonstrate that P_1 and P_2 are inconsistent by adding P_8 and P_9. These premises are as follows:

> P_1. God possesses the attributes of omniscience, omnipotence, and omnibenevolence.
>
> P_2. Some persons do not accept the forgiveness that is available via receiving Christ and are thus damned.
>
> P_8. God will necessarily not allow persons to exist who are lost in their actual circumstances but who would have been saved if placed into different circumstances.

P_9. Some persons who freely reject the grace that God offers them in their actual circumstances and are lost would have freely accepted God's grace and been saved in different circumstances.[1]

We examined in the first chapter how the defender of the PCL contends that the truth of P_8 and P_9 brings out an implicit contradiction between P_1 and P_2 such that God's attributes are incompatible with the purported reality that some of the lost are contingently lost.[2] So, refuting the PCL requires one to show that P_8 or P_9 (or both) should be rejected. One must show that at least one of these two premises is neither necessarily true nor required by Christian doctrine.

Although Craig's theodicy aims to show that P_9 is not necessarily true, I have made the case that this premise ought to be accepted on the basis of certain biblical teachings. The theodicy that I will flesh out and defend in this chapter will allow that some people are contingently lost (thus accepting the truth of P_9). I will instead attack P_8 by contending that there are (for all we know) only two types of contingently lost persons that God permits and that both of these are types that God would plausibly allow because neither type conflicts with God's omnibenevolence or with any other divine attribute.

My theodicy may be summarized as follows. God has sovereignly arranged the world in such a way that nobody is lost due to lack of information (e.g., not hearing the gospel) or due to the sin and corrupting influences of those around them (i.e., being in the wrong circumstances to accept the gospel when they hear it). It is possible that every lost person is lost as a consequence of his or her *own sin* and not epistemological or circumstantial limitations, and my theodicy aims to show how this may be the case even if one must hear the gospel and respond to it in this life to be saved (i.e., even if Christian exclusivism is true). As far as we know from Scripture (especially considering the statements of Jesus concerning

---

1. Refer to Table 1.1 at the end of chapter 1 for a summary of all of the premises that were introduced in the first chapter when I examined various key arguments that are part of the soteriological problem of evil.

2. As noted in the first chapter, the PCL does not call into question God's justice, as justice does not demand that God save anybody. God's decision to forgive any of us through Christ's sacrifice is more than anyone deserves and more than justice demands. The focus of the PCL is instead on God's omnibenevolence (as well as God's omnipotence and omniscience). The idea is that God would not be maximally loving if he allowed people to be lost when he was capable of putting them into circumstances in which they would be saved. We saw in the first chapter that the PCL alleges that P_8 follows from P_1, and P_9 is plausibly unavoidable given P_2.

the wicked cities in Matthew 11 and the many biblical warnings throughout Scripture against apostasy), it seems that we only need to make room for two types of contingently lost people. I propose that God has used his middle knowledge to arrange the world so that there are only the following two types of contingently lost people. The first type is one who would not accept the gospel under any *sufficiently non-pressured* circumstances but would accept it if given revelation that would be unacceptably overt in terms of the sort of impact that it would have on that person. In order for such a person to repent and accept God's grace, he or she would *have to be given* revelation that is so overt that it places excessive pressure on him or her to turn away from sin and towards God. I propose that the Sodomites who would have repented if they had seen Jesus' miracles fall under this first type. The second type of contingently lost person is anyone who willfully rejects God's grace after previously accepting it (i.e., one who apostatizes). My suggestion is that these are the only two types of contingently lost persons, and I will argue that in neither of these cases should God's omnibenevolence or other divine attributes be called into question.[3] I will also suggest that God is so good that he uses his middle knowledge to optimize the balance of saved versus lost—but this soteriological balance is optimized only within the bounds of (at least) two key parameters that I will contend are important to God. Although upholding these parameters—which include God's (relative) hiddenness and God's allowing Satan to tempt us—may result in a less optimal balance of saved versus lost over the course of human history than might otherwise

---

3. Although Scripture does not seem to require me to make room for a third type of contingently lost person and a God who possesses middle knowledge could certainly ensure that the above two types of contingently lost persons are the only two types of contingently lost persons, it is worth mentioning that there is a third sort of contingently lost person that we could probably allow without it being any threat to God's attributes. This third type of contingently lost person is one who is thoroughly evangelized and has all sorts of opportunities to accept the gospel in the actual world but continually rejects it, yet this person would have accepted the gospel in some feasible world. It is hard to see how it would be a strike against God's goodness or love to allow such a person to be lost in the actual world. The most important thing in a theodicy against the PCL is to show how it may be the case that no lost person who is put into disadvantageous circumstances would have freely chosen to be saved if only he or she were given better (but non-coercive) circumstances. The key thing is to ensure that nobody "slips through the soteriological cracks" like the inner-city teen mentioned earlier or like an unevangelized person who would have immediately accepted the gospel if only a missionary had delivered the gospel to her village. So, although nothing that I see in Scripture requires one to do so, one could probably add to my theodicy that God may also allow this third type of contingently lost person.

be achieved if God did not uphold these parameters, I will argue that the soteriological balance may well be as optimal as it can be given the two parameters and that these two parameters are consistent with God's perfect goodness and love. They are consistent with God's goodness and love because they ensure an environment that allows humans to make a morally significant choice to love God, and this is a great good.

A key feature of my theodicy is its utilization of a slightly modified version of Reformed epistemology to propose a process by which the Holy Spirit might break down a person's sinful resistance to accepting the gospel. This process, which also draws upon God's middle knowledge, is put forth as a plausible and biblically-consistent way of showing how God might go about ensuring that: all people who would accept the gospel without undue pressure will come to accept it; nobody is lost due to lack of information or the sin of others; and everyone has an opportunity to be saved even given the truth of exclusivism. Let us, therefore, begin by introducing Reformed epistemology and the two modifications to it that I will propose. After that, I will be in position to unpack my theodicy in even more detail and defend it.

A Modification to Reformed Epistemology

Alvin Plantinga's Reformed epistemology plays an important role in my theodicy. A slightly modified, or qualified, version of this epistemology will provide a structure for how my theodicy achieves key objectives while accounting for the role of sin, propositional evidence, God's providential direction of our lives, and God's design of our cognitive faculties in our coming to faith. Plantinga, along with Nicholas Wolterstorff, began formulating and defending Reformed epistemology in the early 1980s. Plantinga most fully explicates and defends his epistemology in his 2000 book *Warranted Christian Belief*. His aim is to show that both theistic belief and Christian belief are warranted and that this warrant does not depend upon propositional evidence. Warrant is what sets genuine knowledge apart from mere true belief. Plantinga holds that a belief has warrant if four key criteria are met. First, one's cognitive faculties must be working properly in the way that they are designed to work (i.e., one's faculties must not be experiencing any dysfunction in producing the belief in question). Second, when producing the belief in question one's cognitive faculties must be operating within the sort of environment in which they are designed to work properly. Third, one's cognitive faculties must be aimed at producing true beliefs (rather than being aimed at some other purpose, such as merely aiding in survival) as one arrives at this belief. Fourth and finally, the design plan for one's cognitive faculties must be such that the cognitive faculties are designed to produce true beliefs.[4]

Plantinga first lays out his model for warranted *theistic* belief before extending his model to address warranted Christian belief. In agreement with John Calvin, Thomas Aquinas, and Plantinga's interpretation of Romans 1:18–20, Plantinga holds that we all have a *sensus divinitatis* (i.e., a sense of God).[5] Plantinga understands the *sensus divinitatis* to be a cognitive faculty[6] by which we know in a properly basic way certain truths about God (including the existence of God) so long as this faculty is not damaged or blocked by sin. A properly basic belief is one that is foundational and that we rightly hold in a natural and immediate way rather than by inferring it on the basis of other beliefs. For example, we rightly

---

4. Plantinga, *Warranted Christian Belief*, 155–56.
5. Plantinga, *Warranted Christian Belief*, 170–71.
6. Plantinga, *Warranted Christian Belief*, 170–74. Plantinga says that the *sensus divinitatis* is "a disposition or set of dispositions to form theistic beliefs in various circumstances, in response to the sorts of conditions or stimuli that trigger the working of this sense of divinity" (p. 173). He then explores the sort of experiences of general revelation that may naturally trigger in us the formation of belief in God (pp. 173–74). William Lane Craig, although a proponent of Reformed epistemology, rejects the idea that humans have a cognitive faculty that recognizes the truth of theism *apart from the testimony of the Holy Spirit*. See Craig, "A Classical Apologist's Response," 285–87. Craig finds no biblical justification that theistic belief is grounded in "a natural instinct or inborn awareness of the human mind rather than in the witness of the Holy Spirit." He does, however, find "wide biblical support" for there being an inner witness of the Spirit (p. 285). Plantinga does appeal to the testimony of the Holy Spirit when he extends his model to argue that Christian belief (and not just theistic belief) is properly basic, but Craig thinks Plantinga should bring the testimony of the Holy Spirit into the picture when it comes to theistic belief as well. For further discussion of this, see also Moreland and Craig, *Philosophical Foundations*, 153–54. Craig is correct that Scripture does not make it clear that God has given humans an innate cognitive faculty that recognizes the existence of God apart from the testimony of the Holy Spirit. Our cognitive faculties may be designed to work in conjunction with the testimony of the Spirit to recognize in a properly basic way that God exists (i.e., we may not have a cognitive faculty that would recognize the truth of theism apart from the testimony of the Spirit). In any case, what is crucial to Reformed epistemology on this point is that God has designed our cognitive faculties and has placed us into an environment in which we can come to know in a properly basic way that God exists (i.e., we can have an immediate recognition of God in response to our environment that need not be inferred) so long as sin does not prevent our cognitive faculties from recognizing this truth.

believe that the external world exists even though we cannot know this via inference; unless there is a defeater for thinking the external world exists, we seem to be justified in believing this in a natural and immediate way. It is a basic belief that is not inferred, and it seems proper to hold it. Theistic belief, Plantinga contends, is properly basic with respect to both justification (i.e., one does not fail in any epistemic responsibilities in holding this belief) and warrant (i.e., we can know it). This is because if God exists, then God plausibly designed our cognitive faculties to work properly and to arrive at true beliefs concerning the existence of God in the environment in which God has placed us. If this is the case, then we will naturally come to know that God exists in a properly basic way when our cognitive faculties are working properly and are not impeded by sin. Sin, Plantinga contends, is the only reason why anyone does not naturally believe in God.[7] So if God exists, then the four criteria for knowledge are met and theistic belief seems warranted. Moreover, Plantinga's model agrees with the biblical teaching that sin can blind us to the things of God and that there is no excuse for atheism (e.g., Rom 1:18–20; Ps 14:1).

Plantinga thus argues that the ontological issue of whether or not God exists is the determining factor in whether or not theistic belief is warranted. Plantinga explains that if God does not exist, then there is no basis he can see for theistic belief having warrant. It certainly could not have warrant that rises to the level of knowledge, since knowledge requires true belief. Indeed, theistic belief would seem to have no warrant at all if theism is false because there would be no God who designed our cognitive faculties and our environment so that we will recognize God's actual existence. If atheism were true, it is hard to see how any of our cognitive faculties could be both aimed at truth and leading us toward belief in God.[8] But if theism is true, then there is good reason to think theistic belief is warranted. This is because it is most likely that God would design our cognitive faculties in such a way that we would be able form true beliefs about God.[9] So, the question of whether theistic belief is warranted "is not, after all, independent of the question whether theistic belief is true."[10] Plantinga has made a strong case that one would have to show that theism is false in order to show that theistic belief is irrational.

7. Plantinga, *Warranted Christian Belief*, 175–86.
8. Plantinga, *Warranted Christian Belief*, 186–88.
9. Plantinga, *Warranted Christian Belief*, 188–90.
10. Plantinga, *Warranted Christian Belief*, 190–91.

Next, and in a similar way, Plantinga extends his model to show that Christian belief—and not just theistic belief—is warranted if Christianity is true. By "Christian belief," he means the core beliefs that comprise the Christian gospel or that are accepted by all Christians (i.e., "mere Christianity"). Here he brings into the picture both Scripture (i.e., the gospel message, which may either be read or heard) and the prompting of the Holy Spirit. Through these, God communicates to us the truth of the gospel. If Christianity is true, then belief in the gospel has warrant because the belief is formed by properly working cognitive faculties that are designed by God to detect truth and that are aimed at detecting truth; moreover, God ensures that our cognitive faculties are put in the right environment to recognize the truth of the gospel (an environment that includes the beauty of the gospel message and the witness of the Holy Spirit). In addition, if Christianity is true then belief in the truth of the gospel can be held strongly enough to be genuine knowledge.[11]

So, according to Plantinga's model, one comes to know that the gospel is true by hearing it and then becoming convicted that it is true via the testimony of the Holy Spirit. This belief in the gospel, Plantinga stresses, is properly basic and not inferred on the basis of arguments and evidence.[12] As with theistic belief, sin may block us from coming to believe the Christian gospel. Sin corrupts both our cognitive faculties and our will, damaging them so that one can fail to recognize the Holy Spirit's self-authenticating witness that the gospel is true.[13] Pride, envy, disobedience, distrust of God, and pursuit of our own selfish ambition over the good things of God are all factors.[14] Plantinga stresses that "were it not for sin and its effects, God's presence and glory would be as obvious and uncontroversial to us all as the presence of other minds, physical objects, and the past."[15] Plantinga allows that both our own sinful choices and the sin of those in our environment that are beyond our control (e.g., being indoctrinated with anti-Christian ideas by one's parents or growing up in

---

11. Plantinga, *Warranted Christian Belief*, 205–6.
12. Plantinga, *Warranted Christian Belief*, 250–52.
13. Plantinga is correct to recognize the importance of the will. As William Wainwright points out, the fact that intelligent people disagree on the force of the same evidence for the truth of Christianity lends strong support to the important role that our passions and desires seem to play in accepting the Christian faith. Sin can certainly corrupt both the will and the mind. See Wainwright, *Reason and the Heart*, 147.
14. Plantinga, *Warranted Christian Belief*, 206–13.
15. Plantinga, *Warranted Christian Belief*, 214.

a culture of self-indulgence and immorality) can corrupt our minds and wills.[16] So unless we are impeded by sin, upon hearing the great truths of the gospel, "the Holy Spirit teaches us, causes us to believe that that teaching is both true and comes from God."[17] Through Scripture and the prompting of the Holy Spirit, God communicates to us the good news of what Jesus has done to fix our sin problem and restore us. If Christianity is true, then Christian belief has warrant.[18]

Plantinga defends his Reformed epistemology against some common objections. In response to the objection that any crazy belief (e.g., belief in the Great Pumpkin or the Flying Spaghetti Monster) would have to be considered properly basic with respect to warrant if Christian belief is considered properly basic with respect to warrant, Plantinga points out that it is obvious that not just any belief qualifies as properly basic. Just because certain beliefs are properly basic (and some—such as the existence of the external world—certainly do seem to be), it does not follow that any belief whatsoever may be regarded as properly basic.[19] Plantinga then responds to the further objection that epistemologists within a community that hold that some bizarre belief is properly basic with respect to warrant (e.g., epistemologists of the voodoo community who regard their beliefs in voodoo to be properly basic with respect to warrant) would have just as much basis for claiming this as do Christian epistemologists who make this claim about Christian belief. Plantinga's rejoinder first of all stresses that warrant only occurs if the belief in question is true. If the bizarre belief in question (whether it is voodoo or something else)

---

16. Plantinga, *Warranted Christian Belief*, 213–17.

17. Plantinga, *Warranted Christian Belief*, 260.

18. Plantinga also goes on to argue that both the agnostic and the evolutionary naturalist have no warrant for knowledge at all. The agnostic's belief that she cannot know the origins of her cognitive faculties forces her to conclude that there is no reason to think that it is probable that her cognitive faculties reliably produce true beliefs. This means the agnostic has a defeater for her belief in the reliability of her cognitive faculties and must be skeptical of all of the beliefs that she holds. The evolutionary naturalist also has a defeater for the reliability of her cognitive faculties. If evolutionary naturalism is true, then our cognitive faculties are aimed at survival and not necessarily truth. There is no reason to have confidence that any of the beliefs produced by our cognitive faculties are true. So Plantinga concludes that while there is warrant for Christian belief, the agnostic or evolutionary naturalist who understands the undercutting arguments Plantinga has given will not have warrant that is sufficient for knowledge. She will have a defeater for all of her beliefs. See Plantinga, *Warranted Christian Belief*, 218–40.

19. Plantinga, *Warranted Christian Belief*, 344–45.

is false, then belief in it would not be warranted. The same is true for Christian belief. If Christianity is false, then Christian belief is not warranted.[20] Secondly, not just any belief system—even if true—would be warranted. For example, Plantinga argues that belief in philosophical naturalism—even if philosophical naturalism is true—would not be warranted because Plantinga thinks the truth of philosophical naturalism would entail that our cognitive faculties are not reliable.[21]

Plantinga's model for warranted Christian belief has much to commend it. It is a brilliant philosophical defense of the fact that warranted Christian belief follows if Christianity is true—regardless of whether the Christian believer can provide arguments and evidence for her belief. He incorporates into his model the biblical teaching that the Holy Spirit is responsible for convicting the world concerning sin, righteousness, and judgment (John 16:7–11) and that none of us choose to seek God on our own (Rom 3:10–11). God must draw us to himself (John 6:44). Plantinga is surely correct that one's knowledge that Christianity is true does not depend upon one's ability to gather evidence and evaluate its plausibility.[22] God has designed us so that in our environment—when our cognitive faculties are working properly and are not impeded by sin—we are able to know that the gospel is true when presented with the Holy Spirit's self-authenticating testimony that it is true. Since Jesus died for all people (John 3:16; 1 Tim 4:10; 1 John 2:2), Plantinga's view is attractive in that it shows how one need not have the ability and resources to reason one's way to faith. If gathering and weighing out propositional evidence were absolutely essential for anyone to be warranted in accepting the gospel, then a rather small percentage of people in the history of Christianity would be warranted in accepting the gospel. If God did not design us so that we could know that God exists in a properly basic way, then far fewer people in the world would be in a position to come to faith in Christ.

Although Plantinga's model is insightful, I will make two slight modifications to it. The first modification is not really a disagreement with Plantinga's model; rather, it is agreeing with a point that he makes but going beyond it. Plantinga is thoroughly biblical in highlighting the role of sin in blocking one's receptivity to the gospel, and he is correct that both one's own sin and the sin of those in one's environment may

---

20. Plantinga, *Warranted Christian Belief*, 347–49.
21. Plantinga, *Warranted Christian Belief*, 350–51.
22. Plantinga, *Warranted Christian Belief*, 271–80.

impede one from responding to the gospel.[23] Plantinga, however, does not expound upon this point to address whether it is always one's own sin and not the sin of others that is *decisive* in one's failure to accept the gospel. Is it possible that the moral or intellectual or spiritual influences resulting from the sin of others could ever be the decisive factor in one failing to accept the gospel? I propose for theological reasons that God ensures that it is *only one's own sin* and not the influence of the sin of others that is *ultimately* and *decisively* responsible for one never responding to the gospel. The sin of others may temporarily impede one's receptivity to the divine invitation and make it more difficult to accept, but in what sense could Jesus have died for all people (1 Tim 4:10; 1 John 2:1–2; 2 Pet 2:1–2) if some are fully prevented by their environment from accepting God's grace? How could God genuinely want all people to be saved (2 Pet 3:9; 1 Tim 2:4) if God allows some to be placed into circumstances in which the sin of others is the decisive factor in their being lost rather than their own sin? Plantinga's model would do well to put the ultimate onus for rejecting the gospel on each individual; however, given his Reformed leanings, it may be that he does not consider it theologically important to do so.

The second modification to Plantinga's model is to emphasize that arguments, evidences, and certain life experiences might in many cases be necessary for removing the barriers that result from sin. This does not deny that anyone who comes to accept the gospel does so on the basis of the self-authenticating witness of the Holy Spirit, and it does not deny that belief in the gospel is properly basic. Plantinga is insightful on these points. However, room should be left for evidences and experiences to be among the means by which the Holy Spirit removes the obstacles caused by sin so that the gospel and the Spirit's testimony can be seen for what they are and the gospel can be believed in a properly basic way. Reformed epistemology may be accepted by both Calvinists and Arminians. A Calvinist will see the testimony of the Holy Spirit as irresistible for the elect such that one lacks libertarian freedom with respect to choosing whether or not to accept the Holy Spirit's testimony, whereas the Arminian will allow that one has the ability to resist the Holy Spirit and must choose whether to follow the Spirit's promptings. Plantinga says his model "need take no stand" on the question of whether, for a particular unbeliever, the Holy Spirit might be unable to cause that unbeliever to accept the

---

23. Plantinga, *Warranted Christian Belief*, 213–17.

gospel. While he does say that "traditional Christian teaching" holds that the person must be willing to "accept the gift of faith" by in some way "acquiescing" to it,[24] Plantinga never clarifies what is involved in this acquiescing. He often seems to portray the Holy Spirit as directly causing the unbeliever's will and mind to be changed in a way that makes the unbeliever seem passive in the process. He speaks of faith being "given" to the unbeliever as the Holy Spirit does the work of overcoming the effects of sin.[25] The Holy Spirit "does something special" to the unbeliever so that she supernaturally is put in a state of heart and mind to believe the gospel.[26] So Plantinga is quite vague about *how* the Holy Spirit brings an unbeliever to a state in which the effects of sin on that person's will and mind are overcome and about the role that the unbeliever herself might play in this. Some have interpreted Plantinga as indicating that God "zaps" a person into passively accepting the gospel.[27]

In accordance with the acceptance of divine middle knowledge and the Arminian perspective that atonement is unlimited and grace is resistible, my theodicy will take the following position on the above issue that is left unanswered by Plantinga. The way in which the Holy Spirit works to overcome the barriers of sin in the will and mind of each person is unique to each person. Via middle knowledge, the Holy Spirit knows exactly what particular evidences, life experiences, and promptings of various kinds are needed to make healthy a particular unbeliever's sin-infected cognitive faculties and to soften that unbeliever's sinful will so that she can respond to the self-authenticating witness of the Holy Spirit and come to know in a properly basic way that the gospel is true. Because of one's own sin and that of others, no person would come to God without being drawn by the Spirit (Rom 3:10–11; John 6:44). But this process requires our active participation and willingness to respond to the Spirit's work in our lives. The Spirit will ensure that nobody is lost due to the sin of others or the circumstances into which one is placed. So long as there is some set of *sufficiently non-pressured* circumstances (we will soon discuss further why lack of excessive pressure to accept the gospel is important) in which the unbeliever would freely respond to the gospel, the Spirit will work in that person's life to prepare her will and mind and

24. Plantinga, *Warranted Christian Belief*, 257.
25. Plantinga, *Warranted Christian Belief*, 244.
26. Plantinga, *Warranted Christian Belief*, 252.
27. Pritchard, "Reforming Reformed Epistemology," 55.

ultimately bring her into circumstances in which she will hear and accept the gospel. Her accepting and knowing the truth of the gospel is not based on whatever propositional evidence (if any) or life experiences that the Spirit might have used to overcome the effects of sin; rather, she comes to know that the gospel is true in a properly basic way in response to the Spirit's testimony once sin no longer blinds her to this truth. Even if there are no sufficiently non-pressured circumstances in which a certain unbeliever would freely respond to the gospel, the Spirit—despite knowing it will not lead the person to salvation—plausibly offers various promptings and opportunities that are sufficient in strength such that *the sin of the unbeliever herself*—and not that of others—is the *decisive* reason why she rejects the promptings. Had her own sin not prevented her from responding to the promptings and opportunities, she would have eventually arrived in a state of will and mind to accept the gospel and God would have ensured that she heard the gospel and responded to it. If we are actively involved in this way as the Spirit works with us and through us to realign our passions and our beliefs so that the barriers of sin are overcome and we can recognize in a properly basic way the truth of the gospel just as we were designed to do, then everyone truly has an opportunity to be saved. All who are lost are responsible for resisting the Spirit's work in their lives, and divine middle knowledge allows that there is nothing that the Spirit could have done (short of, perhaps, providing excessive pressure) to bring anyone who never accepts the gospel and is lost into a state of will and mind in which the sin barriers that keep that person from accepting the gospel are removed.

A Theodicy Against the Problem of the Contingently Lost

The necessary foundations have now been laid to finish fleshing out my theodicy against the PCL. If both divine middle knowledge and the above slightly modified (or qualified) version of Reformed epistemology are true, then it is possible to envision a way in which God could—even if exclusivism is true—providentially arrange the world so that nobody is lost due to a lack of information (such as not hearing the gospel) or due to the sin and corrupting influences of those around them. It is also possible to show how God may have ensured that as many people as possible are saved and as few as possible are lost in a world in which humans must make a morally significant choice to love God rather than reject him and remain enslaved to sin. Moreover, it is plausible that P_8 is false because God can do all of this while ensuring that nobody is contingently lost other than in ways that do not undermine God's omnibenevolence.

The details of my proposal are as follows. God only considers actualizing worlds of free creatures that are as soteriologically optimal (i.e., have as good of a ratio of saved to lost) as any other feasible world of free creatures that (at least) meet the following two criteria: (1) the creatures in that world exist in a sufficiently challenging moral and spiritual environment (which minimally includes an adequate degree of divine hiddenness and an adequate degree of temptation from an evil creature like Satan) so that their decision to love God rather than remaining enslaved to sin is a significant one; and (2) no creature in that world is contingently lost other than those who would freely choose to apostatize and those who would require what is (for them) unduly overt revelation in order to be saved. The first criterion has to do with the environment that God desires. God wants a world in which as many people as possible come to be saved and enjoy him forever, but God wants to ensure that the environment in which humans accept or reject his love and grace is a morally rich and challenging one so that all who come to be saved truly do love him and want to be with him forever. God thus only considers actualizing feasible worlds in which the two parameters specified in this first criterion are upheld—even if there are feasible worlds that do not meet this first criterion that have a better soteriological balance than any feasible world that does meet the first criterion. The second criterion upholds God's love by ensuring that no person (like the inner-city teen described earlier) slips through the soteriological cracks; that is, the second criterion ensures that the only people who are contingently lost are contingently lost in a way that is compatible with God's omnibenevolence. With these two criteria in place (along with perhaps many other criteria that are important to God), God then sovereignly chooses to actualize one particular feasible world from among all of the feasible worlds that meet the criteria. The world that God picks will be soteriologically optimal within the bounds of the criteria (i.e., the world that God actualizes will have as favorable of a balance of saved to lost as any of the feasible worlds that meet the required criteria).

The above is a broad view of what I am proposing that God may have done. I will now draw upon Reformed epistemology and divine middle knowledge to suggest a process by which God might ensure that nobody is contingently lost other than the two types of contingently lost persons specified above and that nobody is lost due to a lack of information (such as not hearing the gospel) or due to the sin and corrupting influences of others. As I lay out this process, you will note that it focuses on Christian belief and how the Spirit works on a person to prepare that person to accept the gospel; however, it is also plausible that the same sort of process applies to people living in the Old Testament era as well, and I will go on to address this.

The process is as follows. First, God designs each human and the environment into which God places humans in such a way that one who hears the gospel will come to believe it and embrace the truth of the gospel in a properly basic way if one's will and mind are not impeded from doing so by sin. Second, God middle-knows under what (if any) freedom-permitting circumstances the sin barriers of each person whom God could create would be broken down such that the person would freely respond to the gospel in a properly basic way if he or she heard it. Third, God providentially ensures that each person in the world is placed into circumstances in which that person's sin barriers are broken down *unless*: the person is TD (if there are any such persons) *or* the only circumstances in which the person's sin barriers are broken down require what is (for that person) unduly overt revelation. For each person who is placed into circumstances in which the Spirit breaks down the sin barriers in his or her heart and mind, the Spirit does this by carrying out steps in that person's life that are tailored specifically to that person to accomplish this task—steps which may involve propositional evidence and particular life experiences. This divine arrangement of the world also involves the Spirit providing every person in the world (whether that person is ultimately saved or not) with promptings and opportunities such that these will only be resisted as a result of the person's *own* sin and not because of the sin of others. Fourth and finally, God ensures that each person in the world whose heart and will are prepared to accept the gospel are ultimately presented with the gospel, and all such persons then accept it in a properly basic way. Some of these people, however, may go on to apostatize. Such a process is at least consistent with biblical teaching concerning the Holy Spirit's role in convicting the world of sin and drawing them toward faith in Christ (e.g., John 15:26; 16:7–11).

If the above process is true, then every lost person is lost as a consequence of his or her own sin and not epistemological or circumstantial limitations. Notice that this process assumes that the Holy Spirit even offers promptings and opportunities to those whom God knows will never respond to them. These promptings will not always (in the case of every person) include hearing the gospel, but they will be strong enough and of just the right type that they will only be resisted as a result of the person's own sin and not because of the sin of others.

Consider, for example, an unbeliever who remains unevangelized throughout her life. Despite being unevangelized, *she herself* is responsible for never hearing the gospel. That is because she is responsible for responding to the promptings and opportunities that the Holy Spirit gives to her so that her sinful mind and heart are softened. Although God knows that she cannot be placed into any circumstances (short of, perhaps, excessive pressure) in which she would exercise her libertarian freedom to accept the gospel, the Spirit offers her just the right promptings and opportunities such that—had her own sin not prevented her from responding to the promptings and taking advantage of the opportunities—she would have been led by the Spirit down a path that would result in her sin barriers being overcome to the point that she would accept the gospel in a properly basic way and without excessive pressure if she were to hear it. It is also true that she (like any person in this world who never hears the gospel) is resistant to God to the point that there is no feasible world in which she can be placed into circumstances (short of, perhaps, excessive pressure) in which she is brought by the Spirit to a state of mind and heart in which she would freely accept the gospel and ultimately be saved. In this way, it can rightly be said that anyone who remains unevangelized throughout one's life had an opportunity to be saved. Such a person's own sin is decisive in preventing her from being led by the Spirit to a state of heart and mind in which she would respond to the gospel and be saved. The same is true of those who are evangelized but are ultimately lost. Those who never accept the gospel are only lost because there are no circumstances lacking excessive pressure in which they can be brought by God to a state of mind and will in which their sin barriers would be overcome and they would freely accept the gospel. Thus, there is also no feasible world in which a person who never accepts the gospel in the actual world and is lost in the actual world would be brought by the Spirit into a state of mind and heart in which that person would accept the gospel and be saved—except for, perhaps, feasible worlds in which the person accepts the gospel as a result of more pressure being placed upon that person to accept the gospel than God considers to be acceptable.

Now, with regard to those in the actual world who are unevangelized for a time but will eventually be brought to a state of will and mind in which they will accept the gospel once the Spirit prepares them and presents it to them, it is important to note that some such persons may have rejected theism and may have responded little (if at all) to general revelation and to the Spirit's various promptings prior to them hearing the gospel. The gospel is "the power of God for salvation to everyone who believes" (Rom 1:16), and there is more power in the gospel than in general revelation or in the Spirit's promptings sans the gospel. So one need not first become a theist or have a particular response to general revelation before God will bring her the gospel—though general revelation no doubt serves as one of the various ways that the Spirit prompts the unbeliever's heart. Instead, all that is needed is that *God knows it is possible* for him to bring the unbeliever to a state of her will and mind in which her sin barriers are overcome so that she will freely respond to the gospel in circumstances that are acceptable to God. Indeed, an unbeliever who has yet to hear the gospel and has given no response to general revelation or the promptings of the Spirit may need to be presented with the gospel (perhaps multiple times and in various ways) *as part of the process of breaking down her sin barriers* before she eventually is sensitive to the Spirit's testimony that the gospel is true and recognizes this truth in a properly basic way. So, while my theodicy holds to Christian exclusivism and contends that all people have an opportunity to be saved, it does not simply hold that God will bring the gospel to those unevangelized persons who respond to general revelation—the position that I described in the first chapter that has been defended by a number of scholars.[28] My position is more nuanced than that, as it recognizes that the Spirit prompts people in a host of ways that are tailored specifically to the person and that God's middle knowledge of how a person would respond to various promptings is the crucial factor that determines what sort of revelation God provides to the person. The key factor is not merely the response that the person has given to general revelation and to whatever other revelation he or she already has.

Since the process I propose above focuses on Christian belief and how the Spirit works on a person to prepare that person to accept the gospel, it is also important to note how this same sort of process can be applied to people living during the Old Testament (OT) period. Clearly,

---

28. Sanders, *No Other Name*, 163. He provides a helpful list of some contemporary advocates of this view.

in the OT one did not need to hear the gospel in order to be saved since Jesus had not yet come into the world to die for the sins of humanity. Although nobody was saved in the OT era by placing faith specifically in Christ with a full understanding of what Christ would do for them, the Bible is clear that people in the OT were saved by God's grace through faith. In addition, this faith is not mere belief that there is a god; rather, it involves putting one's trust in the true God and following him. The premiere example of faith in the OT is the faith of Abraham. The Bible says that Abraham "believed in the Lord; and He reckoned it to him as righteousness" (Gen 15:6). As Paul makes clear in Romans 4, Abraham was saved by God's grace through faith, and this faith was centered upon trusting in God's promises (Rom 4:13–21). The Bible also teaches that Christ's death is an atoning sacrifice for the sins of all people—even those who lived before the time of Christ (Heb 10:1–18). Hebrews 11 recounts the faith of many OT persons, and their faith always involves some knowledge of the true God (not just any god) and some level of active obedience to God and trust in God's promises. One who comes to God in faith, the author of Hebrews says, "must believe that He is and that He is a rewarder of those who seek Him" (Heb 11:6). Moreover, faith is "the assurance of things hoped for, the conviction of things not seen" (Heb 11:1). So, faith involves belief content and conviction, and this is seen in the examples of faith given by the author. Noah believed God and prepared the ark by faith (Heb 11:7). Moses believed God and was willing to endure hardship, oppose Pharaoh, and cross the Red Sea out of a trust in God (Heb 11:23–29). Abraham showed his faith by obeying God on many occasions: moving to a foreign land; believing God that, despite his old age, he would have many descendants and a seed that would bless the whole world; and being willing to sacrifice Isaac (Heb 11:8–19). Even Rahab, who was not an Israelite, followed the one true God and demonstrated her trust in God by hiding the Israelite spies (Heb 11:31). Rahab knew some information about the true God and how He had delivered Israel out of Egypt, and she recognized that Israel's God must be "God in heaven above and on earth beneath" (Josh 2:11). So even though OT saving faith does not require the exact same content as the gospel, it is analogous in that there seems to be a need for trusting God, having confidence in God's promises, and following God. A strong case can be made that, even in the OT, one must accept some sort of special revelation that goes beyond a mere belief in monotheism that one gathers from general revelation.[29] In any case, for the purposes of this project there is no need to explore OT saving faith in great detail. It is sufficient to recognize that people in the OT were saved by God's grace through faith. My proposal is that there is a process[30] that God used in the OT that is like the NT process I have proposed above in which the Spirit offers promptings to all people and draws them to himself in such a way that—unless their own sin prevents the Spirit from doing so—they will ultimately be brought to a state in which they are prepared to place saving faith in God (whatever such faith might require in the OT). If any OT person resists the Spirit's promptings and is never brought to such a state and never saved, then I propose that God would only allow that person to be lost if there are no circumstances (short of, perhaps, providing excessive pressure) in which that person would freely be saved. That means that in any feasible world (even feasible worlds in which that person lived after Christ and heard all about the gospel) such a person would not freely come to saving faith (except, perhaps, for worlds in which the person required unduly overt revelation that God considers unacceptable to provide to that person).

Having laid out my theodicy, it is now necessary to defend certain aspects of it in a bit more detail in order to solidify my attack on P_8. First, it is important to examine carefully the two types of contingently lost individuals that my theodicy allows and show why it is no threat to God's omnibenevolence to allow them. After that, I must defend my contention that a good and loving God would plausibly uphold the two key parameters that are part of the moral and spiritual environment that exists in the actual world—ensuring an adequate level of divine hiddenness and allowing humans to be tempted in certain ways and to a certain degree by

---

29. Kaiser, "Holy Pagans: Reality or Myth?," 275. Kaiser denies that there are examples of OT people coming to faith by believing in a generic monotheism that can be derived merely from general revelation apart from some sort of special revelation. He rejects cases of "holy pagans." Little also addresses this topic, arguing that even in the Old Testament it was necessary to have special revelation to come to saving faith and receive God's grace. See especially the second and third chapters of Little, *The Revelation of God Among the Unevangelized*.

30. Little, *The Revelation of God Among the Unevangelized*, 70. Little contends that Scripture describes a sort of "process in which the patriarch's faith was developed and nurtured throughout his life (cf. Acts 7:2; Gen. 12:1; 12:7; 13:14; 15:1; 17:1; 18:1; 21:12; 22:1)." God brought Abraham to faith and developed that faith. Beginning with Abraham's initial faith response to God—perhaps in response to hearing of the Noahic covenant (see pp. 59–64)—and then continuing with Abraham's response to God appearing to him "in Ur and then in Haran," Abraham continually showed himself to be a person who was willing to follow God in faith.

an evil creature like Satan—even though it may be the case that eliminating these parameters would allow God to actualize a feasible world that has an even better soteriological balance.

Consider first the two types of contingently lost individuals for which my theodicy allows. I have contended that there is biblical evidence that some are contingently lost, so I do not dispute the truth of P_9. Nevertheless, given the enormous providential control that God has via his middle knowledge and the fact that Scripture does not mention any other type of contingently lost person besides the two types that I identify, I have explained that I find no reason to suppose that there any other types of contingently lost persons. Now I will make my case for why neither of these two types undermines God's omnibenevolence, which is critical if I am to show that P_8 is false. Let us begin by examining one of these types: those who apostatize.

Those who commit apostasy "have once been enlightened and have tasted of the heavenly gift and have been made partakers of the Holy Spirit, and have tasted the good word of God and the powers of the age to come" (Heb 6:4–5). Thus, it is hard to see why God's omnibenevolence should be questioned if he allows such persons to live long enough for them to make the free choice to spurn his love and reject the grace that they once accepted. Although such a person is contingently lost in the sense that God could have taken her life while she was still saved, it may be that doing so would rob her of the opportunity to change her mind and make her final choice. Given that God knows that such a person would freely choose to reject his love and grace if given time to do so, prematurely taking the life of such a person would seem to result in someone being saved who ultimately does not want to be saved and does not want to spend eternity with God. God's sovereign choice to grant us the freedom to reject the greatest gift of love that anyone will ever be offered after having previously accepted this gift surely does not detract from his perfect love and perfect goodness. If Plantinga's epistemological model is true, then a person who has come to accept the gospel *knows* that the gospel is true *on the basis of the divine testimony*. Thus, the one who apostatizes willfully rejects this great gift of love that she knows God has revealed to her. It is not hard to see why such a rejection amounts to "trampling underfoot the Son of God" and "insulting the Spirit of grace" (Heb 10:29). Even if there is a feasible world in which a person who apostatizes in the actual world would have freely chosen to be saved and would not have apostatized despite living a full life in that world, it does not seem that God's omnibenevolence can reasonably be questioned. God's love and goodness ought not be impugned because he led such a person to know and accept the truth about him and that person committed the grievous sin of trampling on Christ and insulting the Holy Spirit. If one finds this objectionable and thinks that an omnibenevolent God should only allow a person to live long enough to apostatize in the actual world if that person would apostatize in any feasible world of free creatures in which he or she accepts the gospel and lives a full (normal) lifespan, then one can add to my theodicy the stipulation that God does this. I could easily add this stipulation to my theodicy; however, I do not consider such a stipulation necessary in order to uphold the omnibenevolence of God. If a person apostatizes in the actual world, then God's perfect goodness and love cannot reasonably be questioned for allowing it to happen regardless of what choices that person would make in other feasible worlds. It may be that there are some apostates in any world of free creatures that has an optimal soteriological balance and meets God's other (non-soteriological) requirements, so that may be one good reason why God permits apostasy. Another good reason is simply the incredibly serious nature of the sin of apostasy. Given the knowledge that the apostate has of God's love and grace, God's omnibenevolence ought not be questioned if he allows some people to throw that away.

The other type of contingently lost person is one who would not freely accept the gospel under any sufficiently non-pressured circumstances but would accept it (at least temporarily) if she were given what for her would be unacceptably overt revelation. In this case, too, it does not seem that God's omnibenevolence should be called into question, for such a person has not responded to the promptings that the Holy Spirit gave her that would have overcome her sin barriers so that her will and mind would have been prepared to recognize the truth of the gospel without undue pressure being placed upon her. She would not repent and turn to God apart from God providing some revelation that is for her unduly overt. Although God could bring it about that such a person accepts the gospel in response to an excessively overt sign, this may well not be the sort of acceptance that an omnibenevolent God desires. Such acceptance would be the result of the person receiving revelation that God may consider to be coercive in some sense. God may want to ensure that all persons who come to him are ones who will do so without him having to prod them excessively. Although there are some people who are so hardened against God that they would even reject miraculous revelation (e.g., the people of Capernaum who rejected the miracles of Jesus in Matthew 11), it may be the case that this same revelation would exert excessive pressure upon other people; that is, such revelation may be so powerful to certain people that they would respond to God only because of the potent impact that it has on them. It may even be the case that God knows that these people would genuinely turn to him only for a short time in response to such overt revelation and that they would not persist over time in their genuine desire to remain committed to God after the intense initial impact of this dramatic experience begins to wane. Paul Moser rightly contends that if God were to coerce or exert too much pressure on a person to repent and turn to him, it would "suppress the will, and thus the personhood, of that person, thereby excluding that person as a genuine candidate for a loving relationship."[31] What is excessive pressure for one person may not be excessive for another, and a God who possesses middle knowledge would know what precise impact any particular revelation would have on any free person. So, the fact that some people are so hardened that they would resist even highly overt or miraculous revelation does not preclude the possibility that others would be pressured in an unacceptable way by that same revelation. It is not obvious that a good and loving God ought to offer highly overt revelation to a person if God knows that such revelation is the only sort of revelation to which the person would respond—especially if God also knows that the person receiving it would not persist in genuine faith over time.

One might, however, raise the following objection to my suggestion that God may allow some people to be contingently lost who would have responded (at least temporarily) only to (what is for them) unduly overt revelation: If that is the case, then why did God provide miraculous revelation to many people who did respond to it (e.g., the Apostle Paul on the road to Damascus or those who followed Jesus after seeing his miracles)? There is a plausible response to this objection. It could be that any persons who see divine miracles or other highly overt forms of revelation and turn to God would have turned to God even if God had drawn them to himself in a different way—a way that is not excessively overt; in this way, nobody who comes to faith after seeing miracles or other highly overt revelation does so *only because* of the power of that overt revelation. It may well serve God's purposes in any number of ways to have the world play out in such a way that certain people come to faith

---

31. Moser, *The Elusive God*, 243.

after seeing miraculous signs as Paul did on the Damascus road in Acts 9, but that does not mean that such people would only have come to saving faith via such revelation. For example, perhaps Paul's coming to faith so suddenly and dramatically after having previously persecuted the church led many more people to turn to Christ than would have otherwise occurred. Nevertheless, it may be the case that God could have led Paul to Christian faith slowly and less dramatically over time. One must remember that my suggestion is that God may not want to give miraculous or highly overt revelation to any person who would *require* such revelation in order to turn to God. Such a suggestion does not entail that God would not offer miraculous or overt revelation to other sorts of people. Why, for example, did God not give miraculous revelation to the Sodomites? Perhaps God arranged the world so that all those in Sodom who would have repented in response to the miracles of Jesus are people who *only* would have responded to such overt revelation (and perhaps they would not have wanted to be with God throughout eternity even if they had seen these miracles and at that moment repented and turned to God). God did not want to pressure them into repentance in that way, so God did not provide them with such revelation. Likewise, it is possible that God arranged the world so that every person who saw the miracles of Jesus and did repent is a person who would have responded to non-miraculous revelation as well. God providentially ordered the world so that neither the Sodomites nor anybody else who would only repent if given (what is for them) excessively overt revelation would receive such revelation, and God likewise ordered the world so that anybody who does see miraculous or overt revelation and subsequently comes to faith is a person who would have come to faith even without being given such revelation.

While all of the above would be simple for a God who has middle knowledge, a key question remains: Why should God punish the Sodomites less severely on account of the fact that they would have responded to miraculous revelation if God considered such revelation to be too overt to give to them? Perhaps it is the case that any person who is contingently lost and would have at least responded to excessively overt revelation had he or she been given it will receive some reduced punishment from God in comparison to those who are lost and would not have responded even to such extreme revelation. The latter sort of person (perhaps Pharaoh, who ignored the many plagues in the book of Exodus, or the people of Capernaum who saw Jesus' miracles and rejected them) may deserve even greater punishment than the Sodomites because such persons are hardened against God even to the point of rejecting such incredible signs.

I will now move to a defense of my contention that a good and loving God would plausibly uphold the two key parameters of the moral and spiritual environment that exists in the actual world even though it may be the case that eliminating these parameters would allow God to actualize a feasible world that has an even better soteriological balance than the actual world. Even if I undermine P_8 by showing that the types of contingently lost persons that God permits are consistent with his omnibenevolence, it would seem that God's omnibenevolence also entails that God would not want to allow more people to be lost than is necessary to bring as many people as possible to salvation. As I have indicated, my theodicy agrees in part with Craig that God would plausibly seek to use his middle knowledge to optimize the balance of saved and lost; however, unlike Craig, I emphasize that there may be certain features of the world that God wants to uphold and that these features may reduce the balance of saved versus lost from what would otherwise be feasible for God to achieve in worlds of free creatures. These features include God's (relative) hiddenness and God's allowing Satan to tempt us. My proposal is that God does actualize a world that has as good of a soteriological balance as any other feasible world in which these two parameters (as well as, perhaps, other parameters) are in place, but I allow that there may well be feasible worlds of free creatures lacking these parameters that are more soteriologically optimal than the actual world. Although—all things being equal—God no doubt desires as many people as possible to be saved and as few as possible to be lost, it is plausible that God also desires that those who are saved make that decision without excessive pressure and are sufficiently tempted by sin such that they must make a significant moral decision to choose God over sin. If God had eliminated either (or both) of the above parameters from the moral and spiritual environment, then it may be the case that the Holy Spirit could bring the will and mind of even more people to the point where sin does not blind them to knowing the gospel. Perhaps, for example, fewer people would apostatize in feasible worlds in which a creature like Satan is not in the world bombarding them with temptations. Moreover, perhaps many people who would only respond to revelation that is (for them) excessively overt in any world in which they are exposed to Satan's temptations would have responded to revelation that is not too overt for God to give them in a world without Satan. Despite the potential negative impact that these two parameters might have on the soteriological balance, let us consider why each parameter seems to be consistent with God's omnibenevolence.

Consider first God's relative hiddenness. There can be little doubt that God is far more hidden from us than he could be. God could manifest himself before each person daily, reminding us all of the gospel and the dire consequences for rejecting it. God could ensure that his existence and the truth of the gospel are facts that cannot reasonably be denied by anyone. But regardless of what impact such a divine unveiling might have on reducing the proportion of persons who will be lost, I have already indicated why a good and loving God would plausibly not want to do this. God's goal is not merely for us to believe that he exists or that the gospel is true. As James 2:19 states, even the demons believe in God. Instead of mere belief, God wants us to turn to him, accept forgiveness in Christ, and embrace him out of love and not as a result of excessive pressure. God wants us to give our lives to him and allow him to sanctify us so that we become morally transformed and love and enjoy him forever. Hiding himself to the degree that he does may be the only way that God can achieve such great goods as: increasing our trust in him and our reliance upon him; increasing our desire for him; allowing us to have the chance to accept the gospel for the right reasons; and ensuring that we do not take God and his plan of salvation for granted.[32] So, the fact that God's hiddenness may[33] reduce the balance of saved versus lost from what it perhaps would have been in some feasible world of free creatures in which God is less hidden is in no way incompatible with God's omnibenevolence.

Turning now to the second parameter, it is also far from obvious that an omnibenevolent God would not allow Satan to tempt us—even if God could have achieved a better soteriological balance by eliminating Satan's temptations. It seems plausible that an omnibenevolent God may still create a world in which an evil being like Satan exists and is

---

32. Moser, *The Elusive God*, 107. These potential reasons are insightfully suggested by Moser.

33. Moreland and Craig suggest that if God revealed himself more directly to all people, it might actually have a negative impact on the number of people who are saved because many may come to resent God's direct presence in their lives. Even if God's regular and direct presence might move some people to faith in Christ, it may push many more away from Christ. There is no way for us to know what impact this would have on the soteriological balance. See Moreland and Craig, *Philosophical Foundation*, 144–45.

permitted to tempt humans because of God's overriding desire to place us into an environment that requires us to make a morally significant choice to love him and embrace the good rather than to love what is evil. The Bible teaches that, in this world, "the evil one comes and snatches away what has been sown" in the hearts of some people before God's truth can take root at all (Matt 13:19); still other people are not willing to pursue God because of "affliction or persecution" (Matt 13:21); and in some other cases God's truth is choked out of a person's heart by "the worry of the world and the deceitfulness of wealth" (Matt 13:22). The temptations and trials that Satan puts in our lives in this world certainly do filter out many people who are not willing to pursue God through those challenges. Even believers are attacked by Satan and must struggle with sin and allow God to refine them and discipline them so that they become the sort of people that God desires (Heb 12:1–11). God assists us in our struggles and helps us to resist the power of sin if we allow him to do so. It certainly seems reasonable that a good God would want our present lives to play out in a moral environment in which there is enough temptation that one must make a meaningful and difficult decision to choose God over sin and in which moral and spiritual growth will occur as we learn to resist Satan's temptations with God's assistance. Allowing us this morally significant choice and this opportunity for moral growth is important for moral agents who are made in God's image. Providing this environment is plausibly a great good even if it means that more people will choose to reject God than in a world without Satan's temptations.

Three Attractive Features of This Theodicy

Although Scripture does not provide a specific solution to the PCL and I do not claim that the theodicy put forward in this chapter is necessarily true, my theodicy is both plausible and consistent with Scripture. I have responded to the PCL by making the case that P_8 is neither necessarily true nor required by Christian doctrine. If I have succeeded in showing that P_8 fails, then the PCL fails to demonstrate that P_1 and P_2 are inconsistent. Having fleshed out my theodicy, I will highlight three of its attractive features as I conclude this chapter.

First of all, this theodicy allows for the truth of P_9 and avoids Craig's biblically problematic proposal that all of the lost are TD. It makes room for what may well be instances of contingently lost persons in the Bible. If

Matthew 11 does indicate that certain people in Sodom, Tyre, and Sidon are contingently lost, then this theodicy has the advantage of handling this difficult passage. Likewise, if one holds (as many Christians do) that apostasy is possible, then this theodicy provides a way to show that apostasy is no threat to God's omnibenevolence. It may be that there are some people who are TD, and my theodicy does not take a stance on whether anyone is TD. Perhaps, for example, some of the people who are so bent against God that they even rejected the miracles of Jesus are TD, but it may be the case that even these people are not TD. It may be that they would freely repent and turn to God if they were put in a different circumstance in which God provided them with revelation that he deems too overt for them to receive. Even though it seems to be unbiblical to hold that all of the lost are TD, I see no reason why some of the lost could not be TD.[34] My theodicy thus takes no stance on this issue.

Second, this theodicy—unlike Craig's theodicy and the theodicies of others who appeal to inclusivism—upholds Christian exclusivism while showing how it is possible that everyone has a legitimate opportunity to be saved and nobody is lost due to a lack of information or due to the sin and corrupting influences of other people. By leveraging divine middle knowledge and a slightly modified Reformed epistemology, I offer a plausible process for how it is possible that every lost person is lost as a consequence of his or her own sin. This process recognizes that an unevangelized person need not respond to general revelation in order to be brought the gospel, making it more nuanced than the common exclusivist position that God brings the gospel to those who respond appropriately to general revelation or to whatever revelation they have. Also, according to my proposed process, one need not have the time, ability, or resources to reason one's way to knowing that the gospel is true, yet I leave room for the Spirit to use apologetic arguments and various evidential means to break down a person's sin barrier and prepare a person's heart and mind to accept the gospel. Ultimately, I show how God can ensure that every single person who is never put into a circumstance in which she repents and turns to God was not placed into such a circumstance because of her own sin.

---

34. As I have contended previously, I do not consider it theologically important to make room for unconditional election (as MacGregor does in his theodicy). One who wants to offer a theodicy that takes into account unconditional election cannot allow the possibility that anyone who is lost in the actual world is TD—or, for that matter, that anyone in the actual world who is saved is transcircumstantially saved.

Third (and most importantly), this theodicy undermines the PCL by attacking P_8. I take this to be the only biblically-consistent strategy. Although Craig opts to attack P_9, I think that doing so is wrongheaded and unnecessary. Not only does my theodicy defend the omnibenevolence of God in the face of two sorts of contingently lost people that many Christians would agree are indicated in Scripture, but it also contends that God's omnibenevolence remains intact despite two thorny features of the world that may seem to count against soteriological optimality—God's relative hiddenness and the temptations of Satan. This is an especially advantageous feature of my theodicy (and one that Craig's lacks). If successful, my theodicy reconciles Craig's insight that God has plausibly optimized the soteriological balance with these two features of the world in a way that upholds God's perfect goodness and love.

5

The Applicability of This Theodicy to the Broader Problem of Evil

AT THIS POINT I have laid out and defended my theodicy against the PCL. However, before drawing together the key points of my overall project and providing a final summary and conclusion, I will offer in this chapter an argument that my soteriological theodicy—or really any Molinist soteriological theodicy that, like my own or Craig's, suggests that a key soteriological aim of God's is to leverage his middle knowledge to optimize the balance of saved versus lost—offers great benefit in responding to the broader problem of evil (POE). Although my theodicy is aimed at dealing with the PCL, which is an aspect of the soteriological POE, I will show how my theodicy might be leveraged in responding to the broader POE in terms of accounting for the vast amount of suffering and evil in our present earthly existence and offering insight into why some evil might appear to be gratuitous.

I will first contend that one can more effectively utilize a Free Will Defense (FWD) of the sort given by Alvin Plantinga in response to the claim that theism is made unlikely by the *amount* of evil in the world if one recognizes that God may allow so much suffering and evil largely because God is using his middle knowledge to optimize the soteriological balance. This will involve: examining Plantinga's defense that God may have brought about the feasible world that has the best balance of moral good and evil; considering the value that is added to defending Christian theism against the charge of excessive evil by including soteriological considerations in the balance of overall good and evil; and showing that

Molinism is critical to running this useful defense. Some contend that Molinism is a hindrance to the FWD, as it increases the responsibility of God for what creatures do with their free will. In response, I will argue that God's possible goal of soteriological optimization blunts the charge that God has an unsavory role in evil if Molinism is true. I also make the case that rejecting the providential control that Molinism furnishes seems to strip God of his ability to guide humanity toward the best outcomes and requires that God gambles by not knowing logically prior to creating free creatures what sort of ratio of good and evil would result.

I will then show how the truth of a Molinist soteriological theodicy that appeals to God arranging the world to achieve an optimal soteriological balance can aid in the defense of God's omnibenevolence against the charge that God ought not allow gratuitous evil. The concern about gratuitous evil is illustrated well by the famous argument given by William Rowe. I will briefly explain Rowe's argument and then show how the truth of my soteriological theodicy allows one to give a powerful response to Rowe.

I will conclude the chapter by arguing that two prominent responses to the POE that (unlike Plantinga's FWD) do have an eschatological and soteriological focus would be strengthened if they drew upon Molinism and allowed that God uses his middle knowledge to carry out soteriological optimization. Doing so would aid them in explaining why God would plausibly allow evil in order to achieve the most favorable soteriological outcome. These two theodicies include Eleonore Stump's Thomistic theodicy and John Hick's soul-making theodicy. Both of these rightly appeal to God molding humans via suffering in order to achieve benefits that are not fully realized within this earthly life, but their proposals are strengthened by the providential control that Molinism affords.

Molinism and Soteriological Optimization Strengthen the Free Will Defense

It is widely recognized that Alvin Plantinga's FWD has shown that theism is logically compatible with the existence of some evil. This aspect of his FWD does not depend upon the truth of Molinism, since God need not have middle knowledge in order for it to be possible that all free creatures that God might create suffer from transworld depravity (which is how

Plantinga shows the compatibility of God with some evil).[1] Yet Plantinga goes on to contend that the *amount* of evil present in the world (i.e., its severity and frequency) does not even render theism unlikely, and this aspect of his FWD does depend upon the possible truth of Molinism. This section will focus upon the benefit that Molinism and God's optimization of the soteriological balance offer to this aspect of the FWD that addresses the amount of evil in the world.[2]

In response to the concern that God's existence may be incompatible with—or at least made unlikely by—the amount of evil in the world, Plantinga suggests that it may not be possible for God to actualize a world with a better balance of moral good and evil than is found in the actual world. Plantinga rightly stresses that the real concern is not the amount of evil (since evil could be eliminated entirely simply by not creating free creatures); rather, the real issue is whether God could have achieved as much good as there is in the actual world with less evil. There are many possible worlds that have as much good as the actual world and less evil, but Plantinga points out that it may not be feasible for God to actualize any of them. It may be that God knows that the balance of moral good and evil achieved in this world is as good as in any feasible world. Of course, this possibility requires an appeal to divine middle knowledge. Besides

---

[1]. If all free creatures that God might create suffer from transworld depravity, then this would be true even if God lacked middle knowledge and did not know that it is true. See Plantinga, *God, Freedom, and Evil*, 48–51. Recall that Plantinga's concept of "transworld depravity," which he uses in his FWD against the POE, is a property that one has if one will do evil in every world in which one is a morally free agent. It is a condition a person P has in which P would err with regard to at least one morally significant action in every world in which God could create P with libertarian freedom. If P suffers from transworld depravity, then in every world W in which "is significantly free in W" and "never does what is wrong in W" are included in P's essence, God could not actualize W. So if all creaturely essences suffer from this condition, then there is no world that is feasible for God to create that is composed entirely of free creatures who never sin. Even though worlds of free creatures who never sin are logically possible, Plantinga points out that the fact that it is at least possible that all creaturely essences suffer from transworld depravity means that there may be no way that God could bring about such worlds. For more on how Plantinga unpacks this concept, see Plantinga, *God, Freedom, and Evil*, 51–53.

[2]. My argumentation in the remainder of this section (on the FWD) and in the section that follows (on the problem of gratuitous evil) draws heavily upon an article that I published in *Philosophia Christi* 22 (2) 2020: 257–72. The full title of the article is: "A Case for How Eschatological and Soteriological Considerations Strengthen the Plausibility of a Good God." Permission has been granted by the editor of *Philosophia Christi* to draw upon material from this article. More information about *Philosophia Christi* can be found at www.epsociety.org.

Plantinga's argument that God possibly actualized a feasible world that has an optimal balance of *moral* good and evil, Plantinga also raises the possibility that natural evil may be the result of the free actions of demons so that all evil (both moral and natural) is "broadly moral" and God may be achieving an optimal balance of broadly moral good and evil. Ultimately, Plantinga argues that the amount of evil in the world does not even make theism unlikely because one can have no confidence that there is so much broadly moral evil that God probably lacks a good reason for permitting it.[3]

Note that Plantinga's focus is on the balance of broadly moral good and evil *in this earthly life*. He never aims to draw into the discussion good and evil actions or good and bad states of affairs that might occur postmortem. His argument does not involve soteriological outcomes or how the balance of broadly moral good and evil on earth relates to the balance of saved versus lost. His proposal certainly makes no attempt to appeal to postmortem conditions that are part of Christian theism. His appeal to demons would not apply to the postmortem conditions that are described in Scripture because demons will not cause natural evils in the new heavens and new earth. God will also no longer have any need to balance moral goods and evils, as those who will do moral evil will be consigned to hell and those in the new heavens and new earth will be sinless (Rev 20:10—21:27).

Plantinga's defense concerning the amount of evil is brilliant, and it effectively defends theism by showing that God's existence is compatible with the amount of evil observed in the world. This is all he sought to do. Yet it is possible to bolster the defense of *Christian* theism against the charge that there is too much evil in the world by expanding his focus to consider not only earthly goods and evils but *all* goods and evils and all good and bad states of affairs that will *ever* come about if Christian theism is true—especially the ultimate good state of eternally enjoying the presence of God and the ultimate bad state of suffering eternal punishment in separation from God. In selecting which world to actualize, it might be that God considers the balance of moral and natural goods and evils found in this earthly life to be far less significant than the balance of those who are ultimately saved and lost. If so, then the Christian theist can allow that it may be necessary for God to permit a worse balance of moral and natural goods and evils in this earthly life than God could feasibly achieve because doing so might be integral to achieving what is

---

3. Plantinga, *God, Freedom, and Evil*, 55–63.

most important: an optimal balance of good and evil *over the course of eternity* (which depends upon the balance of saved versus lost). Making this argument not only draws into the discussion a crucial aspect of the balance of good and evil in the world (soteriological outcomes), but it also adds an element of plausibility to the bare possibility Plantinga offers in his FWD—an element of plausibility that is helpful in responding to evidential forms of the POE. While Plantinga's defense effectively shows that theism is logically compatible with the amount of evil observed in the world, one might find his proposal so implausible that it seems not to reduce the sting of the concern that the amount of evil makes theism unlikely. One might find it hard to imagine that the balance of good and evil could not be better in this earthly life. So adding the soteriological element makes it even more plausible that God could be providentially achieving the best overall (eternal) balance of good and evil. This element makes it all the more difficult for one to assess the likelihood that such an overall balance is being achieved by God simply by observing the amount of suffering in this earthly existence.

This proposal also fits well with biblical teaching. Scripture indicates that the ultimate human good is not fully realized until after this earthly life and is incomparably greater than the suffering experienced on earth (Rom 8:18) in terms of quality and duration. The wretched state of the lost also swamps any pleasures experienced in this brief life (Matt 16:26). Since the balance of earthly goods and evils carries less weight than soteriological outcomes (which are eternal), the optimal balance of *overall* good and evil seemingly hinges largely on the balance of saved and lost. The soteriological theodicy that I have put forth in this project stresses that Scripture attests that God desires for none to be lost (2 Pet 3:9; 1 Tim 2:4) and that a God who possesses middle knowledge would likely aim for soteriological optimality (or at least an optimal balance of saved versus lost within the bounds of certain key parameters—such as divine hiddenness and Satan's temptations—that God considers important to uphold). God's providential arrangement of the world to achieve soteriological optimality may well require a suboptimal balance of broadly moral good relative to broadly moral evil in this earthly life, and it seems quite plausible that this is a fair trade for an omnibenevolent God to make. My proposal that God may well allow a suboptimal balance of broadly moral good relative to broadly moral evil in this earthly life in order to achieve an optimal balance of saved versus lost for all of eternity is consistent with the recognition that it may be the case that "only in a world suffused with natural and moral evil would the optimal number of people come to know God freely" and be saved.[4]

Since achieving an optimal balance of saved versus lost (within the bounds of certain key parameters) appears to be something the Christian God would aim to do and since it affords the Christian theist the option of allowing that there may be a suboptimal balance of moral and natural goods and evils in this world, this proposal has great force against the charge that God's existence is made unlikely by the vast amount of evil observed in the world. Like Plantinga's own defense concerning the amount of evil, the possibility of Molinism must be allowed in order to run this twist on his argument. As I have argued, God surely cannot actualize a feasible world that has an optimal soteriological balance unless God knows logically prior to creation all feasible worlds and is able to select one that is as soteriologically optimal as any other feasible world that has all of the key features that God requires (including non-soteriological ones).

While the above seems to show that a Molinist soteriological theodicy that affirms God's optimization of the soteriological balance helps to strengthen a FWD of theism—and especially Christian theism—against the concern that there is too much evil in the world, some have contended that divine middle knowledge only makes the POE knottier. Their objection is that God's responsibility for what creatures do with their free will would be greatly increased if God has middle knowledge because such knowledge affords God enormous providential control over creaturely free acts. The concern is that the Molinist God providentially guarantees all that happens and thus bears much culpability for the evils that occur. Greg Welty contends that, if Molinism is true, then "God ordains whatsoever comes to pass, and this includes ordaining that acts of moral evil come to pass."[5] While God is not the sufficient cause of evil even if he providentially arranges the world via his middle knowledge, "created agents are God's gun (or at least his bullets)." Since the "bullets are sentient" and free, they bear some blame. Yet God's ordering of the circumstances and knowing exactly what the free agents will do in those circumstances means that God fires the gun and bears moral responsibility.[6] For this reason Christopher Bernard holds that the FWD without Molinism "seems to be better off than it would be if Molinism were true.

---

4. Craig and Rosenberg, "The Debate," 32.
5. Welty, "Molinist Gunslingers," 57.
6. Welty, "Molinist Gunslingers," 67–68.

With less knowledge of consequences comes less responsibility for results" in terms of the evil done by free creatures.[7]

According to my proposal, however, the creaturely "bullets" that Welty contends God is responsible for firing in this earthly life may be absolutely necessary in order to achieve soteriological optimality. If God has middle knowledge and is arranging the world in order to achieve an optimal ratio of saved relative to lost over the course of human history (however long that might be), then God ought not be criticized for providentially allowing the amount of moral and natural evils that he allows in this life. It is unclear how one could show that it is implausible that God is doing this (so long as divine middle knowledge is philosophically coherent, as I have argued). Consequently, we are not in a position to criticize the balance of good and evil that we observe in the world. It seems reasonable that the Molinist God may well allow for a suboptimal balance of evil relative to good in this earthly life because doing so is necessary in order to bring about the best overall balance of good and evil (taking eternal states into account). So the argument that Molinism implicates God in an unsavory way in the evils that occur in this life appears to lack force.

Additionally, the falsity of Molinism would raise the important problem of reckless risk-taking with regard to God's care for humanity. The Molinist Thomas Flint points out that a God without middle knowledge "knows only probabilities" and thus "takes enormous risks in creating significantly free beings." God could not know logically prior to his creative decree whether all of his free creatures would "consistently reject him" and "use their freedom to degrade others and themselves."[8] Flint thinks a good God lacking middle knowledge ought not create a world of free creatures, since logically prior to creation God would not know whether the world would turn out to have massively more evil than good. God would lack the providential control to make it better. Flint points out that taking risks, while not always morally problematic, is clearly wrong when: the stakes are high, one's likelihood of success is low, and taking the risk is not necessary. Taking such risks is especially troublesome when it involves the wellbeing of others (e.g., a father who needlessly risks the security of his family by gambling his life savings).[9]

---

7. Bernard, "Views of God and Evil," 96.
8. Flint, *Divine Providence*, 107.
9. Flint, *Divine Providence*, 104–5.

In response, Bernard thinks such risk-taking is not an insuperable problem and that the FWD can be made effectively without Molinism. First, Bernard claims that it is at least possible that God has morally justifiable reasons for taking the risks that God does and that God is able without middle knowledge to predict accurately enough what humans would do in various circumstances based on their tendencies. Bernard suspects that this guesswork by God might allow God to think that he could produce a world with a "favorable [even if not optimal] pattern of moral good to moral evil." So long as it is possible that God has enough predictive ability of creaturely behavior to achieve this, Bernard thinks God is justified in attempting to attain the benefits that come from creating free creatures. Second, Bernard suggests that God could miraculously intervene on special occasions to keep the balance of good and evil in check without unduly undermining human freedom, thus containing some additional risk.[10]

Contra Bernard, Kenneth Perszyk rightly points out that God's goodness seems to demand that God cannot merely get lucky in creating a world with a favorable balance of good and evil. Clearly "creation is serious business" and "caution (not luck) is a moral category." So "if God didn't ('antecedently') know what any (libertarian) free creatures would do," then it is "not at all obvious" that creating such creatures "would be compatible with his perfect goodness."[11] It stretches the imagination to think that the non-Molinist God would have the providential resources to create a world of free creatures that ends up on balance being good without that result being largely a matter of luck. Consider, for example, the comments of the non-Molinist Robert Adams. Adams admits that God must take "trillions of risks" if God lacks middle knowledge and creates a world of free creatures. Adams recognizes that "no matter how shrewdly God acted in running so many risks, His winning on *every* risk would not be antecedently probable."[12] If even a fraction of a percent of those trillions of guesses are wrong, it would plausibly upset God's providential strategies massively. One miscalculation could easily be compounded greatly given the interconnectedness of human lives. Thus, even if the world does contain a relatively favorable balance of moral good and evil, it does not seem reasonable that the non-Molinist God would

---

10. Bernard, "Views of God and Evil," 95–96.
11. Perszyk, "Free Will Defence," 49.
12. Adams, "Middle Knowledge and the Problem of Evil," 125.

be in a position to know logically prior to creation that he could achieve such an outcome without getting lucky. So while Bernard stresses that it only needs to be possible that the non-Molinist God is able to achieve an acceptable balance of moral good and evil in order to run a non-Molinist FWD, Bernard overlooks the moral significance of God not antecedently knowing that he could do this without luck.

More crucially, when one considers that God may be working to optimize the balance of saved and lost, the non-Molinist God's providential task becomes all the more incredible. Even if Bernard is right that the non-Molinist God could miraculously intervene at times without undermining divine hiddenness and human freedom and could predict human behavior well enough to achieve an adequate balance of moral and natural good and evil in this earthly life (and even if God could antecedently know that he could accomplish this without getting lucky), how is God to know what natural sufferings and moral evils would lead to the best balance of saved and lost? How could God possibly know whether allowing horrors like the 2010 Haitian earthquake or the Holocaust would ultimately result in a benefit to the balance of saved versus lost over the course of human history? The complex web of reactions from all humans affected by such events (both in the near-term and as the consequences of the events trickle down through history) and how those reactions affect the soteriological balance is surely far beyond predictable even for a God who lacks middle knowledge but is otherwise omniscient. Moreover, how could the non-Molinist God allow the death of a young non-Christian who never heard the gospel or who faced other major moral and spiritual obstacles? If God lacks middle knowledge and if (as I have argued previously) Scripture leaves little hope for postmortem opportunities for salvation, then the suffering resulting from such tragic and premature deaths—which are not unusual in this world—are utterly baffling. How could a loving God who desires the salvation of such persons end their lives when there seems to be much potential for their salvation and when there is no way to know that the timing and circumstances of their tragic deaths will have a positive impact on the balance of saved and lost?

So if humans have libertarian freedom (including the freedom to accept or reject God's gracious offer of salvation)[13] and their eternal fate

---

13. Of course, I hold to the theological position that humans have libertarian freedom with regard to their choice to accept God's offer of salvation. Were one to adopt a view that denies that humans have this particular freedom (even if one allows that humans have libertarian freedom concerning other choices), it would seem to preclude

The Applicability of This Theodicy to the Broader Problem of Evil 193

is sealed by their decisions in this brief life, then the idea that God possesses middle knowledge and is optimizing the soteriological balance has much value in terms of defending the goodness of God against the charge that there is too much evil relative to good in this life. If time is of the essence and the Spirit must break down our sin barriers and lead us to Christ in the span of this brief earthly life, then the amount of evil that we observe is not necessarily surprising. The non-Molinist God would have to gamble on whether many—or any—of his beloved creatures would freely be saved and must allow that some—likely many—creatures will be lost who would have been saved if only God knew what promptings and circumstances (including particular sufferings) would result in their freely turning to him. But if God has middle knowledge and is working toward the best soteriological ends, then we are in no position to criticize the amount of suffering and evil in the world because that suffering may be just what is needed to achieve what is ultimately best for us.

Molinism and Soteriological Optimization as a Response to Gratuitous Evil

Having seen the value that Molinism and God's optimization of the soteriological balance bring to offering a more robust FWD, consider now how this soteriological proposal can help the Christian theist defend the goodness of God against the charge that God ought not allow gratuitous evil. The concern that some evil seems to be utterly pointless and that this counts against the truth of theism is illustrated well by the following famous argument given by William Rowe: (R_1) "There exist instances of intense suffering which an omnipotent, omniscient being could have prevented without thereby losing some greater good or permitting some evil equally bad or worse"; and (R_2) "An omniscient, wholly good being would prevent the occurrence of any intense suffering it could, unless it could not do so without thereby losing some greater good or permitting

---

one from making this connection between suffering and evil on the one hand and God's providentially aiming for optimal soteriological outcomes on the other. That is because the suffering and evil of this earthly life would be causally disconnected from the balance of saved and lost. If humans lack libertarian freedom with regard to their choice to accept God's offer of salvation, then any balance of saved and lost could seemingly be achieved regardless of what sort of balance of broadly moral evils occur on earth since God's election would not be dependent—even in part—upon human free choices or circumstances.

some evil equally bad or worse."[14] Atheism is true if both R_1 and R_2 are true. We will see, however, that the truth of Molinism and God's optimization of the soteriological balance provide an enormous benefit in responding to Rowe's objection by casting doubt upon the truth of R_1.

Before laying out this response to R_1, it is worth pointing out that some Christian philosophers opt not to reject R_1 and instead attack R_2. David Baggett and Jerry Walls, for example, allow that gratuitous evil may simply be unavoidable in a world that contains free creatures. They stress that things like child abuse and killings are "tragic and pointless," and "the world would have been better off without" such events. They do not focus on the direct consequences of evil and instead suggest that free will may not be possible without also allowing the possibility of gratuitous suffering. Human moral goods require free will, but God's granting us free will opens up the possibility that it can be abused—and, indeed, it is abused by humans. Baggett and Walls contend that, although humans use their free will to carry out pointless evils, this does not mean that God lacks morally sufficient reasons for giving humans free will. They consider it likely that, in a world such as ours that includes free creatures and stable natural laws, God must allow that there will be "more, maybe many more, sufferings than are strictly necessary to produce relevant goods or avoid comparable things that are bad."[15]

Baggett and Walls raise a fair point, and there is value in making the case that it is not necessarily incumbent upon a theist to accept R_2. God may not be able to prevent gratuitous evil in a world of free creatures—or at least in one that is as populated as the actual world. It does seem, though, that making this case would be especially plausible if one contends that humans possess libertarian freedom and if (contrary to the position I take here) one rejects divine middle knowledge; for in that case it is almost inconceivable that there could be no wasted suffering. God would then lack the providential control over free creatures that is needed if God is to eradicate gratuitous suffering, and God would have to take trillions of risks. Of course, we have already seen that denying divine middle knowledge is problematic for the Christian theodicist in important ways.

There is much value in attacking R_1, and this may be accomplished by leveraging the proposal that God might allow much of the evil that

---

14. Rowe, "The Problem of Evil," 127–28.
15. Baggett and Walls, *Good God*, 151–52.

The Applicability of This Theodicy to the Broader Problem of Evil

occurs in this earthly life in order to achieve the eternal outcome of soteriological optimality (within the parameters I have identified). Consider the following. Let AW be the actual world. Let "gratuitous suffering" (GS) be suffering that God could eliminate without losing a greater good or causing an equally bad or worse suffering. Let "pseudo-gratuitous suffering" (PGS) be suffering that does not *in itself causally lead* to any greater good or the prevention of any equally bad or worse suffering, but either the *circumstances* in which a PGS occurs lead to a justifying benefit that outweighs the concomitant PGS or else *multiple instances* of PGS collectively allow a justifying good. Consider: (1) AW contains instances of PGS but no GS; (2) God knew logically prior to creation that AW contains an optimal balance of *overall* good versus evil (including soteriological outcomes) over the course of eternity—a balance significantly better than that of any feasible world devoid of instances of PGS; and (3) God chooses to actualize AW. If these premises are true, then R_1 would be false and yet would appear to humans to be true (i.e., it may seem to us that there is GS when we observe instances of PGS). Instances of PGS are not gratuitous because they are present in a world with a significantly better balance of good and evil than any feasible world lacking them. Concerning instances of GS, there is never a reason for God to permit them since they are both eliminable and detrimental to the goodness of a world.

To see how the *circumstances* in which a PGS occurs can justify God allowing the PGS, suppose that in AW person P freely inflicts harm H on another human upon finding himself in circumstance C (where C is a maximal world segment[16] that neither includes nor excludes P doing H), yet H leads to no greater good and avoids no suffering equal to or greater than H. Suppose that in any feasible world in which C does not arise, the soteriological balance and thus the balance of *overall* good and evil *over the course of eternity* would be worse than in AW; nevertheless, H in itself does not *causally lead* to a good that outweighs H or to the prevention of a suffering that is at least as bad as H since it is some aspect (or aspects) of C that is crucial to the justifying outcomes. (For example, perhaps P never would have met his victim if a certain prior event E had not happened, but E is crucial to the world playing out in a soteriologically optimal way. God could not eliminate E from C without an eternal

---

16. Recall that a "circumstance" here refers to what is often called a maximal world segment—a complete description of the entire history of the world up until the exact moment that the agent who is part of the CCF freely acts.

consequence.) God would thus have good reason to allow this PGS; yet, when we examine H, we see no justifying goods that causally follow from it because there are none.

Additionally, *multiple instances* of PGS may collectively allow a justifying good. Some "apparently unmerited, pointless" suffering may be needed for there to be compassion and sacrificial aid for the suffering. If suffering were always deserved, then there would be less motivation for others to relieve it; moreover, people would do what is right merely to attain beneficial outcomes.[17] Divine hiddenness may also be undermined if all suffering were according to desert, as it may be obvious that a mind behind the universe is meting out rewards and punishments. Additionally, it may require breaking natural laws if God were to ensure that the severity and distribution of suffering is always according to desert. So perhaps it is only possible for God to achieve the best outcomes in developing us morally—*outcomes that may be needed for soteriological optimality and the best overall world over the course of eternity*—in a moral arena in which there are instances of suffering that are unmerited and appear random and perhaps causally lead to no justifying benefit in themselves but are *collectively* beneficial in the above-mentioned way.

So, given that God is plausibly more concerned about soteriological optimality and the overall (eternal) balance of good and evil rather than merely the balance of earthly goods and evils, it is not reasonable to cast doubt upon God's goodness or existence simply because there appear to be many evils that do not causally lead to any greater good or the prevention of a worse (or equally bad) evil. Rowe's argument, it seems to me, has lost much traction. Similarly, contentions like those of atheist philosopher Bruce Russell that the best explanation for why we often do not see justifiable reasons for certain instances of evil is that there are none[18] lose plausibility in the face of the above considerations.

Molinism and Soteriological Optimization Strengthen the Theodicies of Stump and Hick

Finally, I will consider briefly the benefits that Molinism would inject into two prominent theodicies that try to account for suffering and evil by appealing to postmortem considerations: Eleonore Stump's Thomistic

---

17. Hick, "Soul-Making and Suffering," 186–87.
18. Russell, "Defenseless," 196–97.

theodicy and John Hick's soul-making theodicy. Both of these theodicies already appeal to God shaping humans morally and spiritually via suffering to achieve benefits that are not fully realized until after this earthly life, but neither of them recognizes the importance of leveraging divine middle knowledge in order to justify that God can effectively use suffering and evil to achieve the best soteriological ends. The truth of the soteriological theodicy that I propose would be beneficial to both of their responses to the broader POE. Let us begin with Stump.

Stump's theodicy focuses on offering a possible explanation for the suffering of "mentally fully functional" adults who are "unwilling, innocent" sufferers. Following Aquinas, she identifies two types of unwilling sufferers. Unbelievers suffer "involuntary *simpliciter*" (IS). They suffer unwillingly "in every way." By contrast, suffering "involuntary *secundum quid*" (ISQ) means one is unwilling to suffer "only in a certain respect."[19] A Christian suffers only ISQ, for a Christian gives general assent to suffering by accepting that God will use it for her sanctification. Stump suggests that all suffering is used by God to justify unbelievers and sanctify believers. The worst thing one can experience, she thinks, is to become permanently "psychically fragmented" and separated from God in hell. The best thing is sharing eternal union with God in heaven.[20]

Although Stump's theodicy holds that God uses suffering and evil to achieve soteriological aims, she denies that Molinism needs to play any role in her theodicy. Stump is insightful in identifying the best and worst states that a human can experience. She is also correct that "the relational good of union with God is infinitely shareable without diminution, and it is available to every human person no matter what that person's external circumstances might be." But even if union with God is *available* to all people regardless of a person's external circumstances, that does not mean that this good will be *freely accepted* by a person regardless of that person's circumstances. Stump errs when she goes on to say that obtaining this good depends upon one's "psychic state, not his external circumstances."[21] One's psychic state is influenced by one's circumstances. I have argued that one's openness to accepting and loving God depends in part upon the Spirit directing one's life experiences—including one's experience of suffering—to break down the barriers of sin that

---

19. Stump, *Wandering in Darkness*, 378–81.
20. Stump, *Wandering in Darkness*, 383–87.
21. Stump, *Wandering in Darkness*, 397–98.

prevent one from accepting the grace that God makes freely available. Doing this most effectively and without guesswork requires Molinism. If God uses suffering (and other sorts of experiences) to prompt free human responses that lead unbelievers toward justification and believers toward sanctification, it would require (at least in many cases) affecting the person's environment such that the person will respond in a beneficial way. It would also involve God ensuring that each set of circumstances involving suffering and other experiences that improves one person's psychic state is compossible with circumstances that God needs to bring about in the lives of others to improve their psychic states. This requires enormous providential control over free creatures—control that is surely made possible only by Molinism.

People are not always rational or predictable in their responses to events in their lives—especially emotional events that involve suffering. There may be emotional or psychological baggage that the Spirit must clear away in order for an unbeliever to be made ready in her mind and will to accept the gospel. Without middle knowledge God can only make an educated guess about whether a particular instance of suffering would help a person to overcome that baggage or whether it might only fuel further resistance to God. These complex psychological and emotional factors that play into our free choices are plausibly not fully predictable even for a being who lacks middle knowledge but is otherwise omniscient.

Miscalculations on God's part concerning how a creature would respond to an instance of suffering could have tragic effects—*especially in the case of God's attempts to use suffering to sanctify believers*. In the biblical account of Job, God allows Satan to inflict severe suffering on Job to test him. Stump admits that even if God has simple foreknowledge, he cannot test Job on the basis of knowing that Job would pass the test. Job's passing of the test and God's foreknowledge that this will happen would be logically subsequent to God testing Job. God would be taking a risk.[22] Stump recognizes that, if God lacks middle knowledge and must take risks, Job might have freely responded to the suffering by cursing God. If that had happened, God's attempt to sanctify Job and make Job more glorious via Job's clinging to his faith amidst suffering would have failed; however, Stump thinks that this suffering would then have served a different purpose for Job: it "would have contributed to his justification,

---

22. Stump, *Wandering in Darkness*, 564–65. See endnotes 66 and 67. See also endnote 101 on page 622.

rather than his sanctification."[23] But this characterization of the outcome seems quite odd. Job was, prior to his suffering, a man of faith and character (Job 1:1). He had clearly entered into a faith relationship with God. If Job had died prior to his suffering, surely he would have been saved. So if God's attempt to sanctify Job further via extreme suffering had backfired and resulted in Job cursing and rejecting God, this would not have "contributed to his justification." If (as I have argued) apostasy is possible, then it would seem to have undermined his justification. At the very least, it would have a severely negative impact on his sanctification. Is it credible that the non-Molinist God should take this sort of a risk? Setting a person back in his sanctification is one thing, but risking one's justification just to (possibly) achieve greater sanctification and glory appears to be reckless. If, however, God has middle knowledge, then God takes no risks with anyone's salvation. God could allow enormous suffering in Job's life to achieve greater sanctification for Job, knowing that Job would certainly emerge victorious from the suffering rather than have his faith—and possibly his eternal life—destroyed via the extreme suffering.

Like Bernard, Stump wrongly thinks that God can make the right moves by inductively reasoning based on God's observation of human behavioral tendencies and character[24] and by being the "consummate chess master."[25] But the stakes are far too high for God to be taking such chances with human eternal lives. Laying extreme suffering on a person of faith in the mere hope that this will conduce to greater sanctification and glory for the sufferer while risking that this person might reject his faith is morally dubious to say the least. Since the Bible indicates that God is going to remove all sin from all believers in the afterlife anyway, is guessing about what potential improvements suffering may presently bring to a believer's sanctification worth the risk that is involved?

One might perhaps suggest that the non-Molinist God is justified in trying to use suffering to bring unbelievers to salvation. Perhaps for unbelievers there would be little to lose, as the possible benefits would seem to outweigh the risk of making the unbeliever even more resistant to God. Yet the risk remains that the suffering of an unbeliever may have undesirable and unpredictable effects on others in some way. Even with unbelievers, the non-Molinist God takes risks in using suffering.

23. Stump, *Wandering in Darkness*, 405.
24. Stump, *Wandering in Darkness*, page 622 endnote 102.
25. Stump, *Wandering in Darkness*, 226.

Stump ultimately declines to suggest what particular *mechanisms* God might employ in order to use suffering as a means of improving a person's psychic state.[26] This is a significant omission, however. She needs to be able to justify the sort of providential control that she attributes to God, and it does not seem that she has come close to doing this.

There is one other key way that Stump's theodicy needs to appeal to a God who possesses middle knowledge and is using suffering to direct humans to the best soteriological ends. In responding to the objection that her view implies that one should not help those who suffer, Stump rightly stresses that we must always try to relieve the suffering of others even if God uses it for good purposes. She holds that God's sovereign plan will be achieved whether one tries to ease the suffering of others or not.[27] If one does not help the sufferer and God wants the sufferer to be helped, then Stump suggests that God will have providentially arranged the world to use someone else to provide help. If one does try to help the sufferer and God wants the suffering to continue in order to achieve God's aims, then God will have arranged the world so that the attempted help does not ease the suffering. Stump's response is excellent, but it requires Molinism. Her response highlights that God, in order to use suffering to lead unbelievers to salvation and believers to sanctification in the way she suggests, not only needs to know logically prior to creation how the sufferer will respond to suffering, but God *also* must know how those in a position to help the sufferer would freely respond. God's providential control over the world must be enormous if God is to use suffering to achieve his soteriological purposes for humanity.

Finally, consider Hick's soul-making theodicy (SMT), which centers on God creating the ideal environment for growing mankind morally and spiritually so that we are able to have the eternal union with God that he desires for us. Hick stresses that God does not view humans as his "pets" and does not aim to create a paradise for our comfort here on earth; rather, God is like a good parent who aims to cultivate virtues in children and does not elevate pleasure above all else. So the world, Hick says, must be judged mainly by how well it achieves soul-making.[28]

Hick rightly emphasizes that some degree of divine hiddenness is needed if humans are to have the opportunity to love and follow God

---

26. Stump, *Wandering in Darkness*, 398.
27. Stump, *Wandering in Darkness*, 412–14.
28. Hick, "Soul-Making and Suffering," 169–71.

The Applicability of This Theodicy to the Broader Problem of Evil

without coercion. There must be an "epistemic distance" from God in an "autonomous environment" in which rejecting God and living self-centeredly is possible. Moreover, he stresses that moral significance would be lost from our actions in a world with no chance of real loss or harm coming to people. There would then be no place for virtues like "perseverance, skill, or honesty" that can only be developed in the face of adversity.[29]

Hick thinks the biggest challenge to his SMT is that certain sufferings seem too extreme to be beneficial for soul-making. Some things appear "ruthlessly destructive" and produce "sheer loss" for the sufferer. Hick's response is to appeal to mystery, yet he notes that this mystery concerning why God allows such sufferings may itself point to a general reason why God allows them: their opacity may conduce to greater virtue and faith. A world in which all suffering is deserved and no suffering seems too severe would be flawed. Such a world would lack sympathy and sacrificial aid for the hurting. There needs to be some "apparently unmerited, pointless" suffering, as such seemingly "dysteleological" suffering is likely conducive to soul-making.[30]

Hick adds to his theodicy the possibility of endless postmortem opportunities for salvation. Since so much suffering seems to result in no apparent soul-making, he thinks universalism is needed to preserve "the perfect goodness of God" and the fulfillment of the divine will. There must be no "wasted lives and finally unredeemed suffering."[31] Hick sees the "doctrine of hell, with its implicates of permanently unexpiated sin and unending suffering, as rendering a Christian theodicy impossible."[32]

As it stands, Hick's SMT requires neither Molinism nor God's optimization of the soteriological balance in this life. This is because he appeals to numerous finite lives to achieve soul-making and salvation. This appeal eliminates the need for God to be effective in this life at providentially drawing people to himself. However, if universalism and postmortem opportunities for salvation are excised from Hick's theodicy (as they should be to maintain consistency with the Bible), then Hick needs Molinism as a mechanism to account for God being able to use suffering to achieve soul-making in this life. Apart from Molinism, the

---

29. John Hick, "Soul-Making and Suffering," 177–81.
30. John Hick, "Soul-Making and Suffering," 183–87.
31. John Hick, "Soul-Making and Suffering," 340.
32. John Hick, "Soul-Making and Suffering," 237.

risk-taking concerns raised earlier apply to the SMT as well. If God is going to use suffering effectively to achieve the best soteriological outcomes, then something like the soteriological theodicy that I have proposed is necessary.

Clearly, Hick's SMT is weakened by appealing to postmortem opportunities for salvation. First, this appeal undermines divine hiddenness and human freedom if it is assumed that we retain our memories over the many finite lives that he postulates—an assumption that would seem necessary in order for us to benefit from what we learn in each life. Hick's emphasis on a moral arena that allows sufficient human freedom falls apart if we get recycled into numerous lives as God continues to work on us relentlessly until we all are saved. Second, this appeal makes the extreme amount of suffering that occurs in this life seem much harder to justify. If God has unlimited time to work slowly on our hearts and "chip away" at our rebellion over millennia, he could seemingly do this with minimal suffering rather than press for our salvation in this life via suffering that is often quite intense. Third, I have already made the case that postmortem opportunities for salvation do not square with what Scripture teaches, and thus such an appeal is unhelpful in a defense of Christian theism.[33]

If, however, one's eternal destiny is determined by what one chooses in this life, then God cannot afford to work on us slowly. It would make sense that the Spirit would utilize suffering—even intense suffering—to prompt our wills in an uncoerced way away from rebellion and towards Christ in this one earthly life. Since we have only one life to be drawn to God, the stakes become much higher. Some sort of process like the one that I have proposed (that appeals to divine middle knowledge and Reformed epistemology) seems to be needed in order to show how the Spirit can break down a person's sin barriers and draw a person to Christ in the most effective and efficient manner possible. It is plausible that the Spirit would allow a great deal of suffering at times because that may be precisely what is needed to break down the sin barriers of certain people. Such a process would account for the extreme lengths to which God goes

---

33. Scripture stresses the urgency and finality of repenting and turning to God in this life (e.g., Matt 24:42–51; 25:1–13; Luke 16:19–31; Heb 9:27–28). Also, Jesus says the people of Tyre, Sidon, and Sodom would be punished at the final judgment for their rejection of God rather than given a chance to repent under more ideal circumstances even though they would have repented if they had received different revelation in this life (Matt 11:20–24).

The Applicability of This Theodicy to the Broader Problem of Evil 203

in using intense suffering for soul-making purposes in this life, and it evaporates the charge that God takes excessive risks with our souls.

Chapter Summary

I have made the case in this chapter that a soteriological theodicy like the one I put forward in the previous chapter that includes appeals to divine middle knowledge and God's optimization of soteriological outcomes has benefits beyond responding to the PCL—it is also beneficial in defending Christian theism against the broader POE. Plantinga leverages Molinism effectively in his FWD in response to the claim that theism is incompatible with the amount of evil in the world. Injecting the likelihood that God would use middle knowledge to achieve soteriological optimality further shows how Christian theism is not made less likely by the amount of evil in this life. While some contend that Molinism makes God partially responsible for sin and allege that God can achieve his providential aims through suffering without middle knowledge, this chapter rejects those claims. I have made the point that it may only be in a world in which there is a less than optimal balance of broadly moral good and evil in this earthly life that God can use his middle knowledge to bring about the best overall outcome for humanity—soteriological optimality. If God may be allowing the suffering and evil that he does in order to arrange the world in his perfect sovereignty so as to achieve the best soteriological balance (at least within certain parameters), then one cannot be confident that God lacks justification for allowing circumstances in which so much evil occurs. God's use of his middle knowledge to achieve his soteriological goals also provides a reason to think that we ought to be humble about concluding that certain instances of evil are actually gratuitous simply because they seem to increase (and may actually increase) suffering in this earthly life without bringing about a greater good that occurs within this life. In responding to William Rowe's argument, I suggested that what seem to us to be gratuitous evils may actually be integral to the world playing out in such a way that it is soteriologically optimal; achieving this goal is surely of primary importance, and it may not be possible for us to see how a God with middle knowledge is orchestrating the world to accomplish this goal. So denying divine middle knowledge reduces one's apologetic options in making a FWD concerning the amount of evil and in defending against the alleged gratuitousness of some evils. Denying God's middle knowledge does not seem to offer any clear benefits in responding to the POE, and it raises the specter of reckless risk-taking. A Molinist soteriological theodicy like the one I have put forward would also bolster the theodicies of Stump and Hick by justifying how God can use suffering to mold people morally and spiritually to achieve his soteriological aims. This is instructive in showing the importance of divine middle knowledge in the Spirit's ability to break down effectively the barriers of sin that prevent moral and spiritual growth while upholding human freedom.

Conclusion

THE AIM OF THIS project has been to offer a soteriological theodicy against the PCL that is consistent with Scripture and is also philosophically plausible. Certainly, the PCL is a significant challenge. Many find it difficult to think that the Christian God could be good and loving (much less maximally good and loving) if Jesus is the only path to salvation that God has made available—and especially if Christian exclusivism is true such that one must hear the gospel and respond to it in this lifetime to be saved. Many skeptics and Christians alike struggle to find a way of reconciling divine omnibenevolence with the fact that so many people who are outside of Christ seem to lack a good opportunity to respond to (or perhaps even hear) the gospel. As we have seen, even a scholar like John Hick who once held orthodox Christian beliefs reported that his move away from Christianity and towards religious pluralism was a result of his concerns about the soteriological narrowness of Christianity in the face of religious diversity and the PCL.

In light of our finitude and the fact that God has not revealed in Scripture how he will deal with the unevangelized and others who appear to be contingently lost, anyone who offers a soteriological theodicy against the PCL ought to do so with great humility. Although I have made it clear that I make no claim that my proposed theodicy is true, it does seem to me that it is plausible and may be true for all we know. I humbly offer it as a possible solution to the PCL that does not contradict Scripture and is philosophically coherent and reasonable. That is all that is required in order for it to be a good theodicy. In formulating this theodicy, I have assumed the truth of Christian exclusivism. This is advantageous regardless of whether Christian exclusivism is true. If instead Christian inclusivism were to be true, that would only provide even more options for dealing with the soteriological POE. I have also taken the position that unconditional election, limited atonement, irresistible grace, and perseverance of the saints are not true. It should be noted, however, that the truth or falsity of perseverance of the saints is not especially important to my theodicy. Although I make room in my theodicy for the possibility of apostasy, one could hold that there are no apostates and still make use of my theodicy. In any case, I certainly do come at the PCL from a position that is inconsistent with Reformed soteriology. Those Christians who do not agree with my theological starting points will need to seek a different theodicy to deal with the concerns that are raised by the PCL. However, for the many Christians who do accept my theological starting points, it is my hope that this theodicy will be of great apologetic value and theological interest; moreover, I hope that it will be of great comfort. In the remainder of this concluding chapter, I will highlight the key steps that I have taken in our journey through the preceding chapters before offering some final reflections about the value of what I have proposed.

Retracing the Theodical Journey

In order to make my case that the PCL is the most significant challenge within the soteriological POE, it was necessary to begin by carefully explaining the nature of the soteriological POE and some of the key concerns that arise within it. I emphasized that, within the broader POE, the soteriological POE involves the alleged incompatibility between P_1 (God possesses the attributes of omniscience, omnipotence, and omnibenevolence) and P_2 (some persons do not accept the forgiveness that is available via receiving Christ and are thus damned). Since there is no explicit contradiction between P_1 and P_2, I explained that the only way to demonstrate an inconsistency between these two propositions is to add other propositions to this set such that an inconsistency is revealed. I then briefly examined two key objections within the soteriological POE that are sometimes alleged to show an incompatibility between the Christian God's attributes and the fact that many people will be eternally lost. Each of these preliminary objections add certain propositions to P_1 and P_2 in an effort to reveal a contradiction between them. I needed to explain these preliminary objections and respond to them in order to clear them away and show that the most pressing objection is the PCL. The first preliminary objection that we examined is the claim that a God with the attributes identified in P_1 ought to be both able (P_3) and willing

(P_4) to ensure universal salvation, so the fact that universal salvation is not true (P_2) is alleged to conflict with the sort of God described in P_1. After responding to this first objection, I introduced a second preliminary objection. This second objection makes the case that God ought to provide universal access to salvation but has not done so, and it does this by adding P_5, P_6, and P_7 to P_1 and P_2. After responding to this preliminary objection, the stage was set to introduce the PCL as the key remaining objection within the soteriological POE.[1] The PCL argues that God's possessing the attributes of omniscience, omnipotence, and omnibenevolence (P_1) entails that God would not create persons who are lost in their actual circumstances but who would have been saved if placed into different circumstances (P_8). The PCL further claims that the recognition in P_2 that those who never place faith in Christ are lost plausibly makes it unavoidable—given the lack of access to hearing the Christian gospel and other difficult life circumstances that many non-Christians face—that at least some of the lost are only contingently lost (P_9). Thus, if P_8 and P_9 are both true, then we seem to have a contradiction. God's attributes would then be incompatible with the purported reality that some of the lost are contingently lost. So, if the PCL is to be refuted, one must show that either P_8 or P_9 (or both) should be rejected. One must show that at least one of these two premises is neither necessarily true nor required by Christian doctrine. I eventually go on to attack P_8.

After clarifying the PCL and arguing that it is the most pressing aspect of the soteriological POE, I began to prepare the way for laying out my theodicy. Because of the crucial place that Molinism has in my theodicy, the first step was to provide a thorough explanation of Molinism and unpack the core concept of divine middle knowledge before offering a robust defense of this doctrine's theological and philosophical viability. I also took time to provide a brief history behind the rise of Molinism and examine the way Molina himself applied God's middle knowledge to soteriology. By contrasting the way Molina applied divine middle knowledge to soteriology with the way that Francisco Suarez applied it, I illustrated how it is possible for one to leverage Molinism in a variety of ways in support of the viability of different soteriological perspectives. In addition, I noted how the doctrine of Molinism has seen a revival (largely due to Alvin Plantinga) since the 1970s and how there has been much discussion in recent decades about its biblical faithfulness and philosophical viability.

---

1. See Table 1.1 at the end of chapter 1 for a summary of all the premises that are introduced in the two preliminary objections and in the PCL.

Although an expansive critique of all of the arguments for and against Molinism is far beyond the scope of this project, I aimed to offer a concise but thorough assessment of the most prominent issues surrounding this doctrine. With regard to the biblical evidence in favor of Molinism, I argued that three key considerations in Scripture strongly support its truth even though there is no explicit proof-text for Molinism in Scripture. These include the biblical evidence that: (1) God possesses counterfactual knowledge of how humans would act in circumstances that will never come to exist; (2) humans possess libertarian free will; and (3) God has sovereign control of the world and the ability to achieve his precise plans. I made a biblical case for affirming all three of these points and contended that Molinism appears to be the only way to reconcile them. With regard to the philosophical viability of Molinism, I argued that a defense of the coherence of Molinism is all that is necessary. If Molinism seems to be coherent and at least possibly true, then there can be no objection to its acceptance and to leveraging its significant explanatory power. I pointed out that there are really only two main philosophical strategies for attacking Molinism: denying that a counterfactual of creaturely freedom (CCF) can be true and denying that God can know CCFs logically prior to his creative decree to actualize the world. I then offered a defense against the most prominent philosophical arguments against Molinism that fall within each of these two main strategies.

With my case for the viability of Molinism in place, I began to examine how some thinkers—particularly William Lane Craig—utilize Molinism in an attempt to resolve the PCL. I identified three general categories of strategies that have been adopted in applying Molinism to theodicies against the PCL, and I assessed the theodicies within each of these categories. I made a case that all of the Molinist theodicies that have been put forth have positive aspects, but ultimately none of them are without theological and/or philosophical difficulties.

The theodicy that I identified as most promising is Craig's theodicy. Craig's position is by far the most prominent Molinist theodicy against the PCL, and I carefully laid out and assessed his view. I showed how Craig's theodicy focuses upon three key claims: (1) it may be the case that nobody is contingently lost because God is able to arrange the world such that all of the lost are TD; (2) Romans 2:7 teaches Christian inclusivism, which allows that all persons—even the unevangelized and all of the TD—have an opportunity in this life to be saved; and (3) God may have providentially arranged the world so that it has an optimal balance of saved versus lost. I highlighted a number of strengths in his view. Craig's proposal appears to be philosophically viable so long as God possesses middle knowledge. If all of the lost are TD, then P_9 is false and the PCL is undermined. If God has middle knowledge and it is at least possible that some people could be TD, then there is no apparent philosophical reason why God could not arrange the world so that everyone who is lost is TD. There is also no reason why a God with middle knowledge could not actualize a world with an optimal soteriological balance. God's election would then be purposeful and consistent with his perfect love and universal salvific will. God would be aiming to do the best that he can for humanity as a whole while upholding human free will rather than, as Suarez believed, utilizing middle knowledge merely to ensure the salvation and damnation of specific people. Moreover, unlike the theodicies of Lake and Walls, Craig emphasizes God's sovereignty and providence within this present earthly existence. God does not merely make use of his middle knowledge to clean up the PCL after this present life is over; instead, God providentially arranges the world in such a way that the PCL is resolved. Moreover, if inclusivism were true as Craig suggests, then even those in this world who are TD and lost would have been given an opportunity to be saved (even though they never take advantage of it). So Craig rightly wants to affirm that God grants sufficient grace for all to be saved—even the lost—and genuinely wants all to be saved.

Despite the advantages and insights of Craig's theodicy, I explained why I find biblical grounds for departing from it at certain points. I clarified that my disagreement with Craig is primarily because there appear to be multiple ways in which Scripture contradicts his crucial proposal that nobody is contingently lost. There seem to be two types of contingently lost people identified in Scripture—those who would have turned to God only if they were given unduly overt revelation and those who apostatize. We saw that Craig himself holds to the possibility of apostasy, so it is not clear how he reconciles this with his theodicy. I thus do not think the way forward is to attack P_9. I also disagreed with Craig's appeal to Christian inclusivism, as it seems to be taught neither in Romans 2:7 (as Craig contends) nor anywhere else in Scripture. In addition, Craig's theodicy does not address how God may well have various goals for the world besides soteriological optimality that may place limitations on the balance of saved versus lost that is feasible for God to bring about.

I then laid out my own theodicy. Like Craig's theodicy, it incorporates divine middle knowledge and suggests that God optimizes the soteriological balance; however, there are key differences between our theodicies. With regard to God optimizing the soteriological balance, I emphasize that there might be well-populated, feasible worlds of free creatures that have a better soteriological balance than the actual world. I stress that God may have certain goals that kept him from creating those worlds. Yet I propose that God would plausibly bring about the best soteriological balance that can be achieved while upholding those parameters that are important to God (e.g., ensuring a certain degree of divine hiddenness and allowing an evil being like Satan to have a certain amount of access to tempting humanity). Perhaps the most crucial way in which my theodicy departs from Craig's is that I deny that all of the lost are TD. I allow that there are contingently lost persons who apostatize and those who would have turned to God only if they were given what is for them unduly overt revelation. I attack P_8 rather than P_9, and I do this by arguing that God's omnibenevolence is not undermined despite the fact that he allows some to be contingently lost. This is because God's omnibenevolence is consistent with him allowing both of these two types of contingently lost persons. I see no need to postulate that there are other types of contingently lost persons, since the Bible never indicates that there are other types. As noted, I also depart from Craig by holding to Christian exclusivism. In order to justify that all people have an opportunity to be saved, I utilize a process that draws upon a slightly modified version of Reformed epistemology (which I explained and briefly defended) to show how it may be the case that God gives everyone an opportunity to be saved and how it is only one's own sin and not the sin of others that is decisive in one failing to come to saving faith. Scripture teaches that the Holy Spirit works on the hearts and minds of unbelievers, and my proposed process is helpful in that it shows how the Spirit may utilize divine middle knowledge to provide just the right promptings, experiences, and evidences to break down a person's sin barrier and allow that person to come to Christ. The process not only avoids inclusivism, but it also avoids the oversimplified proposal of many exclusivists that God will bring the gospel to those who respond to general revelation. I also emphasize how this same sort of process may apply in both the OT and NT eras.

Finally, I made the case that my soteriological theodicy also offers benefits in responding to the broader POE—both in terms of the amount of evil and the apparent gratuitousness of some evil in our present earthly existence. If God is using his middle knowledge to optimize the soteriological balance (even within the parameters I identified) over the course of human history (which is surely a more important objective for the wellbeing of humanity than optimizing the balance of good and evil within this earthly life), then this helps to show why an omnibenevolent God may have allowed an even worse ratio of evil relative to good in this earthly life than he feasibly could have brought about. Moreover, if God is using his middle knowledge to achieve the best soteriological outcomes, then I showed why it becomes much harder to have confidence that any particular instance of suffering and evil that occurs in this earthly life is truly gratuitous. I also showed how my soteriological theodicy strengthens the theodicies of Eleonore Stump and John Hick, which appeal to soteriological outcomes in responding to the broader POE.

Concluding Reflections

I will now offer some concluding reflections as I draw this wide-ranging project to a close. With regard to my theodicy making room for there being contingently lost people, which seems to be the proper approach in light of the biblical evidence that there are such people, it is worth noting that there may well be other types of contingently lost people besides the two types that I identify (e.g., a lost person who is thoroughly evangelized and has all sorts of opportunities to accept the gospel in the actual world and yet would have freely and without excessive pressure accepted the gospel in some other feasible world). Although this is possible, there is no way for us to know whether this is the case. Since the two types that I identify seem to be the only types that are indicated in Scripture, I see no reason to speculate about there being other types. What is crucial, however, is that my theodicy eliminates the problematic sorts of contingently lost people; that is, nobody "barely slips through the soteriological cracks" like the inner-city teen that I described at the end of the third chapter. Any theodicy that effectively undermines P_8 must eliminate such problematic sorts of contingently lost individuals.

It is also important to recognize that one need not be confident that either type of contingently lost person that is accounted for in my theodicy actually exists in order for one to find great value in my theodicy. If one thinks, for example, that nobody ever apostatizes, then one could simply excise that from my theodicy. If one understands the comments of Jesus in Matthew 11 about the people of Tyre, Sidon, and Sodom to be merely hyperbolic and one sees no need to make room for contingently lost people who would only have responded to what is for them unduly overt revelation, then one could excise this type of contingently lost person from my theodicy. It is, however, beneficial if one does not excise either type of contingently lost person from my theodicy because it is advantageous to show that they can be handled *regardless of whether or not* Scripture indicates that such persons exist. The fact that my theodicy handles both types and does not require that everyone (or even anyone) is TD will be an attractive feature for many Christians. Yet my theodicy offers a number of advantages besides accounting for these two types of contingently lost individuals. What are some of those advantages?

One advantage is that, if one is an exclusivist, one may find great value in the fact that my theodicy provides a more nuanced account for how God may offer all people an opportunity to be saved than the view that God will bring the gospel to those who respond appropriately to general revelation. One may value the process proposed in my theodicy in which Molinism and Reformed epistemology combine to suggest how the Holy Spirit could be drawing all people to himself in a way that is uniquely tailored to each individual. This process ensures that all people—regardless of their circumstances—will be saved unless their own sin prevents them from allowing the Spirit to draw them to himself. It allows that one need not have the time, ability, or resources to reason one's way to knowing that the gospel is true, yet I leave room for the Spirit to use apologetic arguments and various evidential means to break down a person's sin barrier and prepare a person's heart and mind to accept the gospel.

Another advantage of my theodicy is that it upholds God's omnibenevolence and his efforts to optimize the soteriological balance while recognizing that this optimization may be within the bounds of certain limiting parameters. God's relative hiddenness and his allowing Satan to tempt humanity may seem to rest uncomfortably with the suggestion that God has actualized the feasible world that has the most optimal balance of saved versus lost. If, however, one allows that an omnibenevolent God may well optimize the soteriological balance within the limits of these parameters, then this tension is relieved. By making this case, my theodicy increases the plausibility of God working toward optimal soteriological ends.

Aside from the above advantages, I have highlighted in this study the powerful way in which a soteriological theodicy such as mine can be applied to the broader problem of suffering and evil. This has enormous apologetic value because the amount of evil in this life and the seeming gratuitousness of so much suffering and evil may well be the most prominent intellectual hurdles that stand between unbelievers and the Christian faith. There is great value in a theodicy that alleviates concerns about the contingently lost (thus fighting against the pull of religious pluralism) while at the same time strengthening the case that theism is compatible with the amount and types of suffering and evil in the world (thus fighting against the pull of atheism).

Apart from its value for Christian apologetics, my proposal is also beneficial for soteriology. The soteriological outcome God brings about on this view is purposeful, loving, and consistent with God's omnibenevolence and other attributes. It takes divine sovereignty and providence seriously while preserving human freedom. It upholds Christian exclusivism. It accepts the biblical evidence that some will be lost who would have been saved in different circumstances. It also accounts for the reality of spiritual warfare and the biblical teaching that God desires the salvation of all people. By accomplishing all of the above in a way that is biblically consistent and philosophically reasonable, I believe my project offers insights for Christian theology.

Ultimately, it is my hope that this theodicy will encourage those who are already Christians to be strong in their faith in the face of these significant challenges and to be better-equipped witnesses for Christ. I believe this theodicy can also help unbelievers to see that the Christian faith is true and reasonable. Perhaps God will use this project as a weapon to demolish one more argument "that sets itself up against the knowledge of God" (2 Cor 10:5). If it is the Lord's will, the proposal offered here may be at least a small part of God's eternal plan of drawing all who are willing into a saving relationship with Christ.

Bibliography

Adams, Robert Merrihew. "An Anti-Molinist Argument." In *Philosophical Perspectives*. Vol. 5, edited by James Tomberlin, 343–53. Atascadero: Ridgeview, 1991.

———. "Middle Knowledge and the Problem of Evil." In *The Problem of Evil*, edited by Marilyn McCord Adams and Robert Merrihew Adams, 110–25. Oxford: Oxford University Press, 1990.

———. "Plantinga on the Problem of Evil." In *Alvin Plantinga*, edited by James Tomberlin and Peter Van Inwagen, 371–82. Dordrecht: D. Reidel, 1985.

———. *The Virtue of Faith and Other Essays in Philosophical Theology*. New York: Oxford University Press, 1987.

Attridge, Harold W. *The Epistle to the Hebrews: A Commentary on the Epistle to the Hebrews*. Philadelphia: Fortress, 1989.

Baggett, David, and Jerry L. Walls. *God and Cosmos: Moral Truth and Human Meaning*. Oxford: Oxford University Press, 2016.

———. *Good God: The Theistic Foundations of Morality*. Oxford: Oxford University Press, 2011.

Barrett, David B., and Todd M. Johnson. *World Christian Trends, AD 30—AD 2200: Interpreting the Annual Christian Megacensus*. Pasadena: William Carey Library, 2001.

Bernard, Christopher William Thomas. "Views of God and Evil: A Perspective Approach to the Argument from Evil." PhD diss., University of Maryland, 2008.

Black, Allan, and Mark Black. *The College Press NIV Commentary: 1 & 2 Peter*. Edited by Jack Cottrell and Tony Ash. Joplin: College, 1988.

Breitenbach, Zachary. "A Case for How Eschatological and Soteriological Considerations Strengthen the Plausibility of a Good God." *Philosophia Christi* 22 (2020) 257–72.

Brown, Rick. "Brother Jacob and Master Isaac: How One Insider Movement Began." *International Journal of Frontier Missions* 24 (2007) 41–42.

Bruner, Frederick Dale. *The Christbook: Matthew 1–12*. Vol. 5 of *Matthew: A Commentary*. Rev. ed. Grand Rapids: Eerdmans, 2004.

Calvin, John. *Institutes of the Christian Religion*. Translated by Henry Beveridge. Peabody: Hendrickson, 2008.

Carson, D. A. *The Gagging of God: Christianity Confronts Pluralism*. Grand Rapids: Zondervan, 1996.

———. *Matthew Chapters 1–12*. The Expositor's Bible Commentary Series. Grand Rapids: Zondervan, 1995.

Clotfelter, David. *Sinners in the Hands of a Good God: Reconciling Divine Judgment and Mercy*. Chicago: Moody, 2004.

Cottrell, Jack. *The Faith Once for All: Bible Doctrine for Today*. Joplin: College, 2002.

———. *Romans*. Joplin: College, 2005.

Craig, William Lane. "A Classical Apologist's Response." In *Five Views on Apologetics*, edited by Steven B. Cowan, 285–90. Grand Rapids: Zondervan, 2000.

———. *Divine Foreknowledge and Human Freedom: The Coherence of Theism: Omniscience*. Leiden: Brill, 1991.

———. "God's Middle Knowledge." In *A Faith and Culture Devotional: Daily Readings in Art, Science, and Life*, edited by K. Monroe Kullberg and L. Arrington, 167–68. Grand Rapids: Zondervan, 2008.

———. *Hard Questions, Real Answers*. Wheaton: Crossway, 2003.

———. "Middle Knowledge: A Calvinist-Arminian Rapprochement?" In *The Grace of God, the Will of Man*, edited by Clark H. Pinnock, 141–64. Grand Rapids: Zondervan, 1989.

———. "Middle Knowledge and Christian Exclusivism." *Sophia* 34 (1995) 120–39.

———. "Middle Knowledge, Truth-Makers, and the Grounding Objection." *Faith and Philosophy* 18 (2001) 337–52.

———. "The Middle-Knowledge View." In *Divine Foreknowledge: Four Views*, edited by James K. Beilby and Paul R. Eddy, 119–43. Downers Grove: InterVarsity, 2001.

———. "'No Other Name': A Middle Knowledge Perspective on the Exclusivity of Salvation Through Christ." *Faith and Philosophy* 6 (1989) 172–88.

———. *On Guard: Defending Your Faith with Reason and Precision*. Colorado Springs: David C Cook, 2010.

———. *The Only Wise God: The Compatibility of Divine Foreknowledge and Human Freedom*. Eugene: Wipf & Stock, 2000.

———. "Politically Incorrect Salvation." In *Christian Apologetics in the Postmodern World*, edited by Timothy R. Phillips and Dennis L. Ockholm, 75–100. Downers Grove: InterVarsity, 1995.

———. *The Problem of Divine Foreknowledge and Future Contingents from Aristotle to Suarez*. New York: Brill, 1988.

Craig, William Lane, and Alex Rosenberg. "The Debate: Is Faith in God Reasonable?" In *Is Faith in God Reasonable?: Debates in Philosophy, Science, and Rhetoric*, edited by Corey Miller and Paul Gould, 13–42. New York: Routledge, 2014.

Craig, William Lane, and Joseph E. Gorra. *A Reasonable Response: Answers to Tough Questions on God, Christianity, and the Bible*. Chicago: Moody, 2013.

Dekker, Eef. *Middle Knowledge*. Leuven: Peeters, 2000.

———. "Was Arminius a Molinist?" *The Sixteenth Century Journal* 27 (1996) 337–52.

Engelsma, David. *Hyper-Calvinism and the Call of the Gospel: An Examination of the Well-Meant Gospel Offer*. Grandville: Reformed Free, 1994.

Erickson, Millard. *Christian Theology*. Vol. 2. Grand Rapids: Baker, 1984.

———. *The Concise Dictionary of Christian Theology*. Rev. ed. Grand Rapids: Crossway, 2001.

Flannery, Austin, ed. *Vatican Council II: The Conciliar and Post Conciliar Documents*. Vol. 1 of *The Vatican Collection*. Northport: Costello, 1996.

Flint, Thomas P. *Divine Providence: The Molinist Account*. Ithaca: Cornell University Press, 1998.

———. "Whence and Whither the Molinist Debate: A Reply to Hasker." In *Molinism: The Contemporary Debate*, edited by Ken Perszyk, 37–49. Oxford: Oxford University Press, 2011.

Bibliography

Freddoso, Alfred J. "Introduction." In *On Divine Foreknowledge: Part IV of the Concordia*, 1–81. Translated by Alfred J. Freddoso. Ithaca: Cornell University Press, 1988.
Geisler, Norman. *Baker Encyclopedia of Apologetics*. Grand Rapids: Baker, 1999.
Geivett, R. Douglas, and W. Gary Phillips. "A Particularist View: An Evidentialist Approach." In *Four Views on Salvation in a Pluralistic World*, edited by Dennis L. Okholm and Timothy R. Phillips, 211–45. Grand Rapids: Zondervan, 1996.
Greenlee, David H. *From the Straight Path to the Narrow Way: Journeys of Faith*. Waynesboro: Authentic Media, 2005.
Guthrie, Donald. *The Letter to the Hebrews: An Introduction and Commentary*. Grand Rapids: Eerdmans, 1983.
Hackett, Stuart. *The Reconstruction of the Christian Revelation Claim*. Grand Rapids: Baker, 1984.
Hasker, William. *God, Time, and Knowledge*. Ithaca: Cornell University Press, 1989.
———. "Molinism's Freedom Problem: A Reply to Cunningham." *Faith and Philosophy* 34 (2017) 93–106.
———. "The (Non-)Existence of Molinist Counterfactuals." In *Molinism: The Contemporary Debate*, edited by Ken Perszyk, 25–36. Oxford: Oxford University Press, 2011.
———. "A Refutation of Middle Knowledge." *Nous* 20 (1986) 545–57.
———. "Response to Thomas Flint." *Philosophical Studies* 60 (1990) 117–26.
Helm, Paul. "Are They Few That Be Saved?" In *Universalism and the Doctrine of Hell*, edited by Nigel M. de S. Cameron, 257–81. Grand Rapids: Baker, 1992.
Hick, John. "Jesus and the World Religions." In *The Myth of God Incarnate*, edited by John Hick, 167–85. London: SCM, 1977.
———. *The Metaphor of God Incarnate: Christology in a Pluralistic Age*. 2nd ed. Louisville: Westminster John Knox, 2006.
———. "A Pluralist View." In *Four Views on Salvation in a Pluralistic World*, edited by Dennis L. Okholm and Timothy R. Phillips, 29–59. Grand Rapids: Zondervan, 1996.
———. "Soul-Making and Suffering." In *The Problem of Evil*, edited by Marilyn McCord Adams and Robert Merrihew Adams, 168–88. Oxford: Oxford University Press, 1990.
Hunt, David P. "Middle Knowledge and the Soteriological Problem of Evil." *Religious Studies* 27 (1991) 3–26.
Johnstone, Patrick. *Future of the Global Church: History, Trends, and Possibilities*. Downers Grove: InterVarsity, 2011.
Kaiser, Walter C. "Holy Pagans: Reality or Myth?" In *Faith Comes by Hearing: A Response to Inclusivism*, edited by Christopher W. Morgan and Robert A. Peterson, 123–41. Downers Grove: InterVarsity, 2008.
Keathley, Kenneth. *Salvation and Sovereignty: A Molinist Approach*. Nashville: B&H, 2010.
Keener, Craig S. *Miracles: The Credibility of the New Testament Accounts*. 2 vols. Grand Rapids: Baker Academic, 2011.
Kenny, Anthony. *The God of the Philosophers*. Oxford: Clarendon, 1979.
Knight, George William. *The Pastoral Epistles: A Commentary on the Greek Text*. Grand Rapids: Eerdmans, 1992.
Kvanvig, Jonathan. *The Possibility of an All-Knowing God*. New York: St. Martin's, 1986.

Lake, Donald M. "He Died for All: The Universal Dimensions of the Atonement." In *Grace Unlimited*, edited by Clark H. Pinnock, 31–51. Minneapolis: Bethany Fellowship, 1975.

Leske, Adrian. "Matthew." In *The International Bible Commentary: A Catholic and Ecumenical Commentary for the Twenty-First Century*, edited by William R. Farmer, 1253–1330. Collegeville: Liturgical, 1998.

Lightner, Robert P. "For Whom Did Christ Die?" In *Walvoord: A Tribute*, edited by Donald K. Campbell, 157–68. Chicago: Moody, 1982.

Little, Christopher R. *The Revelation of God Among the Unevangelized: An Evangelical Appraisal and Missiological Contribution to the Debate*. Pasadena: William Carey Library, 2000.

Luther, Martin. "On the Bondage of the Will." In *Luther and Erasmus: Free Will and Salvation*, edited by Rupp, Ernest Gordon, Philip S. Watson, and Desiderius Erasmus, 101–334. Louisville: Westminster John Knox, 1969.

MacGregor, Kirk R. "Harmonizing Molina's Rejection of Transworld Damnation with Craig's Solution to the Problem of the Unevangelized." *The International Journal for Philosophy of Religion* 84 (2018) 345–53.

———. *Luis de Molina: The Life and Theology of the Founder of Middle Knowledge*. Grand Rapids: Zondervan, 2015.

———. *A Molinist-Anabaptist Systematic Theology*. Lanham: University Press of America, 2007.

Mackie, J. L. *The Miracle of Theism*. Oxford: Clarendon, 1982.

Maitzen, Stephen. "Divine Hiddenness and the Demographics of Theism." *Religious Studies* 42 (2006) 177–91.

Marsh, Jason. "Do the Demographics of Theistic Belief Disconfirm Theism? A Reply to Maitzen." *Religious Studies* 44 (2008) 465–71.

Marshall, I. Howard. "Universal Grace and Atonement in the Pastoral Epistles." In *The Grace of God, the Will of Man: A Case for Arminianism*, edited by Clark Pinnock, 51–70. Grand Rapids: Zondervan, 1989.

Mbogu, Nicholas Ibeawuchi. *Christology and Religious Pluralism: A Review of John Hick's Theocentric Model of Christology and the Emergence of African Inculturation Christologies*. Piscataway: Transaction, 2006.

McKnight, Scot. "The Warning Passages of Hebrews: A Formal Analysis and Theological Conclusions." *Trinity Journal* 13 (1992) 21–59.

Molina, Luis. *Concordia*. In *On Divine Foreknowledge: Part IV of the Concordia*. Translated by Alfred J. Freddoso. Ithaca: Cornell University Press, 1988.

Moreland, J. P., and William Lane Craig. *Philosophical Foundations for a Christian Worldview*. 2nd ed. Downers Grove: InterVarsity, 2017.

Moo, Douglas J. *Romans: The NIV Application Commentary: From Biblical Text to Contemporary Life*. Grand Rapids: Zondervan, 2000.

Moser, Paul K. *The Elusive God: Reorienting Religious Epistemology*. New York: Cambridge University Press, 2008.

Mounce, William D. *Mounce's Complete Expository Dictionary of Old and New Testament Words*. Grand Rapids: Zondervan, 2006.

Murray, Michael J., and Michael C. Rea. *An Introduction to the Philosophy of Religion*. New York: Cambridge University Press, 2008.

Nash, Ronald H. *Is Jesus the Only Savior?* Grand Rapids: Zondervan, 1994.

———. "Restrictivism." In *What About Those Who Have Never Heard?: Three Views on the Destiny of the Unevangelized*, edited by John Sanders, 107–39. Downers Grove: InterVarsity, 1995.

Netland, Harold A. *Encountering Religious Pluralism: The Challenge to Christian Faith & Mission*. Downers Grove: InterVarsity, 2001.

Oropeza, B. J. *Jews, Gentiles, and the Opponents of Paul: Apostasy in the New Testament Communities*. Vol. 2. Eugene: Cascade, 2012.

Osborne, Grant R. "A Classical Arminian View." In *Four Views on the Warning Passages in Hebrews*, edited by Herbert W. Bateman IV, 86–128. Grand Rapids: Kregel, 2007.

Perszyk, Kenneth J. "Free Will Defence with and without Molinism." *International Journal for Philosophy of Religion* 43 (1998) 29–64.

———. "Introduction." In *Molinism: The Contemporary Debate*, edited by Ken Perszyk, 1–24. Oxford: Oxford University Press, 2011.

———. "Recent Work on Molinism." *Philosophy Compass* 8 (2013) 755–70.

Peterson, Robert, and Michael Williams. *Why I Am Not an Arminian*. Downers Grove: InterVarsity, 2004.

Picirilli, Robert E. *Free Will Revisited: A Respectful Response to Luther, Calvin, and Edwards*. Eugene: Wipf and Stock, 2017.

Pinnock, Clark. "An Inclusivist View." In *Four Views on Salvation in a Pluralistic World*, edited by Dennis L. Okholm and Timothy R. Phillips, 93–123. Grand Rapids: Zondervan, 1996.

———. *A Wideness in God's Mercy: The Finality of Jesus Christ in a World of Religions*. Grand Rapids: Zondervan, 1992.

Piper, John. "Are There Two Wills in God?" In *Still Sovereign: Contemporary Perspectives on Election, Foreknowledge, and Grace*, edited by Thomas Schreiner and Bruce Ware, 107–32. Grand Rapids: Baker, 2000.

Plantinga, Alvin. *God, Freedom, and Evil*. Grand Rapids: Eerdmans, 1974.

———. *The Nature of Necessity*. Oxford: Clarendon, 1974.

———. "Reply to Robert M. Adams." In *Alvin Plantinga*, edited by James Tomberlin and Peter Van Inwagen, 371–82. Dordrecht: D. Reidel, 1985.

———. *Warranted Christian Belief*. New York: Oxford University Press, 2000.

Pohle, Joseph, and Arthur Preuss. *Grace, Actual and Habitual: A Dogmatic Treatise*. St. Louis: B. Herder, 1915.

Pritchard, Duncan. "Reforming Reformed Epistemology." *International Philosophical Quarterly* 43 (2003) 43–66.

Rowe, William L. "The Problem of Evil and Some Varieties of Atheism." In *The Problem of Evil*, edited by Marilyn McCord Adams and Robert Merrihew Adams, 126–37. Oxford: Oxford University Press, 1990.

Sanders, John. *No Other Name: An Investigation into the Destiny of the Unevangelized*. Grand Rapids: Eerdmans, 1992.

Selby, Pauline. *Persian Springs: Four Iranians See Jesus*. London: Elam Ministries, 2001.

Spencer, Duane Edward. *Tulip: The Five Points of Calvinism in the Light of Scripture*. Grand Rapids: Baker, 1979.

Sproul, R. C. *Chosen by God*. Wheaton: Tyndale House, 1994.

———. *The Truth of the Cross*. Lake Mary: Reformation Trust, 2007.

Strange, Daniel. *The Possibility of Salvation Among the Unevangelized: An Analysis of Inclusivism in Recent Evangelical Theology*. Eugene: Wipf and Stock, 2002.

Strong, Augustus Hopkins. *Outlines of Systematic Theology*. Vol. 3. Philadelphia: Griffith & Rowland, 1908.

Stump, Eleonore. *Wandering in Darkness: Narrative and the Problem of Suffering*. Oxford: Oxford University Press, 2010.

Swinburne, Richard. *The Coherence of Theism*. Oxford: Clarendon, 1977.

———. *Providence and the Problem of Evil*. Oxford: Clarendon, 1988.

Taylor, Charles. *A Secular Age*. Cambridge: Harvard University Press, 2007.

Tiessen, Terrance L. *Who Can Be Saved?: Reassessing Salvation in Christ and World Religions*. Downers Grove: InterVarsity, 2004.

Vallicella, William F. *A Paradigm Theory of Existence: Onto-Theology Vindicated*. Norwell: Kluwer Academic, 2002.

Volf, Judith M. Gundry. "Apostasy, Falling Away, Perseverance." In *Dictionary of Paul and His Letters: A Compendium of Contemporary Biblical Scholarship*, edited by Gerald F. Hawthorne, Ralph P. Martin, and Daniel G. Reid, 39–45. Downers Grove: InterVarsity, 1993.

Wainwright, William J. *Reason and the Heart: A Prolegomenon to a Critique of Passional Reason*. Ithaca: Cornell University Press, 1995.

Walls, Jerry L. *Hell: The Logic of Damnation*. Notre Dame: University of Notre Dame Press, 1992.

———. "Is Molinism as Bad as Calvinism?" *Faith and Philosophy: Journal of the Society of Christian Philosophers* 7 (1990) 85–98.

Walls, Jerry L., and Joseph Dongell. *Why I Am Not a Calvinist*. Downers Grove: InterVarsity, 2004.

Welty, Greg. "Molinist Gunslingers: God and the Authorship of Sin." In *Calvinism and the Problem of Evil*, edited by David E. Alexander and Daniel M. Johnson, 56–77. Eugene: Wipf and Stock, 2016.

Wierenga, Edward R. *The Nature of God: An Inquiry Into Divine Attributes*. Ithaca: Cornell University Press, 1989.

Witherington, Ben, III. *Letters and Homilies for Jewish Christians: A Socio-Rhetorical Commentary on Hebrews, James and Jude*. Downers Grove: InterVarsity, 2007.

Wolterstorff, Nicholas. *Reason within the Bounds of Religion*. 2nd ed. Grand Rapids: Eerdmans, 1984.

Wright, R. K. McGregor. *No Place for Sovereignty: What's Wrong with Freewill Theism*. Downers Grove: InterVarsity, 1996.

www.ingramcontent.com/pod-product-compliance
Lightning Source LLC
Chambersburg PA
CBHW070250230426
43664CB00014B/2483